# Lecture Notes in Computer Science 1670

Edited by G. Goos, J. Hartmanis and J. van Leeuwen

D0286563

Springer

*Berlin*
*Heidelberg*
*New York*
*Barcelona*
*Hong Kong*
*London*
*Milan*
*Paris*
*Singapore*
*Tokyo*

Norbert A. Streitz   Jane Siegel
Volker Hartkopf   Shin'ichi Konomi (Eds.)

# Cooperative Buildings

## Integrating Information, Organizations and Architecture

Second International Workshop, CoBuild'99
Pittsburgh, USA, October 1-2, 1999
Proceedings

PROPERTY OF ALUMNI LIBRARY
WENTWORTH INSTITUTE OF TECHNOLOGY

 Springer

725.23
.C63
1999

AEM-3097

Series Editors

Gerhard Goos, Karlsruhe University, Germany
Juris Hartmanis, Cornell University, NY, USA
Jan van Leeuwen, Utrecht University, The Netherlands

Volume Editors

Norbert A. Streitz
Shin'ichi Konomi
GMD - German National Research Center for Information Technology
IPSI - Integrated Publication and Information Systems Institute
Dolivostr. 15, D-64293 Darmstadt, Germany
E-mail: {streitz/konomi}@darmstadt.gmd.de

Jane Siegel
HCI Institute, Carnegie Mellon University
5000 Forbes Avenue, Pittsburgh, PA 15213, USA
E-mail: jane.siegel@cs.cmu.edu

Volker Hartkopf
Center for Building Performance and Diagnostics
School for Architecture, Carnegie Mellon University
Pittsburgh, PA 15213, USA
E-mail: vh02@andrew.cmu.edu

Cataloging-in-Publication data applied for

Die Deutsche Bibliothek - CIP-Einheitsaufnahme

**Cooperative buildings** : integrating information, organizations and architecture
; second international workshop ; proceedings / CoBuild '99, Pittsburgh, USA,
October 1999 / Norbert A. Streitz ... (ed.). - Berlin ; Heidelberg ; New York ;
Budapest ; Hong Kong ; London ; Milan ; Paris ; Singapore ; Tokyo : Springer,
1999
(Lecture notes in computer science ; Vol. 1670)
ISBN 3-540-66596-X

CR Subject Classification (1998): B.4, C.3, H.1.2, H.4, H.5, J.4, K.4, K.6, J.7

ISSN 0302-9743
ISBN 3-540-66596-X Springer-Verlag Berlin Heidelberg New York

This work is subject to copyright. All rights are reserved, whether the whole or part of the material is
concerned, specifically the rights of translation, reprinting, re-use of illustrations, recitation, broadcasting,
reproduction on microfilms or in any other way, and storage in data banks. Duplication of this publication
or parts thereof is permitted only under the provisions of the German Copyright Law of September 9, 1965,
in its current version, and permission for use must always be obtained from Springer-Verlag. Violations are
liable for prosecution under the German Copyright Law.

© Springer-Verlag Berlin Heidelberg 1999
Printed in Germany

Typesetting: Camera-ready by author
SPIN: 10705432    06/3142 – 5 4 3 2 1 0    Printed on acid-free paper

# Preface

This volume constitutes the proceedings of the "Second International Workshop on Cooperative Buildings (CoBuild'99) – Integrating Information, Organizations, and Architecture" held at the Carnegie Museum of Art in Pittsburgh on October 1–2, 1999. The success of the First International Workshop on Cooperative Buildings (CoBuild'98), held at GMD in Darmstadt in February 1998, showed that there is a demand for an appropriate forum to present research about the intersection of information technology, organizational innovation, and architecture. Thus, it was decided to organize a follow-up event. The decision of where to organize CoBuild'99 was straightforward. Since we had many high quality contributions from the United States (U.S.) presented at CoBuild'98, we wanted to hold the second workshop in the U.S. reaching out to a large audience and at the same time turning it into an international series of events held in different places in the world. Due to the excellent work carried out at Carnegie Mellon University, it was an obvious choice to ask Volker Hartkopf from the Department of Architecture and Jane Siegel from the Human Computer Interaction Institute to be conference co-chairs for CoBuild'99. The workshop is organized in cooperation with the German National Research Center for Information Technology (GMD), the Integrated Publication and Information Systems Institute (IPSI) in Darmstadt, in particular, providing continuity between the events. Furthermore, the workshop is held in cooperation with the following scientific societies: the German Gesellschaft für Informatik (GI), the European Association of Cognitive Ergonomics (EACE), and the American Institute of Architects.

The theme remains the same, "integrating information, organizations, and architecture," because it still reflects the existing challenges. The basic issues have not changed. Although we see promising approaches addressing these issues and developments pointing towards possible solutions, there is still a need for research and development towards the goal of cooperative buildings constituting the workspaces of the future. The papers of this volume show that this is an interdisciplinary endeavor requiring a wide range of perspectives and the utilization of results from various areas of research and practice.

The technical program of CoBuild'99 presented in this volume is the result of the review and selection process of the international program committee. From 33 submitted contributions, we selected 15 to be presented as full papers, two as short papers, two as posters, and one as a demonstration. I want to express my sincere thanks to the members of the program committee for their careful reviews and for constructive comments that often helped to improve the final versions of the papers.

Finally, I want to express my sincere thanks to Shin'ichi Konomi for compiling and copy-editing the camera-ready manuscript, and to Tom Pope and Jack Moffett for creating the workshop's website. I extend special thanks to Volker Hartkopf and Jane Siegel as conference co-chairs and to the people working with them for their efforts in taking care of all those additional issues that are essential for a successful workshop.

Darmstadt, August 1999                                 Norbert A. Streitz
                                                               Program Chair

# Supporting/Cooperating Societies

American Institute of Architects

European Association of Cognitive Ergonomics (EACE)

German Computer Science Society / Gesellschaft für Informatik (GI)
    Special interest groups / Technical Committees
    2.3    Human Factors in Computing
    2.3.1 Software Ergonomics
    4.9.1 Hypertext and Hypermedia Systems
    5.14  CSCW in Organizations

# Conference Committee

## Conference Chairs
Volker Hartkopf      Carnegie Mellon University, Pittsburgh
Jane Siegel      Carnegie Mellon University, Pittsburgh

## Program Chair
Norbert A. Streitz      GMD-IPSI, Darmstadt

## Program Committee

| | |
|---|---|
| Paul Allie | Steelcase, Grand Rapids |
| Bernd Brügge | Technical University München |
| Hans-Jörg Bullinger | FhG-IAO, Stuttgart |
| Heinz-Jürgen Burkhardt | GMD-TKT, Darmstadt |
| Ernest Edmonds | University of Loughborough |
| Tom Finholt | University of Michigan, Ann Arbor |
| Jonathan Grudin | Microsoft Research & University of California, Irvine |
| Volker Hartkopf | Carnegie Mellon University, Pittsburgh |
| Ludger Hovestadt | University of Kaiserslautern |
| Hiroshi Ishii | MIT MediaLab, Cambridge |
| Simon Kaplan | University of Queensland, Brisbane |
| David Kirsh | University of California, San Diego |
| Saadi Lahlou | Electricité de France, Paris |
| Steve Lee | Carnegie Mellon University, Pittsburgh |
| Scott Mainwaring | Interval Research, Palo Alto |
| William Mitchell | MIT School of Architecture, Cambridge |
| Gale Moore | University of Toronto |
| Tom Moran | Xerox PARC, Palo Alto |
| Steven Poltrock | Boeing Company, Seattle |
| Ralf Reichwald | Technical University München |
| Jun Rekimoto | SONY Computer Science Lab, Tokyo |
| Burkhard Remmers | Wilkhahn, Bad Münder |
| Eric Richert | SUN Microsystems, Palo Alto |
| Mike Robinson | University of Jyväskylä |
| Ken Sakamura | University of Tokyo |
| Gerhard Schmitt | ETH Zürich |
| Jean Schweitzer | Siemens STZ, Saarbrücken |
| Jane Siegel | Carnegie Mellon University, Pittsburgh |
| Ralf Steinmetz | Darmstadt University of Technology |
| Konrad Tollmar | Royal Institute of Technology, Stockholm |
| Terry Winograd | Stanford University |

## Publication

Shin'ichi Konomi          GMD-IPSI, Darmstadt
Norbert A. Streitz        GMD-IPSI, Darmstadt

## Website

Jack Moffett             Carnegie Mellon University, Pittsburgh
Tom Pope                 Carnegie Mellon University, Pittsburgh
Jane Siegel              Carnegie Mellon University, Pittsburgh

# Table of Contents

**Methodology and Empirical Studies**

**Networked Home Environments**

**Demo and Poster Presentations**

Keynote Speech

# A Time for Talk and a Time for Silence

## Herbert A. Simon

Richard King Mellon University Professor of
Computer Science and Psychology
Carnegie Mellon University
5000 Forbes Avenue
Pittsburgh, PA 15213
Herb.Simon@cs.cmu.edu

## Abstract

The computer stores mountains of information which it communicates worldwide through an enormous bandwidth. We must learn to exercise severe, intelligent selectivity in mining our data mountains, and to communicate information in ways that will inform and not bury the recipients.

This is today's task of organizational design. Organizing combines human efforts efficiently, dividing the undertaking into separate but interdependent tasks and securing good coordination in their performance. An effective organization and its buildings balance opportunity for reflective deliberation against opportunity for mutual exchange of ideas and information. That balance is lost if talk drowns out silence. In our time, silence is unlikely to drown out talk.

## Biographical information

Herbert A. Simon's research has ranged from computer science to psychology, administration, and economics, with a focus upon human decision-making and problem-solving, especially in organizations. He uses the computer both to simulate human thinking and to augment it with artificial intelligence.

Simon received his B.A. (1936) and Ph.D. (1943) in political science at the University of Chicago. Since 1949, he has been on the faculty of Carnegie Tech, now Carnegie Mellon University, where he is Richard King Mellon University Professor of Computer Science and Psychology.

In 1978, he received the Alfred Nobel Memorial Prize in Economic Sciences, and in 1986 the National Medal of Science.

His books include *Administrative Behavior, Human Problem Solving*, jointly with Allen Newell, *The Sciences of the Artificial*, and his autobiography, *Models of My Life*.

# Boeing Operations Fleet Support:
# A Case Study in Integrated Workplace Design

Robert Hunt

Barclay Dean Interiors
Bellevue, WA, 98105 USA
bobdhunt@aol.com

Steven E. Poltrock

The Boeing Company
Seattle, WA, 98124 USA
steven.poltrock@boeing.com

**Abstract.** To investigate ways to improve organizational performance, The Boeing Company designed a pilot workplace for an engineering group in Everett, Washington. The concept for the project was to deploy physical space and technology in a manner that both mirrored core work processes and provided an environment facilitating complex teamwork and collaboration. The Future@Work, an experimental laboratory in Seattle, Washington that explore emerging trends in the workplace, significantly influenced the project design concept. The methodology used to support the design process was influenced by the workflow principles used in Boeing's airplane design and manufacturing processes; these processes draw heavily on the Lean Enterprise Model developed by the Massachusetts Institute of Technology in conjunction with a consortium of private enterprises. This paper documents the concepts, goals, planning methodology, resulting design, and subsequent performance of the pilot space.

**Keywords.** cooperative buildings, teamwork, workplace design, Lean manufacturing

## 1 Background

With technology revolutionizing the way people work, work process becoming more team based, real estate costs rising, and regional infrastructures stretched to the breaking point by population increases, the office must adapt. An experimental exhibit called Future@Work explored ways of employing integrated workspace design to improve effectiveness while reducing costs (Hunt, Vanecko & Poltrock, 1998). This exhibit inspired some large organizations, including The Boeing Company, to investigate how integrated workspace design could improve the functionality of their office environments while maintaining or reducing costs. This paper presents the methodology, design, and results of a pilot project at The Boeing Company.

The overall goal of the project was to explore creating white-collar environments utilizing a design methodology based upon Lean manufacturing principles (Womack, Jones, Roos, 1990). The project's sponsors believed this approach would develop work environments that more effectively leverage the integration of physical space and technology to enhance the organization's effectiveness and desired culture. The project was not intended to push the frontiers of technology, as in Streitz, Geißler, and Holmer (1998), but was expected to address collaboration and mobility using available commercial technology.

The organization selected for the pilot project was Operations Fleet Support (OFS), which manages airplane repair and kit modifications for Boeing's wide body aircraft. The scope of the pilot included approximately 200 people who were occupying 2,200 m$^2$ of office space. The organization had 13 m$^2$ per person, which is compliant with their space utilization targets. A key goal of the project was to avoid increasing the overall amount of real estate use. Another goal was to re-deploy as much of the existing furniture as possible.

The underlying factors causing the need for a redefinition of physical space are found in advances in information technology and changes in organizational structures and processes. Some of these trends are as follows:

- Information technologies are changing the ways people work together. Boeing teams often collaborate across distances (Mark, Grudin, & Poltrock, 1999).
- Companies such as Boeing have significantly re-engineered their business processes and their cultures are changing.
- Companies are placing more emphasis on the group work of multi-disciplinary teams over the individual work of people performing functional tasks.

## 2 Design Approaches

This project integrated three related design approaches: Lean manufacturing, activity-based planning, and integrated planning.

Lean manufacturing is a set of principles, concepts, and techniques used to improve production systems. It involves changing a work area to maximize efficiency, improve quality and safety, eliminate unnecessary motion and inventory, and save time. The initial step is often an Accelerated Improvement Workshop where the people who do the work identify improvements. Then they make the improvements right on the factory floor, resulting in improved employee morale and enhanced ability to deliver value to customers. In theory, the techniques of Lean can be applied to office environments. The major principles are to find out exactly what the customer wants, eliminate all waste, and make value flow continuously as pulled by the customer. The Lean approach was applied in this project, involving the organization in examining their processes and designing the environment to support their processes. Activity-based planning was the primary tool for gaining their involvement.

This project approached the design utilizing activity-based planning (Duffy, F., 1997). Traditionally Boeing's allocation of real estate has been based on status, not function. Space allocations are determined by rank, and individuals of similar rank receive basically the same space and same layout whether they spend most of their day in meetings, team activities, individual activities, or travel 80% of the time.

Activity-based planning is a methodology for determining the appropriate mix of individual and shared workspaces needed to best support the work processes of an organization. It begins with studies of the frequency, importance, content and location of individual and teamwork activities. Also studied are strategies to achieve overall organizational goals, existing use of space and technology, core work processes, ergonomic considerations, and the organization's current and desired cultural attributes.

Lean involves using the findings from activity-based planning to maximize performance. Organizational performance is the result of *people* organized by *business processes* supported by *technology* performing work in a *workplace*. In the design and manufacture of aircraft and other aerospace systems, Boeing embraces cross-functional integrated product teams. In the design and deployment of office systems, however, Boeing has not used an integrated planning methodology. Real estate and facilities, information systems, and human resources operate as independent functions. These groups may all support the same strategic vision or business process, but they rarely collaborate on how the interrelationships between their disciplines could be leveraged to impact organizational performance. In this pilot project, however, we formed an integrated team of expertise that included the Customer, Facilities, Information Systems, and Organizational Development.

# 3  Project Goals

Without discounting the influence of culture and status in the organization (Schein, 1992), the premise of the pilot was that effective environments should first serve the diverse activities of organizational populations, regardless of rank. The expected outcome was an improvement in productivity and more efficient space utilization.

The Boeing Facilities organization had the following goals for the project:
- Develop and explore a methodology for applying lean principles to the design of an office environment.
- Manage the construction costs within established Boeing benchmarks.
- Execute the solution within a space utilization target of 13 $m^2$ per employee.
- Design a solution that re-deploys as much of the existing assets as possible.
- Measure the results.

OFS, the customer organization had the following goals:
- Bring together the people who should be working together.
- Better facilitate interaction and teamwork.
- Provide an environment that better facilitates capture and transfer of knowledge.
- Leverage technology to enhance organizational productivity.
- Remove physical barriers to interaction.
- Create a sense of community.
- Align the physical movement of people and the electronic movement of information with the process structures of the organization.
- Build inherent flexibility and adaptability into the space.
- Improve the overall quality of the work environment.

# 4 Project Scope and Guidelines

The Operation Fleet Support group included about 190 people. The intent of the project was to redesign 2,200 m$^2$ using activity based planning methodology. Some general project parameters and constraints included the following:
- Design a concept suitable for large-scale system integration.
- Benchmark all costs against current Boeing cost models.
- Maintain a cost structure that adheres to established Boeing cost parameters for real estate and technology.
- Use life cycle costing to evaluate all relevant costs.

# 5 Organizational Findings

The work done by OFS runs a spectrum from the fairly routine development of standard kits for aircraft modification and repair, to highly complex work that results from urgent airplane repair requirements. Despite this variance in complexity, the workflow processes are similar for most groups within the organization. A key challenge is to efficiently balance a highly reactive, complex workload that requires multiple disciplines.

Work is coordinated and performed through a variety of mediums: face to face, electronic, and telephone. In general, the organization's work process is highly collaborative and face-to-face interaction is critical, with over 50% percent of the people spending over 50% of their time in face-to-face group activities. Most of these interactions are informal.

The majority of the work is performed on site, with the exception of incident repair teams, which on a moment's notice may go anywhere in the world for extended periods of time.

Despite the importance of cross-functional coordination in successfully executing their work, the organization was somewhat divided into functional camps and little informal cross-functional interaction occurred. As a result there was some disagreement between job functions over the roles of each functional unit. Furthermore, large amounts of undocumented "tribal knowledge" existed within different groups and management felt the efficient transfer of this knowledge was key to their productivity. However, the functional alignment of the organization and the isolating nature of the work environment impeded the transfer of this knowledge.

The initiation of the pilot project coincided with a major re-structuring of the organization from functional units to a series of integrated product teams termed *work cells*. These multi-disciplinary teams were to be organized around the major categories of work performed, and team members would be periodically rotated to facilitate overall organizational collaboration and the transfer of knowledge.

# 6 Old Office Environment

Operational Fleet Support was in a space filled with systems furniture workstations 1.7 m high. These workstations were allocated to individuals who were collocated by function, not by process. The workstations were in regimented groupings (see Figure 1). The uniform layout of these workstations did not consider individual differences in work process, and the space was isolating. Long orthogonal corridors led to pockets of rectilinear workstations. Co-workers could not see outside the confines of the 4-station clusters and anyone 1.8 m or less tall could not see anything but corridors. This spatial isolation created inefficiency as people wasted time searching for one another.

Seven senior managers were located in private offices distributed along the perimeters of the space. These offices were typically 15 m$^2$ and contained a desk, credenza and table.

There were many dysfunctional and unattractive features of this work environment. Although the organization's processes are predominately team based there were only two conference areas that serviced all 190 people and there were no informal meeting areas. Despite the complex process coordination required by the organization there was little ability to display shared information. The design was highly inflexible and did not accommodate any realignment of work processes or groups. There was poor access to shared storage, which resulted in redundant storage within individual workstations. There was no spatial, color, or lighting variation. This resulted in a lifeless, homogenous environment that emphasized monotony and anonymity.

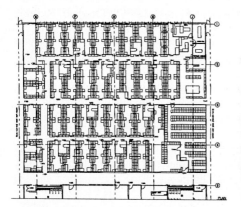

**Fig 1.** Floorplan of the original space

**Fig 2.** Photograph of the original space

# 7 Conceptual Design

The design team made the following conceptual recommendations for the design of the new space:

- Increase the amount and diversity of space available for team activities.
- Open the environment for better communication.
- Mirror the core business processes in the design of the space.
- Build an environment that can easily change as the organizations needs and processes change
- Improve the overall quality of the space through use of light, color and architectural features.
- Provide a sense of identity for OFS.
- Re-deploy as many assets as possible.
- Improve the access to and mobility of technology for both individuals and teams.
- Consolidate resources and provide better access to shared information and work tools.

With these recommendations in mind, the planning team developed a concept that envisioned providing a centrally located public area or "town square" that would become the hub of group activity for the OFS community. We approached the design as if building a city. There would be a centrally located main street providing for primary circulation and housing the community resources. Building outward from the main street, resources would become more individually allocated; just as in a city we move from shared group resources (stores, parks, etc.) to individually owned or controlled residences outward in the suburbs. The Main Street and town square would support informal and formal meeting areas, shared storage, equipment, etc., and the suburbs would house the work cells.

One of the main problems in the existing state was that the panel heights isolated people from one another. We determined that the height of the partitions should be lowered to provide better visual access to co-workers to facilitate the efficient flow of information. After examining several different options of work-cell layouts, the four-station cluster shown in Figure 4 was selected for the work cells. This design re-utilized approximately 40% of the existing assets.

Senior managers elected to move from working in a private office environment to open-plan workstations. There were three factors behind this decision.

1. They had the most space allocated and felt the performance of the organization would be better served if they sacrificed some individual space in order to provide more group spaces.
2. Senior managers are the core strategic support group and instead of being disbursed in private offices they wanted to be centrally collocated in the new environment. They believed this central collocation would facilitate improved strategic decision-making and reduce cycle time.
3. They wanted to lead by example and have their actions demonstrate "openness" to the organization.

PROPERTY OF ALUMNI LIBRARY
WENTWORTH INSTITUTE OF TECHNOLOGY

8

# 8 Final Design

Figure 3 shows the floor plan of the final design. Note the centrally located main street, which houses the majority of the shared resources of the organization. The work cells are distributed surrounding the main street and are grouped by the major types of work performed by OFS.

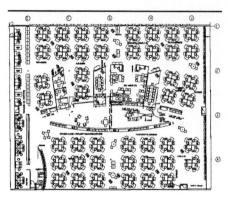

**Fig. 3** Floorplan of final design

Figure 4 shows a west facing view of the Main Street. This area serves dual functions as informal team space and as the central circulation corridor through the space. A 4.7m coffee counter serves as a central informal meeting point. All the furniture shown in Figure 4 is mobile and is designed to be moved to support ad-hoc team requirements. Multiple data drops built into the area facilitate access to data from a variety of locations.

Figure 5 shows a view of the work cell area with the wall defining the town square on the left. Each work cell is defined by a series of 4 workstation clusters. In order to facilitate immediate communication between team members, the divisions between workstations are only 1.4 m high. Each workstation consists of .79 x 1.7m primary worksurface and a mobile secondary worksurface. The user can choose where to locate the mobile worksurface. Additionally, these mobile worksurfaces can be pulled together for ad-hoc conferences.

Figure 6 shows the area for the management team. In the new design all senior managers share an open area that is centrally located off of the

**Fig. 4** Town square

**Fig. 5** Work Cell area

**Fig. 6** Senior Management area

town square. As with the work cells, each of the manager's workstations has a mobile table that can be configured in a variety of ways and can also be ganged together to form an ad-hoc conference space. The managers are bracketed on either side by enclosed conference rooms, providing ready access to privacy when needed.

Table 1 quantitatively compares attributes of the new design against the prior design. The variety of spaces available for individual and group work has increased significantly, but the overall real estate usage has not. Another key element of this comparison is the change in the overall percentage of space allocated for group activities. This reflects a better alignment of the space to support the highly collaborative nature of the organization's core work processes.

| Benchmark | Old Design | New Design |
|---|---|---|
| Population density | 13 m$^2$ | 12 m$^2$ |
| Average m$^2$ per manager | 19 m$^2$ | 7 m$^2$ |
| Average m$^2$ per non-manager | 4.2 m$^2$ | 3.6 m$^2$ |
| Percentage of space allocated to group activities | 10% | 35% |
| Percentage of space allocated to individual activities | 90% | 65% |
| Amount of enclosed meeting areas | 3 | 5 |
| Amount of non-enclosed meeting areas | 0 | 5 + |
| Ability to change configuration of individual and group spaces | None | High flexibility |
| Number of private offices | 7 | 0 |
| Access to, and mobility of technology to support group work | Data support confined to workstations and 1 conference room. 1 digital projection unit | Multiple plug and play locations in infrastructure |

## 9 Business Case Analysis

The project is being evaluated for its results in three major areas:
- Cost
- Impact on Productivity
- Impact on Morale/User Satisfaction

One of the goals for the project was to develop it within established Boeing cost benchmarks. Both initial costs and life cycle costs were evaluated against established benchmarks. The overall cost for the entire project was $962,000 or $437 per m$^2$. These figures include architectural design costs (exclusive of the activity based planning analysis) and all costs associated with the construction, furnishing, and provision of a new technological infrastructure for the space.

Even when considering the additional costs associated with any first time pilot project, most of these costs are in line with established industry benchmarks for space design and construction (IFMA,1997). Furthermore, many of these costs could be reduced if the concept was adopted on a large scale. Project costs exceeding normal Boeing targets predominately were in design fees, technology infrastructure and in upgrades in the environment's acoustic performance. It is likely that these costs would remain somewhat higher then in traditional designs.

A major goal of this pilot project was to investigate whether the resulting work environment would generate gains in productivity and improvements in morale. We evaluated the results as follows:
1. We measured the overall output of the organization against the amount of workers required to support the workload
2. We used pre and post occupancy surveys that measured people's impressions of the environment's effectiveness in supporting both individual and group work.
3. We benchmarked existing OFS productivity metrics and then compared their performance in the new environment against similar metrics in the old environment.

At the time of this paper the group has occupied the space for 4 1/2 months. In this short time the influence of the new environment on organizational performance has been dramatic.

The most significant finding has been the improvement in OFS's capacity to handle workload. Shortly after the organization moved into the space they had a headcount reduction of twenty (20) percent. Subsequent to the headcount reduction the organization's overall workload increased slightly. Although one might expect that such a dramatic downsizing would have negative impacts on work capacity and on quality, the reverse seems to be true. Workload has increased and quality metrics have generally maintained at prior levels and have improved in some cases.

Although the process change to multi-disciplinary work cells also occurred during this time, it is the spatial rearrangement of the organization that empowers the work cell's ability to operate. If the organization is able to maintain its workload and quality standards at reduced workforce levels this results in a savings to the Company of approximately $3.5 million a year. The only significant organizational changes that have occurred have been the spatial redesign and the process change to work cells. If only 25 percent of the improved performance is as a result of the environmental changes it would still mean that the project had a payback period of only a little over 1 year. Over time, the new design generates significant revenue for Boeing over the performance generated by the prior work environment.

The organization's management team believes unanimously that the new environment has significantly contributed to the improvement in the organization's workload capacity. The management team also believes that the collocation of senior managers in an open plan environment has improved strategic coordination between functional groups and enabled faster decision making.

For the most part, user satisfaction levels with the new environment have also increased; particularly in overall satisfaction with the quality of the environment and its ability to support collaborative activities. The one significant negative finding involves complaints about the reduced size of the individual work cell stations, which have 1m less worksurface then the old individual workstations. These complaints are valid and result from a last minute change in the computing solution for the work environment. Initially the plan had the occupants of the work cells utilizing laptop computers instead of desktop computers. This was mainly to support flexibility and information mobility. Another benefit was that the reduced size of the laptops allowed us to design smaller workstations. At the last minute the budget for the laptops was cancelled, and the workers now have large desktop monitors and CPU's taking space on worksurfaces that were designed to support laptops.

# References

1. Hunt, R., Vanecko, A., & Poltrock, S. (1998). Future@Work: An Experimental Exhibit Investigating Integrated Workplace Design. In *Proceedings of the First International Workshop on Cooperative Buildings* (CoBuild'98), Darmstadt, Germany (February 25-26, 1998). Lecture Notes in Computer Science, Vol. 1370. Springer - Verlag, Heidelberg, pp. 177-190.
2. Womack, J., Jones, D., Roos, D. (1990). The Machine that Changed the World, New York: Harper Collins
3. Duffy, Francis (1997). The New Office, Conran Octopus Ltd.: London
4. Mark, G., Grudin, J., & Poltrock, S.E. (1999). "Virtual Teams" in the Workplace. In *Proceedings of ECSCW'99,* Copenhagen.
5. Streitz, N.A., Geissler, J., & Holmer, T. (1998). Roomware for Cooperative Buildings: Integrated Design of Architectural Spaces and Information Spaces. In *Proceedings of the First International Workshop on Cooperative Buildings* (CoBuild'98), Darmstadt, Germany (February 25-26, 1998). Lecture Notes in Computer Science, Vol. 1370. Springer - Verlag, Heidelberg, pp. 4-21.
6. Schein, Edgar H. (1992). Organizational Culture and Leadership, San Francisco: Jossey-Bass Inc. pp. 115-122
7. International Facilities Management Association (1997). IFMA Research Report #18 Benchmarks III

# The GSA Adaptable Workplace Laboratory

Volker Hartkopf
Vivian Loftness
Azizan Aziz
Jayakrishna Shankavaram
Stephen R. Lee

Center for Building Performance and Diagnostics
School of Architecture
Carnegie Mellon University
Pittsburgh, PA 15213, U.S.A.
vh02@andrew.cmu.edu

**Abstract.** This paper is a progress report on the Adaptable Workplace Laboratory (AWL) within the Headquarters of the General Services Administration (GSA) of the United States of America. GSA owns, operates, leases and rents real estate for major U.S. Government agencies and departments, such as the Environmental Projection Agency, the Department of Energy, and the Department of Commerce. About 1.5 million office workers are housed nationwide in GSA owned, leased or rented buildings. Consequently, GSA is one of the world's largest landlords.

To demonstrate advanced systems integration concepts, to create a platform for experimentation with innovative information technologies, furniture, heating, ventilating, air-conditioning (HVAC), lighting and building control subsystems, and, most importantly, to create organizational know-how with the goal to better serve its clients, GSA is partnering with Carnegie Mellon University's Center for Building Performance and Diagnostics under the auspices of the National Science Foundation. This partnership is to create the Adaptable Workplace Lab (AWL), a evolutionary workspace on the 7th floor of the 3rd wing of the GSA Headquarters in Washington, DC. This 10,000 sq. ft. space will feature raised flooring, plug & play non-imbedded mobile technologies, and provide for individual control of environmental systems, workstations and workgroups.

**Key words:** Adaptable, innovative, flexible, workplace, GSA, systems integration, laboratory, individual control, grids & nodes, plug & play, sustainability

# 1  Purpose

The Adaptable Workplace Laboratory (AWL) is being pursued because:

- GSA should be leading innovations in organizational re-engineering, space planning and infrastructure development and through investing inside existing federal buildings to support innovations and change.

- GSA should use it's market strength to motivate industry to develop new generations of lighting, mechanical, networking controls, and interior systems to improve the quality of the work environment for the American worker. The testing and development of viable solutions will allow GSA to lead by example.

- GSA has an obligation to demonstrate and market the value of life cycle decision-making, where organizational and individual productivity are supported by "mission enabling" work environments, moving beyond least first-cost decision-making and universal solutions.

# 2  Four Major Goals

Workplaces are far more than overhead costs for the business (Figure 1).

- Workplaces support collective decisionmaking and multi-disciplinary projects

- Workplaces support individual concentration with needed resources and working quiet; and

- Workplaces offer social and technically rich environments to potentially attract and retain the most productive workers (Loftness et al. 1996a).

*Annualized Cost for an office employee*

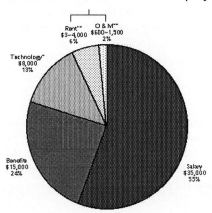

Figure 1: *Chief Financial Officers and stockholders must realize that saving on base building costs can be quickly outweighed by facility/ churn costs, and certainly productivity costs per person. The economic losses due to absenteeism and technical limitation losses in productivity will far outweigh the real estate expenses in the near term (Loftness et al. 1996a)*

14

The four major goals of the Adaptable Workplace Laboratory are as follows:

**Organizational Flexibility**

Demonstrating advances in organizational flexibility will require that the community of workplaces be reconfigurable on both annual and daily levels to ensure "organizational re-engineering" for collaboration – supporting regrouping and sharing for organizational productivity, creativity and innovation (Figure 2).

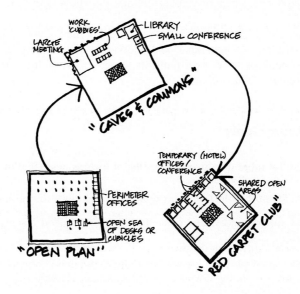

Figure 2: *Organizational flexibility is often reflected in changing space configuration. Dynamic tasks and dynamic organizations need the ability to continuously reconfigure workplace types over time and space.*

**Individual Productivity and Comfort**

Demonstrating advances in individual comfort and productivity will require that both interior system and engineering infrastructures are "plug and play" to ensure that furniture and space reconfigurations for individual productivity and creativity are immediately matched by technology and environment reconfigurations for comfort, health, and corresponding productivity.

### Technological Adaptability

Demonstrating advances in technological adaptability will require that vertical and horizontal pathways for connectivity are accessible and open and that both interior systems and engineering infrastructures support changing technological demands for horizontal and vertical worksurface, lighting, acoustics, thermal conditioning, ergonomics and group spaces.

### Environmental Sustainability

Demonstrating advances in environmental sustainability will require that both energy and materials are used effectively over a life cycle. Concepts such as system efficacy, user controls, micro-zoning for flex-time, just-in-time delivery of infrastructures, environmentally sustainable and healthy materials, natural conditioning should all be demonstrated and comparably measured to standard practice.

## 3  Major Lessons for Success from the Adaptable Workplace Laboratory Project

### 3.1  Assemble the entire team for preliminary design, a team dedicated to industrial design innovation.

Most office design projects are carried through early design without involving the disciplines that carry over 75% of the project budget and play a critical role in the long term flexibility of the solution. Mechanical and electrical engineers, lighting designers, and construction managers are rarely asked to join in the concept and preliminary design stages. Consequently typical engineering practice is reactive to previously made "architectural" and planning decisions. Idiosyncratic and customized "solutions" are the result, preventing adaptable/dynamic workplaces. The AWL design team includes:

#### Adaptable Workplace Design Team

- Architect/ Systems Integrator
- Interior Designer
- Mechanical Engineer
- Electrical/Lighting Engineer
- Telecommunications Designer
- Construction Manager

Presently, the linear process that takes workplace projects from conceptual/layout design through design development to working drawings, bid documents, and eventually shop details does not yield adequate performance in product selection, component integration for performance, or in the resulting aesthetics of the integrated system. Indeed, it is critical for flexible, adaptable and well detailed workplace designs to select or generate working drawings and shop details as a critical subset of preliminary design. A combination of one-to-one details and samples of off-the-shelf products alongside new component details developed collaboratively with the component manufacturer, are critical to the thermal, visual, acoustic, air quality and spatial performance of the workplace, as well as the long term integrity and refined aesthetics of the space.

In the AWL project over twenty components or component assemblies were identified that needed to be fully detailed in early design for performance and for aesthetic resolution of the space. Surprisingly, a significant number of these components have not developed significantly since the 1950's either in performance or aesthetic detailing. It seems that a majority of these products are either hidden from view by the architect or overwhelmed by applied aesthetics so that their visual inadequacies might be ignored. Unfortunately, their performance inadequacies (noise, air quality, ergonomics, glare, thermal discomfort, wear and tear) cannot be overlooked. The AWL project represents a concerted effort to put the best industrialized products on display, with an emphasis on selecting and designing building components in the early design stages, with hopes of greater collaborative involvement of industry in early design decisionmaking.

## 3.2 Begin with optimum workspace standards

The Office of the Future provide productive work environments for each multi-tasking individual, which can only be achieved with careful study of existing work processes and workspaces along with alternative recommendations for improvement (Figure 3). Instead of minimum and universal standards, workspace design standards must include clear commitments for each work setting to the following:

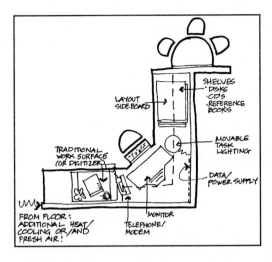

Figure 3: The all-capable knowledge worker who is expected to be creator, producer, manager and promoter at once needs multiple, diverse worksurfaces and storage.

## Setting Optimum Design Standards for Each Individual

- Workspace size
- Linear feet of worksurface
- Linear feet of storage
- Ergonomics
- Acoustics – balancing privacy & interaction
- Connectivity – data, power, voice
- Lighting control
- Thermal control
- Air quality control
- Access to the natural environment

The AWL project has set these optimum standards in a 30-page document that includes: 80 square feet minimum per "multi-tasking" individual with primary residence here; 15 linear feet of work surface and storage; ergonomic chairs and keyboard support; stackable partitions for variable workspace closure; split ambient and task lighting for user control; air to the desk with user control; and, especially important for the US, seated views of a window that opens;  as well as an outdoor work/relaxation space for the workgroup.

18

### 3.3 Generate multiple layouts for the dynamic workplace

Typically, private and governmental renovation projects start with top-down interviews and a series of alternative layouts for furniture and walls for executive approval. After such a limited consensus is achieved, a single floor plan is carried forward and mechanical, electrical, telecommunications and lighting professionals are involved (often linearly) to customize an infrastructure for the accepted plan. Then the client's needs change, and a game of iterative catch-up is started. The result is a redundant and often mismatched assembly of lights, diffusers, outlet boxes, closets and furniture components with no "as-built" documentation and badly located zone controllers. Such an assembly is typically further compromised by value engineering, which eliminates important features to stay within a first cost budget.

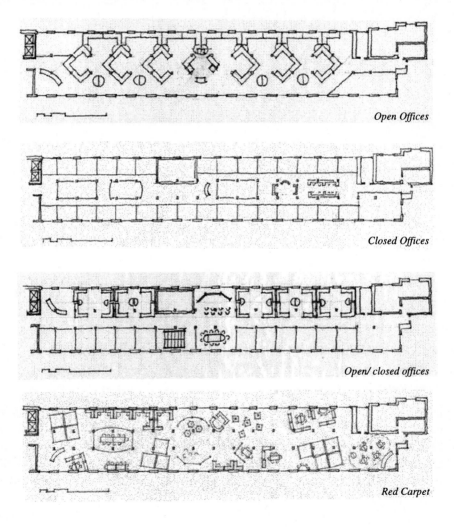

*Open Offices*

*Closed Offices*

*Open/ closed offices*

*Red Carpet*

Figure 4: *AWL project designer's generated multiple workgroup layouts capable of supporting continuous organizational dynamics.*

The AWL is to support individual productivity with organizational and technological change and environmental sustainability. To achieve these goals multiple workgroup layouts and related flexible infrastructures must be designed by the entire architecture and engineering team.

Consequently the AWL project's designers generated multiple viable workgroup layouts representing a range of workstyles. The combination of these layouts were used to generate the flexible infrastructures for the workplace capable of supporting continuous space dynamics. The layouts themselves have continued to evolve as the client's needs evolve, with confidence that the overall kit of parts (furniture and infrastructure) is capable of accepting present and future individual, organizational and technological demands (Figure 4).

### 3.4  Commit to high-performance flexible infrastructures – grids and nodes

Typical workplace renovations select a single floor plan in design development and then proceed to develop a customized and fixed set of engineering drawings for cooling, lighting, networking, fire and plumbing of that set of plans.   Not only are these "embedded" engineering systems obsolete after the organizational change, they are often obsolete before occupancy, as space planning continues to evolve past the first hand-off of drawings to the engineers.

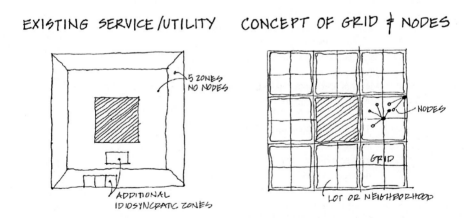

Figure 5: *We must abandon the large zone approaches to thermal conditioning and lighting, which are intended to blanket hundreds of people with adequate environmental quality. The dynamics of technology, workstation density and teaming concepts make these zones even less capable of delivering adequate environmental quality than 20 years of survey have revealed.*

FIGURE 6:   **INTER-DISCIPLINARY DECISIONMAKING TO ENSURE EFFECTIVE, FLEXIBLE, SYSTEMS INTEGRATION**

## Ten Major Decisions:   Interiors

1.   neighborhood clarity & shared services
2.   layers of ownership, multiple work environments
3.   functional support for shared work processes
4.   functional support for individual work processes
5.   layers of closure, open/closed variations
6.   layers of mobility
7.   levels of personalization
8.   infrastructures to support environmental control
9.   infrastructures to support technical control
10.   healthy, detailed, aesthetic environment

## Nine Major Decisions: Connectivity
## Data, power, voice, security, environment, monitoring, controls

1.   central vs. distributed central services
2.   central vs. distributed cores for vertical distribution
3.   central vs. distributed satellite closets
4.   ceiling versus raised floor horizontal distribution
5.   harnessed data, power, voice, environment wiring or independent
6.   terminal units bundling all services - data, power, voice, environment
7.   monitoring and controls
8.   system interfaces
9.   relocatability of shared services

## Six Major Decisions:  Lighting

1.   daylighting as a dominant light source vs. visual interest
2.   split task and ambient vs. combined task-ambient
3.   relocatable fixtures with changing densities
4.   type of fixture
5.   level of user control and automation
6.   integrity and material sustainability

## Ten Major Decisions: HVAC

generation, distribution, terminal units, controls

1.   splitting ventilation and thermal conditioning
2.   air-based vs. water based thermal conditioning
3.   ceiling vs. floor distribution
4.   thermal zone size
5.   user relocatable terminal units
6.   levels of control: directional, speed, temperature, quantity of outside air
7.   load reduction/ energy conservation
8.   load balancing by thermal redistribution or mass
9.   natural conditioning opportunities
10.   system integration opportunities

The Adaptable Workplace Laboratory reflects a simultaneous commitment to changing space configurations, as well as changing infrastructures for air, temperature control, network access, lighting control, exhaust and material management. As a result, the entire design team must be dedicated to high performance, flexible infrastructures, separating out the fixed grid of service from the reconfigurable nodes for delivering that service to the individual (Loftness et al. 1996b, Figures 5 & 6).

The AWL project has established dual demonstrations of flexible infrastructures connected through the raised floor:

**HVAC** - For cooling and heating in the south zone, there are 20 wall-mounted hydronic heat pumps as nodes for individually controlled thermal comfort, fed by the existing chilled and hot water supply "grid' of the building (Figure 7). For ventilation in the south zone, individual fan diffusers at every workstation (a combination of floor and desk diffusers or nodes) is fed by a heat recovering air handler combined with an underfloor plenum (the grid) for supply of conditioned air. For cooling, heating and ventilation in the north zone, there are 24 wall-mounted hydronic induction units as nodes for individually controlled thermal comfort, fed by a ducted supply of conditioned air (the grid) using displacement ventilation to ensure air quality. In order to provide flexibility in modifying or supplementing the HVAC devices, manifold piping with quick-connect valves are being installed at the perimeter (at a seven foot spacing) throughout the length of the facility. In both cases, additional water -based cooling will be required for central spaces - a combination of ceiling-hung radiant cooling elements (possibly utilizing the sprinkler system as the source) and hydronic heat pumps. The central air handlers for each zone have been selected for ventilation with the highest air quality, while considering energy efficiency, noise, and maintainability.

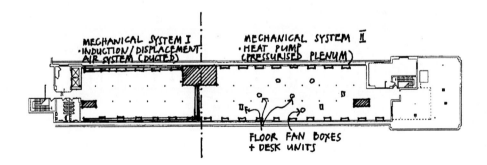

Figure 7: *The AWL will demonstrate high-performance flexible HVAC infrastructures, for individually controlled thermal comfort.*

**Lighting –** The Adaptable Workplace Laboratory demonstrates a split ambient and task lighting strategy to support a high level of spatial dynamics. For ambient lighting, a series of high-voltage/low-voltage tracks have been introduced at every column line to allow the "plug-and-play" addition of uplights for uniform ambient conditions of 30 footcandles and downlights for spotlighting. Relocatable task lights with articulated arms and occupancy sensors will be introduced at every workstation to take light levels up to the 50-80 footcandles needed for detailed work. There are 54 linear tracks (each 12 or more feet in length) hung several feet from the sloped roof/ceiling, 150 uplight fixtures (with some downlighting), and between 50 and 100 task lights depending on user demand. The north and south zone will represent two different lighting track manufacturers and their uplight fixtures, as well as two or more different task light manufacturers. Shared spaces with dedicated functions such as service "pubs", conference rooms and reception areas will have additional specialized fixtures that can plug into the grid of service with relocatability.

**Connectivity-** The GSA Adaptable Workplace Lab will demonstrate plug and play access to data, power and voice (Figure 8). Twelve prefabricated satellite closets feed data, power and voice cabling through underfloor wire baskets to intermediate underfloor distribution modules, establishing the grid of service. Each workstation is then given at least one floor or desktop relocatable outlet box with combined access to data, power, and voice. There are 40 underfloor power distribution boxes and 40 underfloor data distribution boxes to support from 80 to 120 floor and or desk boxes for data, power and voice connectivity. Just as in the lighting and HVAC systems, the location and density of the nodes for "connectivity can be modified on a continuous basis to support workplace dynamics, with the benefit of just-in-time purchasing of additional nodes with growing demand.

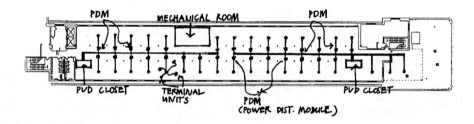

Figure 8: *The AWL will demonstrate plug and play access to data, power and voice.*

### 3.5   Challenge the industry to develop fully prototyped, grid-and-node solutions

The AWL project has taken on the task of challenging both industry and the design professionals to fully design/engineer/specify each building sub-system for performance. All generating, distributing and terminal units are being engineered and realized by forming grids of service and relocatable and addable nodes of service. These systems do not necessarily require fully meshed, embedded or integrated products, but can be a tested assembly of compatible products for building service performance.   In the AWL project, full-system design has included: lighting power tracks as grids for lighting service and relocatable fixtures, sensors, and controllers as nodes; outside air handlers for ventilation combined with strategic duct runs or plenum supply as grids of HVAC service and distributed, relocatable fan boxes and diffusers as nodes; satellite closets, cabling in open wire baskets and power and data distribution boxes as grids of connectivity service, and relocatable and reconfigurable outlet boxes as nodes of service.   Because of the plug-and-play nature of grids, an excessive number of nodes will not need to be installed in this workplace laboratory until needed.  This allows for the just-in-time purchasing of user interfaces for each of the buildings major subsystems and for the possibility of long term ownership and relocation of high performance and aesthetic industrially designed and tested nodes.

### 3.6   Ensure that work process and furniture decisionmaking is both first and last

Even if a client group does not change as dramatically as in the AWL project, changing work processes demand an active regeneration of neighborhood and workstation guidelines during the 6-12 months of infrastructure design, engineering, bidding, and construction.

This regeneration of the performance program is only possible because of the capabilities of the flexible infrastructures to support the environmental and technical requirements of end-of-project space planning. With the design of infrastructures that are capable of supporting multiple layouts, and the selection of grids of service with adaptable and relocatable nodes in an accessible plenum design,  it is possible to address workplace issues both first and last in design.

As a result of this design process, the final selection of the full range of AWL furniture components, worksurfaces, partitions, chairs, task lights, storage, and teaming spaces could be selected at the latest possible moment to meet the needs of the latest individuals and workprocesses.  These furniture components must still meet the performance standards of all of the "base building" components and systems - relocatable, scalable (can be added and subtracted), user customizable, maximum environmental performance (visual, acoustic, thermal, air quality, integrity), and compatible with the other building systems. Moreover, these furniture components should represent the best industrialized products affordable through comparable performance specifications and competition. It is critical that the design team be well versed on innovation in the furniture industry, international space planning approaches, and the latest research on work process and its relationship to workplace planning. As previously described, there are at least 10 major interior design decisions that must be made in a collaborative process.

To make these decisions with the entire design team and client group requires the preparation of a series of 3-D CAD alternatives based on a range of industrial modular components. The intention of these multiple solution sets is to make the initial, move-in decision for space configuration. The alternative approach drawings need to be three dimensional (instead of 2-D line drawings) because neighborhood clarity, layers of closure and mobility, and infrastructures are only apparent in three dimensions. The alternative approach drawings also need to be 3-D because the path out of "Dilbertsville" is not the elimination of square corners which serve a major purpose, but the introduction of dynamics in the third dimension (heights of walls and elements) and the introduction of playful, mobile worktools and personalization components that the industry is rapidly developing today. The development of on-line alternatives can also allow for the rapid substitution of manufactured components to ensure that competitive products can deliver the solution. Finally, the on-line alternatives - made up of a kit-of-parts of interior components - can visualize the capability of the space to evolve after move-in to support changing work processes and individual or group needs.

The AWL project will demonstrate several different workstation furniture approaches with several commonalties. All of the systems will be stackable panel systems with acoustically absorbing panels and appropriate light reflection characteristics. Floor-based worksurfaces will be the standard, with ergonomic keyboard supports, ergonomic chairs and articulated arm task lights, of elegant and sustainable materials. The workstation solutions selected have the capability to stack up to a ceiling level, and some can support doors and a level of closure that will enable the organization to evolve from open to closed planning, and from individual to group workplaces - and back again. In addition, the AWL project will strive to include fun and innovative solutions to a number of shared office amenities - the business center, the service pub, the multi-media conference room, the hoteling center, and the reception area. The availability of an adjacent rooftop terrace for the 7th floor Adaptable Workplace Laboratory will allow the creation of an outdoor work and relaxation space that recognizes a motivational need for access to the natural environment.

# 4 The Adaptable Workplace Lab (AWL) as a Research Platform

The AWL supports research in advanced workplaces in two ways: a) as an experimental building delivery process; and b) as a research platform to test building performance in the occupied setting. Beyond researching the results of the experimental building delivery process, the AWL will serve as a test-bed for a number of research questions pertaining to each of the four major objectives for workplaces of the future:

**Individual Comfort, Health, and Productivity**

AWL will lead to improved worker productivity and high levels of user satisfaction: Determine the benefits for the different levels of control of environmental parameters. Examine the behavioral patterns of use of individual control. Explore the impact of access to the natural environment on user satisfaction, health and well-being. Study the combined effects of ventilation systems and material emissions in an occupied setting. Assess the impact of high performance workplaces on user productivity.

**Organizational Flexibility**

GSA will find the workplace to be easily adjusted to changing organizational requirements: Define, operationalize and validate measures of flexibility in the workplace. Determine the marginal performance benefits resulting from the adoption of advanced interior and infrastructure systems for different types of organizations with varying levels and types of churn.

**Technological Adaptability**

GSA will find the laboratory to be easily adaptable to rapidly evolving computer supported collaborative work environments: Measure the adaptability of advanced workplaces, to the hardware, software and workprocesses affected by work environments.

## Environmental Sustainability

These achievements will come at significant energy and material savings over present good practices: Measure the energy and resource use of the facility compared to norms in practice, as well as the health and well-being of the occupants. Examine the life-cycle impact (pollutant generation, energy use) of advanced systems vs. conventional systems, components and materials, in the occupied setting. Determine the impact of advanced technologies for utility demand side management, particularly in the context of utility deregulation and real time pricing.

### Potential AWL Performance & Productivity Studies

#### a.  Organizational Change and Organizational Effectiveness
- Time & Material Study of Space Change Costs
- Product/Service Timeliness, Innovation, Quality and Learning Studies
- Questionnaire Study of Situational Awareness/ Collaboration & Corporate Identity
- Calendar study of Frequency/Success of  Formal and Informal Meetings

#### b.  Individual Effectiveness/ Productivity
- Questionnaire Study of User Perception of Effectiveness/Productivity/ Motivation
- Keystroke Monitoring of Unbroken Work Effort (e-flow)
- Human Resources record comparison of Absenteeism, Health Costs and Compensation

#### c.  Technological Place and Change
- Questionnaire Study of Appropriateness of Existing Connectivity
- Comparative Study of Material, Cost and Time Records
- Comparative Study of Flexibility of AWL Infrastructure

#### d.  Environmental Place and Change
- Instrumentation & Questionnaire Study of Environmental Quality
- Instrumentation & Questionnaire Study of Acoustical Conditions with Space/Furniture Modifications

#### e.  Sustainability
- Data Mining and Simulation Study of Energy Use – HVAC, Lighting, Process
- LEED/Green documentation and Comparisons of Material Toxicity –
- Literature and Field study of Material/ Resource Use with Churn –
- Literature and Field study of Materials & Maintenance–

The AWL project and the subsequent multi-year research will provide a major stepping stone for the development of improved building practices, considering the entire life cycle of facilities, their materials, components and flexibly integrated systems.

## 5 Conclusion: Flexible, Sustainable, Quality Workplace Environments Is an Obvious Result

Flexible and adaptable work environments are critical to environmental quality and sustainability. User based, relocatable infrastructures help to ensure indoor environmental quality – thermal, visual, air quality, and acoustic quality – critical to occupants' health and productivity (Hartkopf et al. 1997, Hartkopf et al. 1996). These relocatable infrastructures also support organizational and technological change without waste, supporting simple moves of service interfaces with the workstations, in contrast to the demolition required for embedded infrastructures. The just-in-time purchasing of nodes (outlets, diffusers, lights) helps to reduce redundancy and waste, and supports the concept of purchasing quality products in the place of least-cost, throw-away components.

The careful selection of materials and assemblies ensures that there is less pollutant outgassing and fewer "sinks" for absorbing indoor pollutants. The careful selection of furniture for human anthropometric and ergonomic quality helps to reduce muscular-skeletal strain and overall work stress. Access to the natural environment in the form of operable windows and terraces for daylight and natural ventilation also reduce work stress and support the optimum use of natural conditioning energies before the use of mechanical and electrical systems are necessary. This reflects an ascending strategy to cooling and lighting, with significant benefits in energy conservation and human health. Finally, the AWL project has pursued high-performance multi-module HVAC systems: air handlers, heat pumps, induction units, and control strategies for both energy effectiveness and indoor environmental quality.

The combination of indoor environmental quality for health and productivity with material and energy resource conservation makes the Adaptable Workplace Laboratory of the General Services Administration an important demonstration, research and learning environment within the US federal government.

# References

1. Hartkopf V., Loftness, V,, Mahdavi, A., Lee, S., Shankavaram, J., (1997), An integrated approach to design and engineering of intelligent buildings — The Intelligent Workplace at Carnegie Mellon University, Automation in Construction 6 (1997) 401-415, Elsevier Science.
2. Hartkopf, V., Loftness, V., Shankavaram, J., Tu, K., (1996), Facilities Managers as Indispensable Partners in Corporate Strategic Planning,, World Workplace (October 6-8, 1996), (IFMA), Salt Lake City, Utah.
3. Loftness, V., Beckering, J., Miller, W., Rubin, A. (1996a), Re-valuing Buildings – Investing Inside Buildings to Support Organizational and Technological Change through Appropriate Spatial, Environmental and Technical Infrastructures. (1996), Steelcase Inc., Grand Rapids, MI.
4. Loftness, V., Hartkopf, V., Mahdavi, A., Shankavaram, J. (1996b), Flexible Infrastructures for Environmental Quality, Productivity and Energy Effectiveness in the Office of the Future, International Facility Management Association (IFMA) – (Intellibuild 1996), Anaheim, CA.

# The Collaborative Building:
# Mediating between Climate and Interior Quality

Vivian Loftness   Volker Hartkopf   Stephen Lee
Ardeshir Mahdavi  Paul Mathew  Jaykrishna Shankavaram  Azizan Aziz

Center for Building Performance and Diagnostics
School of Architecture
Carnegie Mellon University
Pittsburgh, PA 15213, U.S.A.
vh02@andrew.cmu.edu

**Abstract.** Collaborative environments can be understood to be "enabling" environments, which enable individuals and organizations to be creative and productive. Buildings can be seen to operate as enabling environments at different yet inter-related levels: 1) as mediator between outdoor and indoor environments; 2) as provider of appropriate indoor physical settings; 3) as host to information technology for an organization. This paper focuses on the first level, and describes a range of architectural alternatives for improved indoor environments in commercial buildings. The paper uses illustrative examples of high-performance buildings in the U.S. and Europe, contrasting their respective approaches to the integration of enclosure, mechanical, and lighting systems.

**Keywords.** cooperative buildings, architecture, interior quality, energy effectiveness, environmental sustainability

## Why Are "Enabling" Buildings Important?

In the U.S., the best cost-justification for high-performance office buildings could be employee retention and organizational productivity. Even at companies such as Sun Microsystems, the average turnover rate is as high as 15%. In tight employment markets, workplaces with high indoor quality may be the critical condition to improve both the attraction and retention of knowledge workers. The importance of this is underscored given that *a)* it takes up to one year to effectively integrate a new employee within an organization, and *b)* it takes up to 2-3 years to reestablish a team with new employees (Siegel 1998).

# What Causes "Disabling" Environments in Buildings?

In addition to the potential contributions of inadequate enclosure, and mechanical system engineering or operation, there are a number of architectural factors which contribute to poor indoor environments and high energy use in buildings:

Deep Buildings
Sealed Buildings
Climate-Indifferent Buildings
Basement/Warehouse Workplaces
   (spaces never intended for human occupancy)
"Worst Case" System Sizing
Duct and Control Albatross
Huge Zones, Tiny Workplaces
Fixed Infrastructures
Fast Tracking and Renovation on top of occupants
No System Modifications with Technology & Spatial Changes
Percentage Reductions in maintenance and repair budgets and staff

Each of these factors contributes to conditions that demonstrate poor indoor quality and energy ineffectiveness. These buildings are least-cost, cannot accommodate organizational or technological change, and will become the next generation of obsolete buildings. There is mounting evidence that many buildings in the U.S. do not provide adequate indoor quality (Hartkopf et al. 1994, Collet et al. 1993, Kirkbride et al. 1990, Loftness and Hartkopf 1989, NIOSH 1989, Woods 1989). At the same time, numerous studies have shown that buildings in the U.S. consume at least 30-50% more energy than they need, in order to deliver present environmental qualities (Drake et al. 1991, Mahdavi et al. 1995, Milam 1992, Shavit and Wruck 1993).

The U.S. is the only industrialized country in which deep section buildings and basements or warehouses are legal workplaces, despite the loss of daylight and access to natural ventilation. The fixed nature of the infrastructure makes upgrades rare and maintenance difficult. Moreover, the dynamic building activities that are trademarks of the information age cannot be effectively accommodated. This paper will outline architecturally driven steps towards improved indoor environments, reducing building obsolescence, and improving global environmental sustainability.

# Step 1: Architecture Unplugged - Regionalism

Imagine designing commercial buildings in locations where brown-outs and rolling black-outs were common, as they are in many parts of the world. The architecture that would evolve would be entirely regional in character, would use daylight and natural ventilation to its maximum potential, and carefully balance the assets and liabilities of the climate (HUD 1978).

## Location, Location, Location

Ian McHarg argues that "the quest for appropriate architectural expression should respond to the pressure of natural regions, including ecosystems/ biomes, physiographic regions, energy regions, material regions, and hazard regions" (IEA 1998). Approaching the selection of building sites by careful evaluation of ecological stress and opportunity would significantly change present decisions about where development and growth should occur worldwide.

## Environmental Massing - Height, Depth and Orientation

At the same time, decisions about the building mass, the aspect ratio and orientation of buildings also have a major impact on energy use and indoor environmental quality. Neither the tallest building in the world nor the largest building under one roof offer any gains for either energy or indoor quality. Indeed, these buildings guarantee significantly higher energy loads in almost every climate, since they eliminate any use of daylight, natural ventilation, or internal heat dissipation through building surfaces (Mahdavi et al. 1996). They also guarantee that the building must be abandoned in a power outage. If energy use and indoor quality are a driver for building form, then the next generation buildings would strive for campus planning with limited height and appropriate orientation for achieving environmental comfort for a maximum percentage of the year, "unplugged". The Robert L. Preger Intelligent Workplace at Carnegie Mellon University (Hartkopf et al. 1997) has a cross-section that permits adequate natural ventilation and daylighting, such that the building can run with out any "artificial" thermal conditioning and lighting for 6-8 months in the year, depending on weather conditions (figure 1).

## Regional Enclosure Materials

Regionalism would also require a shift away from the pervasive sameness of building enclosures, away from international styles with unshaded glass and uninsulated concrete, steel and aluminum or the post-modernism of today. "Architecture Unplugged" would require serious attention to the management of solar gain, heat transfer, moisture migration, and day-night load balancing. These mass, color, venting, and thermal insulation characteristics are also key to energy, natural resources and material conservation in buildings, requiring entirely regional solutions.

## Regional Openings and Controls

Finally, regional design requires far more serious attention to opening size, location, materials and controls. Windows are both the weakest elements in an enclosure for heat loss, solar gain, and infiltration and the most critical to heat dissipation, natural ventilation and daylighting – key to both energy conservation and health. Designing for "Architecture Unplugged" would yield a new generation of regionally-appropriate residential and commercial buildings, with openings and windows that recognize the wisdom of native solutions while introducing the opportunities of 21st century innovations.

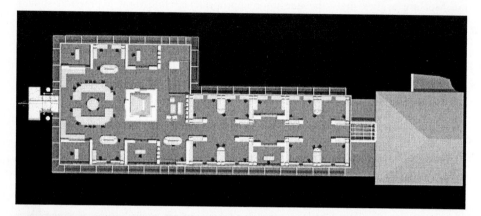

**Figure 1:** Plan (top) and sectional view (above) of the Robert L. Preger Intelligent Workplace at Carnegie Mellon University. The narrow cross section allows for the use of natural conditioning and daylighting throughout the workspace, with no artificial conditioning for 6-8 months in a year.

# Step 2: Windows for Workers (and *not just* Windows NT™)

In North America, it is time to rediscover the importance of the window for commercial buildings - offices, schools, hospitals and clinics, courthouses, laboratories and more. Windows, indeed operable windows, are a key to comfort, health, productivity and resource conservation in the technologically advanced society. Many of the architectural/engineering approaches to improved indoor environments described in this paper are dependent on the access of each occupied space to operable windows - for natural ventilation, daylighting, passive solar heating, and load balancing.

Commercial building energy use in the U.S. is evenly distributed between lighting, cooling and heating (EIA 1995). In the Intelligent Workplace "living laboratory" at Carnegie Mellon University, effective window design has offset over 80% of the electric lighting loads – about 0.2 $W.ft^{-2}$ (2 $W.m^{-2}$) daytime vs. new building standards of 1.0 $W.ft^{-2}$ (10 $W.m^{-2}$). This laboratory has also eliminated over 50% of the ventilation and cooling loads typical to commercial office buildings in the region, and utilizes passive solar heating (figures 2 and 3).

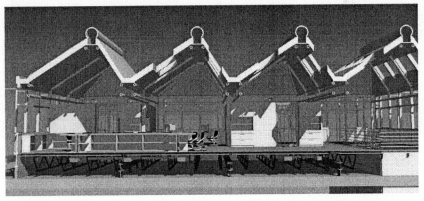

**Figure 2:** Longitudinal section through the Robert L. Preger Intelligent Workplace at Carnegie Mellon University, which incorporates natural ventilation (cross and stack), daylighting and passive solar heating

Windows provide a number of additional opportunities. While the U.S. struggles with 20 cfm/person (9.4 $l.s^{-1}$) outside air requirements through large central systems, European buildings introduce greater air change rates and full "purge" cycles through dedicated ventilation systems, and include windows in the ventilation system design. Scandinavian engineers require that all occupied spaces be provided with operable windows to cope with thermal and pollution overloads. Sunlight entering through windows provide a natural disinfectant, and provides basic "nutrients" for humans and plants alike. Hospital studies have shown that patient recovery times are shorter in rooms that have windows with views (Ulrich 1984). A study in North Carolina schools reveals statistics that link windows and daylight to higher test results, student health and faster growth (Nicklas and Bailey 1996). Wilson and Hedge identified that operable windows, clear glass, and constant volume ventilation systems, correlates with the healthiest building scores in a UK national survey (Wilson and Hedge 1987). This echoes the conviction of the European Community that all occupied spaces should have operable windows, and that no worker should sit more than 7 meters from a window. Indeed, workplaces with windows and views may be the critical condition to improve the attraction and retention of knowledge workers.

**Figure 3:** Interior view of the Robert L. Preger Intelligent Workplace. 75% of the façade area is glazed with high-visibility glass, maximizing daylight use throughout the year.

## Step 3: Architecture as a Mechanical and Lighting System - Shape and Drape Innovations

While the Information Technology industry argues that technology makes worker co-location less necessary, the U.S. real estate industry is trying to promote 30,000 square feet floor plates as the new minimum for organizational re-engineering. While the U.S. is building these megablocks with dominantly internalized spaces, Scandinavian countries have a very different vision of the office of the future (figure 4). These massing issues have major implications on the potential of architecture to act as mechanical and lighting system.

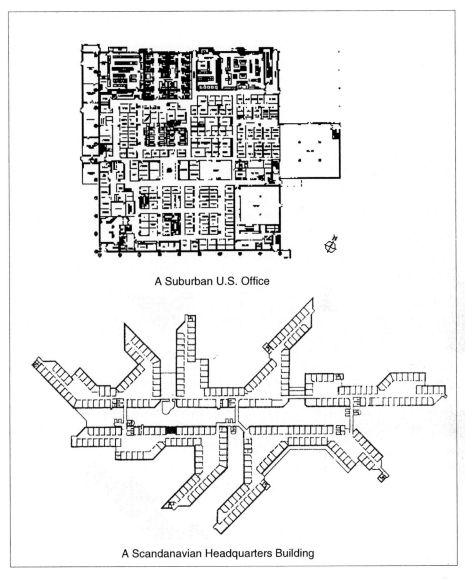

A Suburban U.S. Office

A Scandanavian Headquarters Building

**Figure 4:** Two contrasting approaches to building massing and environmental quality (U.S. vs. Europe)

## Depth, Height, Cross Section and Orientation for Natural Ventilation

In Europe, a number of architects have recently taken on the challenge of designing commercial office buildings without any mechanical system or with a minimum of mechanical systems. These efforts have required collaborative design processes with a major rethinking of the depth, height, cross section and orientation of the buildings. The mechanical system that is typically eliminated first is cooling and, secondly, central ventilation. At the same time, new architectural projects represent a balance of natural conditioning and mechanical conditioning approaches. The Commerzbank (by the Foster/Ove Arup/Josef Gartner team) is one of the tallest buildings in Frankfurt (over 50 floors), yet has operable windows and daylit office spaces (figure 5). Through the ingenious design of stacking open air courts, this high rise breaks down both wind speeds and stack effects to allow office windows to be opened, with refrigerant cooling used only a minority of the time (Herzog 1996).

## Day-Night Load Balancing

A second strategy for eliminating the need for mechanical cooling is the use of day-night load balancing strategies. Explored in the completion of a number of State Office projects in California, under architect Sim Van der Ryn in the 1970s, load balancing through night ventilation can successfully reduce or eliminate cooling loads in climates with diurnal swings. Lloyds of London is possibly the best known building which is utilizing night ventilation of the structure to effectively eliminate cooling for most of the following day - even with the massive influx of up to 6000 trading agents each morning (Hartkopf et al. 1991). A key component of the successful introduction of time-lag cooling, was the underfloor air system and exposed waffle slab ceilings, combined with carefully monitored dew point temperatures for avoiding overcooling and condensation.

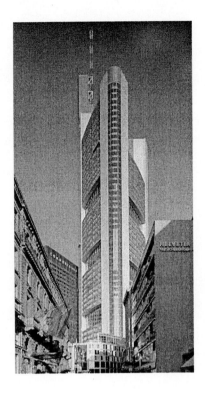 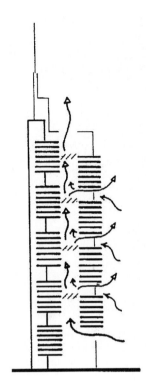

**Figure 5:** The Commerzbank building, by the Foster/Ove Arup/Josef Gartner team is one of the tallest buildings in Frankfurt, yet has natural ventilation up to the top floor. Left: exterior view; Right: Sectional sketch showing ventilation scheme. (Source: Herzog 1996)

## Depth, Cross Section and Orientation for Daylighting & Passive Solar

The shape and enclosure design of buildings (shape and drape solutions) are also critical to the effective use of daylighting and passive solar heating in commercial buildings. Daylight is without question, an abundant, healthy and manageable light source for commercial buildings. Numerous buildings have been completed in the last decade that demonstrate the even, effective distribution of daylight through bilateral lighting, atria and skylights, in combination with light shelves (figure 6). These buildings have dramatically reduced electric lighting loads, and they introduce the full range of daylight attributes into commercial spaces, as previously described.

**Figure 6:** The Robert L. Preger Intelligent Workplace at Carnegie Mellon University has a layered enclosure, with dynamic light-redirection louvers, operable windows, high visibility glass, and internal shading devices, to maximize daylighting and solar control

# Step 4: Mechanical System Innovations for Improved Thermal and Air Quality

The mechanical systems community - both engineers and manufacturers - need to be active players in the continued exploration and development of architectural approaches to cooling, ventilating, lighting and heating commercial buildings. The mechanical industry must also invest in the development of a new generation of flexible, high-performance systems for today's dynamic buildings – both new and retrofit solutions.

### Split Systems - Ventilation and Thermal Conditioning

The most critical move will be the realization that thermal conditioning systems must be separated from ventilation. Combined thermal and ventilation systems, which typically lead to pressurized buildings, has eliminated the opportunity for operable windows, not just in high rises, but in low-rise offices, schools, community centers and more.

Once a commitment has been made to splitting these two infrastructures, numerous mechanical innovations arise. The Europeans have introduced *displacement ventilation* systems with water-based heating and cooling (radiant, fan-coil, induction units or heat pumps). These displacement air systems introduce conditioned outside air in low velocity floor plenums to provide silent delivery of conditioned breathing air. Cooling is then provided through a second system, typically water based fan-coils, heat pumps or radiant cooling elements (figure 7).

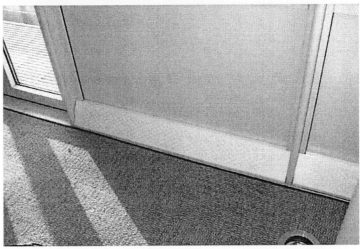

**Figure 7**: Split thermal and ventilation systems provide greater thermal control, and improved ventilation. In the Intelligent Workplace, low-pressure perimeter diffusers provide displacement ventilation (above), with thermal conditioning provided by water mullions (above) and modular ceiling-hung cooling elements (top).

In the Ministry of Finance in France, over 12,000 workers rate very highly the air quality and thermal performance of their constant-volume ceiling ventilation system combined with perimeter fan coil units, which fully supports the opening of windows in offices. For energy efficiency, the perimeter fan coils in these buildings (heating or cooling) shut off whenever the window is opened, with the constant volume ventilation system continuing as a guarantee of ventilation effectiveness.

### Individual or Task Systems with Broad-Band Ambient

A second successful approach to improving indoor quality has been a shift away from blanket, uniform, ceiling based systems to workstation or task based systems. These floor and desktop components deliver conditioned air to the individual, and typically allow for some level of user control. One high performance approach is a system which puts a mixing box at every desk (figure 8). This module allows primary, conditioned outdoor air to be delivered directly to the desk and provide end user control of temperature (by varying the quantity of filtered room air mixed with conditioned primary air).

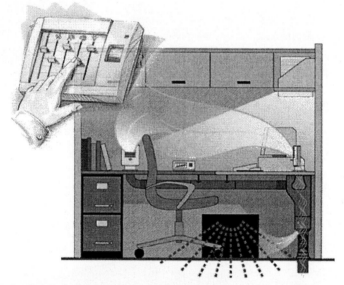

**Figure 8:** The Johnson Controls Personal Environmental Module (PEM) provides an air mixing-box at every desk, such that each user can individually control ventilation, air quantity, speed, direction, and temperature.

A number of other manufacturers have begun to introduce individual/task diffusers for ensuring thermal comfort and air quality. Some manufacturers offer plenum floor system with relocatable air diffusers in the floor. These systems enable the density and location of air diffusers to match the changing needs of workstation layouts and changes in occupant and equipment densities.

# Step 5: Lighting System Innovations for Improved Visual Quality

As in the case of mechanical systems, the electrical lighting systems in high-performance workplaces must provide flexibility and dynamic controls to accommodate the wide variety of tasks in a modern office, while maximizing energy efficiency and daylight usage.

### Split Task-Ambient Lighting with Daylighting

The Intelligent Workplace demonstrates a split-task ambient lighting system – a major shift away from uniform, high-level lighting in the ceiling, which creates visual stress whenever furniture and partitions are reconfigured, and does not accommodate differences in individual visual needs. Ambient lighting in the IW is accomplished with indirect luminaires that have T-8 fluorescent fixtures with electronic ballasts supporting daylight-based dimming (figure 9). Each workstation in the IW will be provided two high-efficiency task fixtures that provide user control of task light location and light direction, as well as on-off control provided by occupancy sensors.

Of course, daylighting will be used to provide both ambient and task lighting needs. As previously described, external light-redirection louvers reduce glare at the window and increase light levels away from the window. The internal blinds provide an additional level of glare control.

**Figure 9:** The ambient lighting system in the Intelligent Workplace incorporates user-controlled indirect luminaires that have T-8 fluorescent fixtures with electronic ballasts to support daylight-based dimming.

**Flexibility and Dynamic Control of Lighting "Scenes"**

Different tasks and moods require different visual environments. In the Intelligent Workplace, the user has control of external light redirection louvers, internal blinds, ambient lighting, task lighting, and accent lighting. The individual adjustment of these multiple devices every time a task changes, can be a cumbersome process. The concept of a "scene" suggests that for each task or mood, a preset configuration of these control devices can be programmed, such that a "scene change" is a single button operation. Intelligent lighting control systems allow each device to be individually addressable and to be combined into groups that correspond to the physical boundaries of the space. The more innovative control systems also allow the user to reconfigure scenes and override a particular device (figure 10).

**Figure 10:** User interface unit for the Luxmate control system in the Intelligent Workplace. The topmost button is to activate the lighting; the two buttons in the middle allow increase/decrease in light levels, and the five buttons below that correspond to five programmable "scenes".

# Conclusion

This paper illustrates the richness of environmental conditioning strategies for improved indoor environments and energy effectiveness. They rely on a complete reintroduction of regionalism in design, through such techniques as "architecture unplugged". These environmental conditioning strategies also rely on a firm commitment to collaborative design, to ensure the level of integration of enclosure, mechanical, lighting and interior systems, needed to realize buildings as mediators between climate and indoor quality.

# References

1. Collet, C. W., J. A. Ross, E. M. Sterling, (1993): "Strategies for the Investigation of Indoor Air Quality Problems and Findings from their Implementation", ASHRAE Transactions, Vol. 99, Part II, pp. 1104-1110, 1993.
2. Drake, P., P. Mill, M. Demeter, (1991): "Implications of User-Based Environmental Control Systems: Three Case Studies", Healthy Buildings, IAQ '91, pp. 394-400, 1991.
3. EIA (1995): Energy Consumption in Commercial Buildings in 1995. Energy Information Administration, U.S. Department of Energy.
4. Hartkopf, V., V. Loftness, A. Mahdavi, S. Lee, J. Shankavaram (1997): "An Integrated Approach to Design and Engineering of Intelligent Buildings – The Intelligent Workplace at Carnegie Mellon University", Automation in Construction 6 (1997) 401-415.
5. Hartkopf, V., V. Loftness, A. Mahdavi, P. Mathew, J. Shankavaram (1994): The Intelligent Workplace Retrofit Initiative, 1994, "Field Studies of the Major Issues Facing Existing Office Building Owners, Managers & Users", DOE Building Studies, Center for Building Performance and Diagnostics, Carnegie Mellon University, Pittsburgh, PA-15213, USA.
6. Hartkopf, V., V. Loftness, A. Mahdavi, P. Mill, P. Drake, G. Rainer, F. Dubin, J. Posner, H. Rosenheck, G. Ziga (1991): Field Studies of Advanced Technology and Intelligent Buildings: Research Report Series; Center for Building Performance and Diagnostics, Carnegie Mellon University, Pittsburgh, PA-15213. Advanced Building Systems Integration Consortium.
7. Herzog, T. (1996): Solar Energy in Architecture and Urban Planning. Prestel. Munich. 1996.
8. HUD (1978): Regional Guidelines for Building Passive Energy Conserving Homes. Prepared by the American Institute of Architects for the Office of Policy Development and Research, U.S. Department of Housing and Urban development, in cooperation with U.S. Department of Energy. 1978.
9. IEA (1998): "Towards Sustainable Buildings – A Workshop on Defining Collaborative R&D Needs", International Energy Agency. Hilton Head, SC. September 1998.
10. Kirkbride, J., H. K. Lee, and C. Moore. (1990): "Health and Welfare Canada's Experience in Indoor Air Quality Investigation", Indoor Air '90. Vol. 5., pp. 99-106, Ottawa, 1990.
11. Loftness, V. and V. Hartkopf, (1989): "The Effects of Building Design and Use on Air Quality", Occupational Medicine: State of the Art Reviews, Vol. 4, Nos. 4, Oct-Dec - 1989.
12. Mahdavi, A., Brahme, R., Mathew, P. (1996): "The 'LEK'-Concept and its Applicability for the Energy Analysis of Commercial Buildings". Building and Environment, Vol. 13 No. 5. pp. 409-415.
13. Mahdavi, A., Mathew, P., Kumar, S., Hartkopf, V., Loftness, V. (1995): "Effects of Lighting, Zoning, and Control Strategies on Energy Use in Commercial Buildings". Journal of the Illuminating Engineering Society. Volume 24, Number 1, Winter 1995. pp. 25 - 35.
14. Milam, J. A. (1992): "Underfloor Air Distribution HVAC Analysis," Environmental Design International Ltd., Marietta, GA., 1992.
15. Nicklas, M., Bailey, G. (1996): "Daylit Students Shine Brighter", SunWorld Vol. 20 No.3, September 1996.
16. NIOSH (1989): "Indoor air quality: Selected references", Division of Standards Development and technology Transfer. Cincinnati: National Institute for Occupational Safety and Health, 1989.
17. Shavit, G. and R. Wruck, (1993): "Energy Conservation and Control Strategies for Integrated Lighting and HVAC Systems", ASHRAE Transactions, 1993.
18. Siegel, J. (1998): Personal Communication  - Jane Seigel, Senior Systems Scientist, Human Computer Interaction Institute, Carnegie Mellon University.

19. Wilson, S., Hedge, A. (1987): The Office Environment Survey: A Study of Building Sickness. London, Building Use Studies, Ltd.
20. Ulrich, R. S., (1984): "View Through a Window may Influence Recovery from Surgery," Science, 224, pg. 420-421, April 27, 1984.
21. Woods, J. E., (1989): "Cost Avoidance and Productivity in Owning and Operating Buildings", Occupational Medicine: State of the Art Reviews, Volume 4, Number 4, October-December 1989.

# Passage: Physical Transportation of Digital Information in Cooperative Buildings

Shin'ichi Konomi, Christian Müller-Tomfelde, Norbert A. Streitz

GMD - German National Research Center for Information Technology
IPSI - Integrated Publication and Information Systems Institute
Dolivostr. 15, Darmstadt D-64293, Germany
{konomi,tomfelde,streitz}@darmstadt.gmd.de

**Abstract.** The Passage mechanism introduced in this paper provides an easy and intuitive way to transport various types of digital objects by using also normal physical objects without any special identification tags. The current implementation of the Passage mechanism utilizes electronic scales and contact-free identification devices and thus allows for identification of arbitrary physical objects as well as immediate and unique identification of certain dedicated physical objects. The mechanism is used in various types of cooperative work scenarios in the i-LAND environment (Streitz, et al. 1999) that provides an essential part of the infrastructure for cooperative buildings.

**Keywords.** augmented reality, ubiquitous computing, sensing devices, databases, information spaces, cooperative buildings, roomware

## 1   Introduction

In order to support people in their communication and cooperation activities, the concept of "Cooperative Buildings" (Streitz et al., 1998) has been proposed. It is characterized by a comprehensive approach on providing information and communication technology throughout the building based on a careful analysis of the tasks and contents, the work practices and organizational structures, and the architectural environment. Initial realizations of parts of this overall approach as, e.g., the i-LAND environment (Streitz et al., 1999), an interactive landscape supporting creative team work, are based on "roomware" components (Streitz et al., 1998) where information technology is integrated in room elements as, e.g., walls, doors, furniture. Examples are the DynaWall, the InteracTable, and the CommChairs (Streitz et al., 1999). Extending the i-LAND approach to the whole building results in spreading roomware components to various parts of the building going beyond offices and meeting rooms to cafeterias, hallways, stairways, foyers, etc.

The devices will be available at multiple places, distributed and embedded in the environment. Thus, computational power and information will be available everywhere (ubiquitous computing, Weiser, 1991). This raises new issues for the design of how people interact with information when using multiple devices. The design has to be aware of the importance of the physical architectural space in which people move around and interact with these devices. Therefore, it is not only designing human-computer interaction but extending the view towards a perspective that "the world around us is the interface". Spreading multiple devices in the building allows to create and view information in almost all places in a ubiquitous way. At the same time, there is the demand that people are also able to "carry" this information with them and transfer it between multiple devices in a very intuitive way. In this paper, we will show how we can support these situations of sharing and exchanging information between multiple devices by assigning digital information objects and also processes to arbitrary physical objects taken from the real world.

The paper is organized as follows. In the next chapter, we will describe three sample application scenarios guiding our design. In the third chapter, we present the *Passage*-Mechanism as our proposal for a solution of the problem introduced above. In the fourth and fifth chapter, we explain how we identify physical objects, which act as *passengers*, in various ways and assign digital information to them via so called *bridges*. This is followed by a description of how data and applications interact with passengers. Finally, we present related work and discuss future plans.


## 2 Sample Application Scenarios

We now describe sample application scenarios resulting from the availability of multiple information devices in the environment of Cooperative Buildings.

### Agenda Planning and Meeting Preparation

Imagine a person who is preparing the agenda of a meeting, sitting at a desktop computer in his office. He creates the agenda and links various background material (documents, presentation slides, pictures, video clips, etc. ) to the different items of the agenda. He has to store the agenda as a file, name the file, select a directory in his or in the team's directory structure on the server and place it there. Later, at the time of the meeting, he walks over to the meeting room. There, he wants to display the agenda and the background material for the meeting on an interactive, electronic wall (e.g., the DynaWall in the i-LAND environment) or by using an LCD projector connected to a networked computer in the meeting room. In order to get access to the agenda file stored on the server, he has to identify himself and log in to the server, navigate to the directory, find and select the file, open and display it. Hopefully, he has appropriate access rights, remembers the directory and file name, etc. Thus, a number of steps, error prone steps, are involved. In the "traditional" case of using paper for the agenda, he writes down the agenda items on a piece of paper, copies it, takes the physical objects "paper sheets" and carries them to the meeting room. We come back to these physical actions.

### Capturing Information from Discussions

Another scenario is where two (or more) people meet in the hallway or the cafeteria and start an informal conversation. This informal conversation evolves into a non-planned discussion of some project issues. They start to illustrate their discussion by drawing a sketch on a whiteboard in the hallway or on a piece of paper on the bistro table. Afterwards, the people want to use the results of their discussions in their offices or in an official, scheduled meeting. In case of the physical whiteboard, this will be difficult. One has to copy this information somehow. In the case of the piece of paper, one can take it but it is not electronically available unless it is scanned and filed, etc. In case they are in a cooperative building, the whiteboard will be an interactive wall (DynaWall) and the bistro table in the cafeteria an interactive table (InteracTable). Sketches drawn on these roomware components can be easily stored as electronic documents. If they want to use this information in a different place, they have to go through similar processes as in the example before. Wouldn't it be nice to take and carry the electronic document around similar to a physical object ?

**Starting Applications**

A third case is the example of starting an application on one device, e.g., the presentation program on an interactive wall, on a computer connected to an LCD projector in a meeting room or a cooperative group application on several devices. Again, it is an awkward and cumbersome process finding the programs, starting one after the other, etc. Wouldn't it be nice to have a "magic" object, place it somewhere and everything is being started without overhead ?

## 3 The Passage Mechanism

While we have described some application scenarios leading to the design of the Passage mechanism in the context of a cooperative building, the problem and our approach to provide a solution is not limited to that application context. The problem of transporting complex information structures created or collected at and from various sources exists and has to be addressed in almost any environment with similar characteristics. Common to all of these situations are a number of awkward tasks: numerous tools have to be started, the material has to be arranged, maybe copied, and

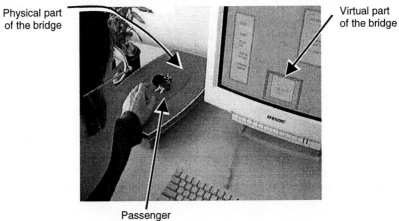

Physical part of the bridge

Virtual part of the bridge

Passenger

**Fig. 1:** Assigning information to a key chain as an example of an arbitrary physical object

48

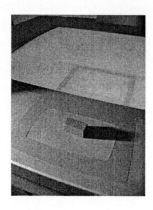

**Fig. 2:** Passenger on a bridge

finally sent to the new location, e.g., by e-mail attachments, ftp or similar services. When the person who sends this information arrives at the new location, a similar activity of finding and unpacking the material begins.

In order to facilitate this process, we developed a concept called *Passage*. Passage describes an elegant mechanism of connecting information structures in the digital, virtual world of computers with a real-world object. This object, which we call a *Passenger*, can be seen as a physical bookmark into the virtual world. One can connect information to a passenger and physically transport it to a new location. Then, by simply putting it on a special device called a *bridge*, the connected information is immediately fetched from a database and displayed on that screen which corresponds to the bridge. It is no longer necessary to open windows, browse hierarchies of folders, worry about mounted drives and doing similar annoying actions.

A *passenger* does not have to be a special physical object. Any uniquely identifiable physical object may become a passenger: a key chain, a watch, a ring, a pen, a wooden block, or many other kinds of objects. You can take whatever you happen to have around at this moment. The only restriction passengers have is that they must be detected by a bridge and uniquely identified by the system. Fig. 1 shows the process for the first scenario, i.e. a person sitting at his desktop computer and using a key chain as a *passenger* by placing it on a *bridge* where sensing devices are embedded. The bridge has a physical part (left side of the picture) where you place the passenger and a virtual part, a window appearing on the screen (see the rectangle on the lower part of the screen). The assignment is done by a gesture, simply by dragging the electronic object on the screen onto the rectangle representing the virtual part of the bridge. Note that the digital information is not stored on the physical passenger object. The passenger functions only as a physical representative. While Fig. 1 shows a stand alone mobile bridge, Fig. 2 shows a bridge integrated in the InteracTable and a wooden block as another example for a passenger. Fig. 3 shows the retrieval and display of information after placing a passenger on a bridge.

**Fig. 3:** Displaying information

# 4 Detection and Identification of Physical Objects

Detection and identification of physical objects play essential roles in the Passage mechanism. The current implementation of the Passage mechanism realizes two different methods to detect and identify objects; one uses the weight of physical objects and the other uses electronic ID tags. When using the weight anything that can be measured by scales can be used as a passenger. When using electronic ID tags, we can take advantage of their capability that allows for immediate, unique and highly reliable detection and identification.

## 4.1 Identifying Objects by Weight

The bridges we built are equipped with electronic scales in order to measure the precise weight of physical objects and send it to computers. Here, the weight is used as an ID for the electronic document/ the digital object. Since the electronic scales are sensitive enough to detect the difference of 0.1 g, they even respond to slight changes of surroundings including air flow and occasional vibrations of the floor. Such environmental disturbances are detected and filtered out by the device manager software. Also, it takes a few seconds for the scales to obtain the precise weight, which could be problematic when users require immediate access to information. In order to solve this problem, the device manager has a heuristic function that reduces the time required to measure the weight of *passengers*. It computes the weight before the value of the scale actually converges in a few seconds while the virtual part of the bridge is launched on the display (see Fig. 1 ).

## 4.2 Identifying Objects with Electronic ID Tags

The bridges are also equipped with contact-free identification devices (MIKRON's EasyKey™) in order to read electronic ID tags (see Fig. 4). The bridges obtain 32-bit identifiers from ID tags when the distance between the bridges and the ID tags is less than 6 – 10 cm, depending on the type of the tags. It is not necessary to insert them in certain dedicated slots but only to place them on top or to hold them close. In

addition, the ID tags can be pasted on or embedded in normal physical objects. The process to detect and identify ID tags is performed much more quickly than the weight. A small ID chip and an induction coil within an ID tag initially receives electric power and a trigger code from a bridge. A few hundred milliseconds after this initial action, the *bridge* receives a 32-bit identifier from the ID tag. The identification devices together with the scales allow for reasonably quick identification of arbitrary objects as well as immediate and unique identification of tagged objects.

**Fig. 4:** Identification device

## 5 Connecting Physical Objects and Digital Information

Fig. 5 shows various components of the Passage mechanism. Physical objects and digital information objects are associated by the Passage agents that manipulate the data in the Passage databases and the device managers. Most of the major components in Fig. 5 can communicate with one another over the network so that they can be distributed across rooms and buildings. Thus, the Passage mechanism can be easily configured for different types of cooperative buildings.

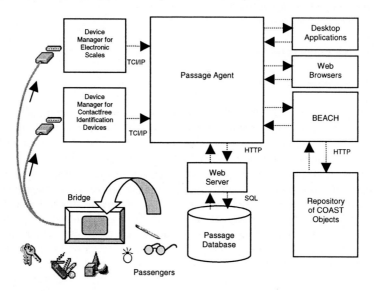

**Fig. 5**: The Passage mechanism

### 5.1 Passage Agents

The Passage agents link physical objects and digital information by using the data received from the device managers and the Passage databases. As soon as a passenger is put on a bridge, electronic signals from the bridge are handled by appropriate device managers according to the types of the devices that are activated by the passenger. The Passage agents obtain the physical properties of the passenger such as the weight and/or the identifier. When the passenger is new to the agents, they associate the passenger with the digital information specified by the user and store the relationship as a record in the Passage databases. When the agents know the passenger already, they simply retrieve a record from the databases and automatically display the digital information corresponding to the passenger. There is no need to manually launch applications or select menu items. The only thing users have to do is to put a passenger on a bridge and wait for the information to be presented on the screen.

## 5.2 Passage Databases

The current implementation of the Passage mechanism utilizes a simple relational database management system that can be accessed via the HTTP protocol. Therefore, Passage agents distributed on the network can easily access the Passage database and manipulate the attributes of passengers including:
- weight
- electronic ID
- information object (or pointer to information object)
- type of information object
- timestamp

## 5.3 Configuring Passage Agents

Passage agents and device managers communicate with each other using TCP/IP sockets. The use of TCP/IP sockets permits to flexibly distribute the Passage agents and the device managers in rooms and buildings, which is a part of the first step towards the ubiquitous collaboration environments.

Fig. 6 shows a sample configuration of passage agents and device managers for selected roomware components as, e.g., in i-LAND. There are six Passage agents $a_1$, $a_2$, ..., $a_6$ in Room A, five of which are connected to the device manager of $Bridge_1$. Under this configuration, a passenger placed on $Bridge_1$ invokes actions on the three computers ($CPU_1$, $CPU_2$, $CPU_3$) behind the interactive electronic wall and the two computers ($CPU_4$, $CPU_5$) integrated with chairs. In contrast, a passenger on $Bridge_2$ or $Bridge_3$ invokes actions on only one computer ($CPU_6$ or $CPU_7$, respectively). All Passage agents access the same Passage database so that digital information can be transported across $Bridge_1$, $Bridge_2$ (in Room A) and $Bridge_3$ (in Room B).

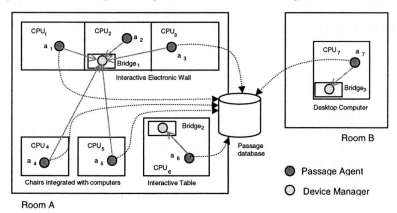

**Fig. 6 :** Sample configuration of Passage agents

# 6 Interacting with Data and Applications via Passengers

Passengers can be used to interact with various types of data and applications. As shown in Fig. 5, Passage agents can control general applications, web browsers and BEACH (Basic Environment for Active Collaboration with Hypermedia), which is the software infrastructure for roomware environments, developed to meet the requirements of i-LAND (Streitz et al., 1999).

## 6.1 Interacting with BEACH

BEACH runs on roomware components such as the *DynaWall* (an interactive electronic wall), the *InteracTable* (an interactive table) and the *CommChairs* (computer enhanced chairs) and provides shared hypermedia functionality, gesture-based interaction methods, and many other functions for collaborative work. Users of the BEACH software can utilize passengers to transport information such as a meeting agenda and results of brain storming sessions across different roomware components which might be placed in different rooms. The only requirements are that they are connected to the network and that they have a bridge. When users put a passenger on a bridge, a small window appears on the screen, sliding up from the physical location of the bridge. Objects can be dragged out of BEACH applications and dropped on the window in order to assign them to the passenger. The objects assigned to the passenger are inserted into a repository and a database. When the passenger is put on another bridge, the objects are retrieved from the database and the repository and displayed in a small window of the display corresponding to this bridge. Then, the objects can be dragged out of the window and dropped on the BEACH applications.

## 6.2 Interacting with the Web and General Desktop Applications

Passengers can also be used to store and display URLs. Since various MIME types are handled by web browsers, this feature augments the Passage mechanism with a simple facility to manipulate applications and multimedia data types.

   In addition, passage agents can directly control regular desktop applications to start and stop word processors, spread sheets, presentation software, etc. The applications and the files that are connected with passengers do not have to be on shared file systems. When they reside on local file systems, they are transferred via the HTTP protocol using the POST method.

# 7 Related Work

We presented the concept and implementation of the Passage mechanism, a novel transport mechanism of information. Our approach is related to and was inspired by certain developments in human-computer interaction, augmented reality, ubiquitous computing and computer-supported cooperative work.

Comparing the Passage mechanism with related work shows that the general idea of using physical objects to move information from place to place is not very new. For example, floppy disks are used to copy and move information around. However, since their storage capacity is severely limited, one often has to go through a complex process to send information by email, ftp, etc.

Informative Things (Barrett and Magilo, 1998) proposes a method to attach network information sources to floppy disks so that they can hold virtually unlimited amounts of information. However, floppy disks, all of which have very similar physical characteristics, have to be inserted into special disk drives and ejected from them.

A related but different approach is the notion of "graspable" user interfaces (Fitzmaurice et al., 1995) and "tangible bits" (Ishii and Ullmer, 1997) which was also inspired by the "marble answering machine" developed by Bishop (Poynor, 1995) where incoming phone calls are indicated by (physical) marbles which can be placed on a specific area for playing the message. MediaBlocks (Ullmer et al., 1998) uses wooden blocks that physically contain ID tags and serve as containers, transports, and controls for online video data (or other media streams). Our Passage approach is not media transport, browsing, and editing but attempts to realize ephemeral binding between physical objects and digital contents considering requirements of cooperative work. Therefore, we made it possible to use arbitrary objects as physical representatives of digital information. Furthermore, our Passage mechanism can easily be configured to support work in cooperative buildings. It provides an intuitive way for transporting information across computers, offices, meeting rooms, etc. as described in the application scenarios in Chapter 2.

# 8 Discussion and Future Work

The first implementation of the Passage mechanism described in this paper convinced us that our approach to use physical objects for representing and transporting digital objects is promising. We utilize two different methods to identify physical objects; identification by weight and identification by electronic ID tags. The use of weight makes the mechanism work without special ID tags. This generally works well when the stored information is immediately transported and retrieved (=> short term memory), e.g., in group work situations. In contrast, passengers with electronic ID tags are always uniquely identified. This requires that ID tags have to be pasted on or embedded in physical objects (=> long term memory).

When passengers are not transported and used immediately, users would need to remember which passenger is connected to which information object. In the future, we will explore the possibilities of storing and/or displaying information on passengers themselves. Small electronic devices including cellular phones, PDAs and palmtop computers will be used as "active" passengers which can send, receive, store, process, and/or display information. The use of such gizmos in the Passage mechanism would support certain types of mobility in various activities in cooperative buildings.

While using the first implementation of the Passage mechanism in our i-LAND environment, we found that the capability of Passage agents to simultaneously start up and quit applications on multiple computers was extremely useful. We are interested in extending this capability besides the primary function of the Passage mechanism as a physical transportation medium.

For future developments, it is essential to design a generic Passage framework, which we call *Open Passage*, in order to provide generic APIs for varieties of devices and data types. In addition, security issues have to be investigated in order to develop a security model for the Passage mechanism.

## Acknowledgments

We would like to thank Jörg Geißler, Torsten Holmer, Peter Seitz, Wolfgang Reischl, Daniel Warth, and Jochen Denzinger for useful discussions of the Passage concept and their help in the realization.

# References

1. Barrett, R. and Maglio, P. P. (1998). Informative things: how to attach information to the real world. In: *Proceedings of UIST '98* (San Francisco, CA, Nov. 1-4). ACM Press, New York, 81-88.
2. Fitzmaurice, G., Ishii, and H., and Buxton, W. (1995). Bricks: Laying the foundations for graspable user interfaces. In: *Proceedings of CHI'95*, Denver, CO, (May 7-11). ACM Press, New York, 442-449.
3. Ishii, H. and Ullmer, B. (1997). Tangible bits: Towards seamless interfaces between people, bits and atoms. In: *Proceedings CHI '97*, Atlanta, Georgia, (March 22-27, 1997). ACM Press, New York, 234-241.
4. Poynor, R. (1995). The hand that rocks the cradle. *I.D. - The International Design Magazine*. May-June.
5. Streitz, N. A., Geißler, J. Holmer, T. (1998) Roomware for Cooperative Buildings: Integrated Design of Architectural Spaces and Information Spaces. In: [7], 4-21.
6. Streitz, N. A., Geißler, J. Holmer, T. Konomi, S., Müller-Tomfelde, C., Reischl, W., Rexroth, P., Seitz, P., Steinmetz, R. (1999). i-LAND: An interactive Landscape for Creativity and Innovation. In: *Proceedings of CHI'99*, Pittsburgh, U.S.A. (May 15-20, 1999). ACM Press, New York, 120-127.
7. Streitz, N., Konomi, S., Burkhardt, H. (Eds.) (1998*), Cooperative Buildings — Integrating Information, Organization and Architecture. Proceedings of the First International Workshop on Cooperative Buildings (CoBuild'98)*, Darmstadt, Germany, February 1998. Lecture Notes in Computer Science 1370. Springer: Heidelberg, 4-21.
8. Ullmer, B., Ishii, H., and Glas, D. (1998). mediaBlocks: Physical containers, transports, and controls for online media. In: *Proceedings of SIGGRAPH '98* (Orlando, FL, July 19-24). ACM Press, New York, 379-386.
9. Weiser, M. (1991). The Computer for the 21st Century. *Scientific American*, 1991, 265 (3), 94-104.

# Complex Construction Kits for Coupled Real and Virtual Engineering Workspaces

Wilhelm F. Bruns

artec – Research Center for Work, Environment, Technology
Bremen University
Enrique-Schmidt-Str. 7, Bremen D-28334, Germany
bruns@artec.uni-bremen.de

**Abstract.** A concept of complex objects, being artifacts that have one real physical part and several virtual parts representing certain aspects of the object, is introduced. These parts are coupled by bi-directional double links of control and view, enabling a synchronous update of all part, if one of them is changed by user action or internal events. With a construction kit, being a set of compatible complex objects for a certain engineering or office application field, it is possible to build a system in reality with real parts, generating synchronously the assembly of virtual parts by means of a universal graspable user interface. The bi-directional double links allow the control of virtual parts by grasping and pointing on real parts and view the virtual parts by light projection into the real scene and vice versa, that is, control and view real parts by grasping and pointing on virtual parts. The concept is being demonstrated with prototypes for the application areas of pneumatic circuit design and flexible assembly systems.

**Keywords.** coupling reality and virtuality, simulation, cooperative system design, universal graspable user interface, augmented reality, tangible objects, complex objects

## 1 Introduction

Coupling tangible objects of real work spaces with information spaces of digital representation has been subject of increasing interest during the last decade. Weiser (1991) set up the vision of a room with information and action generated by a ubiquitous computer. Wellner et al (1993) emphasized the paradigmatic shift of computer-augmented environments: back to the real world. Fitzmaurice et al (1995) lay the foundations for graspable user interfaces. Resnick (1993) introduced behavior construction kits based on real objects. Since then, many prototypical applications have been published. To name only a few: Kang & Ickeuchi (1994) proposed a concept of programming robots by concrete teaching, the MIT Media Lab is hosting a strong research group working on tangible objects (Ishii & Ullmer, 1997), Suzuki & Kato (1995) use real AlgoBlocks for programming, Rekimoto (1998) developed intelligent rooms and a series of workshops now has a focus on the integration of information into real Buildings (Streitz et al., 1998).

All these attempts to couple real tangible objects with digital representations only support one-way-links (manipulating digital representation by concrete handles) or a projection of digital representations into the real scene. In engineering applications, mainly in the area of design of automation devices and systems, it is extremely interesting to have an easy access to both sides of a system, the real physical environment of actors, sensors with their electro-mechanical mechanisms, and its digital representation used in simulation models and its driving control algorithms. We therefore introduce a concept of tight bi-directional coupling to bridge these two worlds.

Some prototypes we developed for the cooperative design and simulation of automation systems, namely flexible assembly systems driven by PLCs (Programmable Logic Controller), robotics and pneumatic circuits are presented and generalized. The derived concept aims at a new kind of distributed work space for systems design in production automation. However, it is also intended to yield a new kind of learning environment allowing the switch between concrete and abstract views on physical and work phenomena to be made easily and quickly.

## 2  Basic Concept

In several industrial simulation projects in the area of production and logistics, we learned from experience, that physical models are very helpful for a common understanding in multidisciplinary design teams and improve the understanding of difficult technical matters. This proved to be true not only for the specification of geometrical and topological features, but also for the intended dynamical behavior of devices or systems. We therefore developed the concept of complex objects, having one real part and several corresponding virtual parts (computer internal representations). In Fig. 1 two different kinds of complex objects are presented, one for a pneumatic cylinder (left) and one for a conveyor belt (right). Computer based links between real and virtual parts ensure the synchronization of their states. They can be realized by video-image-recognition or, as shown in Fig. 1, by data glove tracking. Starting from a reference situation, changes of state are sensed by a graspable user interface and used to update the complementary part (Bruns 1993). The term *complex object* is an allusion to the mathematical notion of complex numbers. Similar to complex numbers, having a real and an imaginary part, the complex object contains an abstract object with enriched possibility of mathematical treatment and behavior (algorithms, data-structures) and the controlled automation device as its projection into reality. Of course, this is only a limited metaphor because we allow different levels of abstraction and perspective for one real part.

With construction kits, containing sets of these complex objects for specific application areas, it is then possible to construct a system in reality and synchronously generate a corresponding virtual model, that can be tested, analyzed and transmitted to remote places (Fig. 2).

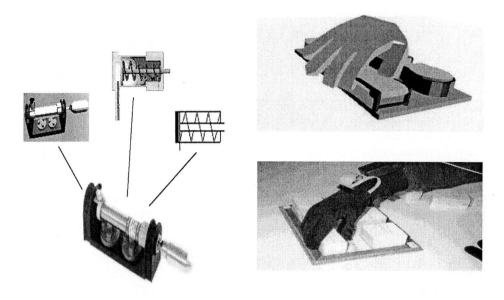

**Fig. 1.** Complex Objects with real tangible parts and various digital representations

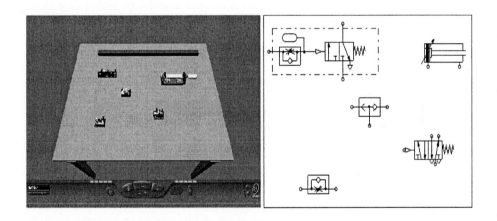

**Fig. 2.** Synchronous Generation of Virtual Reality and Simulation Models

Technical details of the implementation of this concept have been described elsewhere (Bruns 98) but are summarized for convenience. One main characteristic of the approach is the use of our hand as a manipulator of physical objects in a real environment. Appropriate interface devices like data gloves and tracking systems are used to capture the user's hand movements and finger flexions. With the help of gesture recognition algorithms, based on statistical methods (Brauer 94), the raw interface data is analysed and gestures, grasps, or user commands are recognised by the computer in real time. Working with physical objects while being linked to a computer has a certain analogy to the well known Drag & Drop principle of GUIs. When the grasp of an object happens, all following data of the Drag-Phase are recorded. This phase terminates when the user places the object at another location and releases it (Drop). Now, the physical object has a new position and due to this, the virtual computer internal model of the physical environment is immediately updated. By giving the user an acoustic feedback in the moment of grasping and releasing, the graphical output on a display becomes obsolete. So the user can work distinct from the encumbering aura of the monitor, the keyboard and the mouse. The interface becomes a passive observer and is ideally not noticed by its users. This is achieved by linking physical objects to their virtual representation. Because of maintaining objects having both a physical and a virtual representation, we call them *complex objects*.

Complex objects are one of the basic elements of our concept. For both kinds of object representation a number of instances must be available. This means to create a virtual representation consisting of the object's geometry and algorithms describing the dynamic behaviour. The geometric description contains the object's size (length, width, height) and its surface shape. The dynamic behaviour is specified by application specific languages or general purpose descriptions like Petri-Nets. It may be pre-defined and fixed or taught by concrete demonstration (see below). On the other hand, the physical part of an object must be constructed using technical construction kits, wooden bricks or other materials. The object representations may vary in shape, size and level of detail. In initial state, the objects are located in an object box which has a predefined position on the tabletop, such that for each object in the box the position can be computed. A model is created stepwise by taking objects out of the box and putting them on the model ground. This way, several models can be managed synchronously, providing different views on the system to be built. With the help of 3D visualisation software, the geometrical representation can be displayed on a monitor screen. With the help of an application specific simulator, the symbolic, functional and behaviour representation can be displayed in a circuit diagram, a program source-code or a projection of its dynamics on the screen or table. Although the visual feedback is not necessary for those who model with the physical model, it is used for replaying the actions recorded during a modelling session. Furthermore people working in remote locations can observe a modelling process via a network connection to the *Real Object Manager* running as Server.

Working synchronously with two models requires sophisticated communication structures between several software modules in which each of them is responsible for a specific task. These tasks are:

- maintaining a virtual model, keeping track of the actions performed with the complex-objects,
- recognising grasp and gesture events,
- recording data of the object movements,
- abstracting a general description of the recorded data,
- visualising the modelling process and
- persistent storage of data in files.

According to this allocation of tasks, a general software architecture was designed (Fig. 3). A central component of this architecture is the Real Object Modeller (ROMAN). This module maintains an object database which contains geometric object descriptions, keeps track of the state of the model, provides information for the visualisation in a 3D graphical model, handles model-files, and provides an interface for the dynamic data exchange (DDX) with external real or virtual processes. Via DDX and appropriate communication protocols, a connection of external processes, running on different machines, may be established. This is the case for the Gesture-Server task which handles the data glove and sends gesture event messages to the ROMAN. Another example is the Simulation-Converter which acts as a mediator between the ROMAN and standard simulation software products. Fig. 3 shows bi-directional connections between the DDX interface and simulators. This indicates that a model-file (SML) is downloaded from the ROMAN, translated with a converter to a simulator-specific data format, and is then simulated. The dynamic simulation yields to changes in the model, for example a container is transported by a conveyor belt to a new location. These changes are immediately transferred via DDX to the ROMAN where the virtual model is updated. We developed visualisation clients which can be connected to the ROMAN via DDX. By using standard TCP-IP protocols for data exchange a connection via the Internet to the ROMAN is possible. This architecture has several advantages: computational power of various computers becomes available, different hardware and operating system platforms may be used, and remote access and visualisation of dynamic changes to the model is provided.

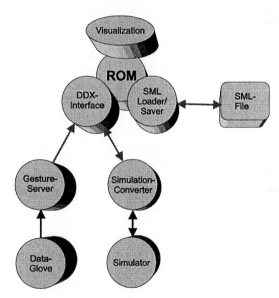

**Fig. 3.** System Architecture of the Modeller

The gesture and grasp recognition algorithm is based on techniques of statistical multi-variate discriminance analysis (Brauer 94). Different grasp- and gesture-patterns can be defined using a teaching software. The user teaches the algorithm with some examples and for each example a set of characteristic features is computed. While acting on the complex objects, the gesture server continually tries to match an actual feature vector with one of the taught patterns in the n-dimensional feature space. In case of a match, the object is bound to the position-path of the data glove. If the bending values of the fingers change significantly (the hand opens), the recognition indicates a release event and the object is left at the actual position. The statistical recognition algorithm performs well and runs in real time on a dedicated 4/86 CPU. The modularity of our concept allows the integration of further improvements in pattern recognition.

To make the computer redo or even derive programs from what was previously demonstrated by the user, is an old issue in human-computer interaction. This research is currently focused on the conventional WIMP (Windows, Icons, Menus and Pointers) interface styles. The 3D interface provided by our concept offers new possibilities for specifying dynamic model behaviour by demonstration. The investigation of this potential is one of our main goals of research.

In a first approach, a scenario out of the domain of production and logistics was constructed. A conveyor belt delivers containers of different types (represented by differently coloured blocks). A robot has to transport these containers to one of three outgoing conveyor belts which convey them to further places of processing. The assignment of a specific container to a target conveyor depends on its type (colour). For a concrete situation these assignments have to be specified by the user. Additionally, a control program for the robot which picks up the containers and places them on the target conveyor must be created. In the following it is described how these tasks can be performed with the interface.

The initial scenario described above was created with our modeller. The containers are located in the object box which in this case is simply a dedicated area on the table-top. Now, the user takes the containers and moves them through the system on individual paths. While putting a container from one conveyor to another the user plays the role of the robot that picks, transports, and releases containers. Furthermore, the modeller recognises the assignment of a specific type of containers to a target conveyor belt. According to our philosophy the movement paths are recorded, can be saved and animated. A path which bridges a gap between different conveyors may be refined with a path editor, and a basic version of a robot control program can be generated.

In addition to continuous path-control programs, rules for the distribution of the typed container belts within the system are generated, for example: „*put green containers always on conveyor A*“. The rules and control programs can be used for simulation. Randomly created containers are moved through the virtual conveyor system according to the taught set of ramification rules and paths. This way, experimental changes of the material flow through the system can be easily and intuitively analysed and optimised. Furthermore, by scaling the model and the paths to the size of a real plant, the control programs for the robot can be simulated. For this purpose a robot simulator (COSIMIR) is employed. It offers various types of robots contained in a library. This simulation tool provides the functions to make unreachable co-ordinates visible and to optimise transport curves.

The overall behaviour of the system can be simulated with a universal simulation tool (simple++). The controlling algorithm for the behaviour of the components can be taught by concrete demonstration of hand movements using real tokens, generating Petri-Nets. These tokens are placed on certain points to mark relevant states of the system (Fig. 4).

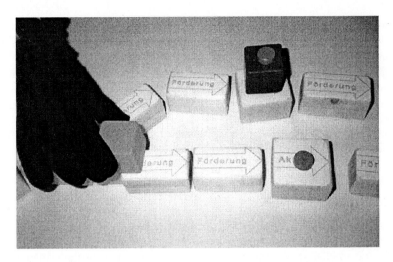

**Fig. 4.** Generating Petri-Nets by Concrete Demonstration

This control algorithm can then be used to drive the real model, enriched by actors and sensors, see Fig. 5.

**Fig. 5.** Model with actors and sensors driven by a Programmable Logic Controller (PLC)

In our modelling environment, physical and virtual objects are tightly coupled by sensored user hands. The experience with prototypical applications shows some major advantages of this concept:

- The similarity between real and virtual objects supports the spatial and dynamic orientation in complex systems. Physical laws are carefully respected (spatial extension of bodies, steadiness of motion, friction, acceleration, synchronisation).

- The physical model can be viewed from different perspectives, without additional technical means like head mounted devices. The context as a whole is always preserved.
- The user senses the hardness and heaviness of the complex objects and uses them intuitively.

The power of this concept compared to conventional Graphical User Interfaces lies in its orientation towards all human senses during the modelling process, especially to the haptic. Instead of sensoring each object, the concept of utilising the hand, yields a universality, because we can use all familiar objects of our surrounding as user interface.

Conceptually our work can be seen as an extension and application of the Model-View-Control concept of Smalltalk80 (Goldberg & Robson 1983). The Model-View-Control concept separates model functionality from the user interface (Fig. 6). Whenever the model changes, it broadcasts a message ("I have changed") to all dependents and they take whatever action is appropriate. The controller tells the models what to change, the view displays the current state of the model from one perspective. We introduce double valued bi-directional links between real objects and their virtual counterparts, mediated by ROMAN, a real object manager, implemented as a software-component. These links are double valued as they allow the submission of state-information (view) and control data (controller) between the virtual and the real world (Fig. 7). They are bi-directional in the sense, that they can be used from the real and the virtual side. From the reality side, one can point on a certain element of the system and get a a video projection of information into the scene (R->V-view) or one can start a simulation in virtuality (R->V-control) having the visualization again being projected into the scene (Fig. 8). From the virtual side, one can point on a certain virtual element of the system and get the video picture of the real system (V->R view). Starting a control program of the generated type, one can not only see the simulation on the screen or projected into the scene but also drive the real actorized model (V->R control).

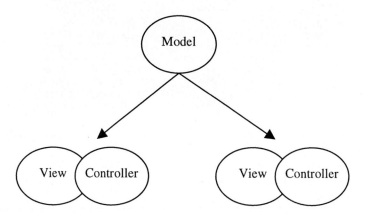

**Fig. 6.** Model-View-Controller Concept of Smalltalk

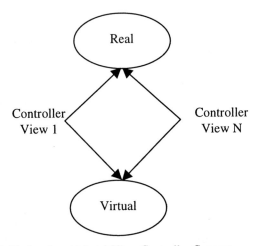

**Fig. 7.** Bi-directional Model-View-Controller Concept

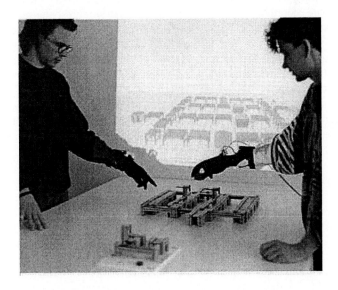

**Fig. 8.** Projection of Information into the Scene

## 3 Applications

In three projects, two funded by the German Research Community (RUGAMS and EUGABE) and one by the European Community (BREVIE) we demonstrate the feasibility of the above concept.

*Project RUGAMS*

First prototypes of a flexible assembly systems designer have been improved in the project RUGAMS (*Computer supported Crossing between concrete and abstract Models of Production Systems*). With a simple data glove and feature based versions of grasp recognition, a "brick world" and a virtual world can be geometrically manipulated as shown in fig. 3 (Bruns 93, Brauer 96, Bruns et al. 97). In addition to geometrical modeling it is now possible to teach dynamic behavior and decision rules by concrete demonstration. Individually taught behavior patterns are abstracted and then used to create machine control programs. The prototype has been demonstrated for a Conveyor System of the type being subject to considerable investigations in the European Simulation Community (Krauth 1992).

For each conveyor belt type we construct a geometrical and functional virtual representation with conventional modeling tools. These virtual building blocks are then imported into the Real Reality modeler. Using a data glove, the user teaches his way of grasping the real objects. He thus associates a grasp pattern to each type of object. After that, the user places the conveyors on the model ground, thus building a conveyor system. Conveyor belts may be connected or gaps between them may be bridged by a robot system. Now, different types of containers can be taken out of their starting position and moved through the system of conveyors on individual paths. These paths are recorded and abstracted to a parametric representation which then can be interactively edited in the virtual scenario. From this internal representation we are able to generate program code for the control of industrial robots and PLCs. The virtual model is now used for systems analysis. Randomly created containers enter the system and pass their way through it, activating the relevant robot programs according to the taught set of ramification rules and pathways.

With this prototype we can demonstrate a new and efficient way of system specification, programming, testing and optimization. Our reality oriented method is especially suited for new forms of communication between customer and system developer.

*Project EUGABE*

In project EUGABE (*Experience oriented Bridges between real and virtual Modeling-worlds for vocational Training*), we apply the idea of coupled modeling to the area of pneumatics and vocational training. This field is difficult, because pneumatic circuits in reality are very disordered and have crossing air tubes connecting the cylinders, valves and switches; furthermore they are flexible, not rigid like conveyors, and the physical laws of pneumatics are complicated enough so it is always possible to find a perspective, where the real and the virtual model differ (Fig. 9). Many students prefer to build a real physical model to understand the principles. On the other hand, the advantages of virtual and abstract modeling show up very clearly as soon, as the models are getting complex enough. We found, that it is a very interesting, yet not enough investigated question, how and when thinking styles may switch from physical to logical orientation and vice versa, depending on the problem and the representing modeling languages. Further pedagogical and psychological research will result from this project.

The technological challenge of not being able to apply our grasp-pattern method to a flexible and bending object (how do you recognize the sliding of a tube in your hand?) may be solved by imposing procedural constraints on the user. When she connects two pneumatic devices she is not allowed to connect one end of a tube, leave the other end, do some other work and then decide to connect the other end. The user always has to do her work in the sequence: 1. grasping a tube, 2. connecting one end to one component and 3. the other end to the other component. This certainly is a restriction which is not acceptable for a free intuitive and experimental work. Therefore we left our pure hand orientation for this application type and switched to a video-image recognition of the modeling parts and actions. This solution is being further investigated in project BREVIE.

**Fig. 9.** Group oriented learning of Pneumatics

*Project BREVIE*

This European project *Bridging Reality and Virtuality with a graspable User Interface[1]* aims at the development of a product, that eventually may replace all conventional pneumatic learning environments. The new learning environment consists of a table for the placement of real pneumatic elements, a camera-system for the recognition of elements and actions and a PC for 3D-VR presentation, simulation, animation and multimedia support for the subject (video films, sounds, demo applications). The real and virtual worlds are coupled, so that the learner can switch between different views and action rooms (Fig. 10).

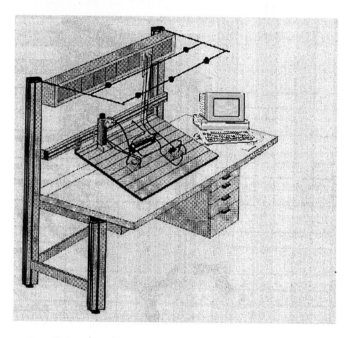

**Fig. 10**. Learning Environment for real and virtual Pneumatics

The Model-View-Control concept allows the distributed use of this environment. One Real Object Manager is assigned to one real workspace, but can offer its services for world wide Internet-Clients that understand VRML.

---

[1] Our partners in this project are Festo Didactic, Virtual Presence, Superscape, Stockport College, Friese Poort Drachten, Escola Superior Leiria, Schulzentrum am Holter Feld, Institut for Work-Psychology ETH Zürich

# 4 Conclusion and Further Work

In this paper, I introduced a concept of complex objects and a kind of reality oriented modeling which is closely linked to virtual modeling. Compared to conventional Graphical User Interfaces the power of this concept lies in its orientation toward a variety of our senses during the modeling process, especially to the haptic one. By using direct manipulation of real objects as a computer interface and by integrating this principle into the learning process, as we do, a new approach to human-computer interaction is followed. It supports the process of concrete modeling and it constitutes a basis for cognitive abstractions, thinking, and the formation of concepts. Our approach raises questions of cognition and system theory. How do we grasp tools and parts? In which way are mental models affected by the acts of grasping and concrete manipulation? What working and learning styles are preferred by students or system designers if they can freely switch between different modes? Some of these questions are investigated in a current evaluation project where we observe three different groups of students: one group is learning pneumatics by blackboard teaching, one by simulator support and one with the new real-virtual modeling environment (Grund 99).

Further technical work will be concentrated on possibilities of tele-modeling and reality oriented distributed cooperation. With devices of light-projections, it is possible to point into the real scene and synchronously into a virtual model at another place. This may considerably improve communication in service work for automation systems.

## Acknowledgments

I would like to thank my colleagues for their valuable contributions: Volker Brauer, Hauke Ernst, Hermann Gathmann, Eva Hornecker, Jürgen Huyer, Dieter Müller, Mario Müller, Bernd Robben, Ingrid Rügge, Kai Schäfer, Kai Schmudlach and all of my group's graduate researchers: Cedrik Duval, Martin Faust, Mladen Ilic, Piotr Kaczmarczyk, Keith-Andre Piedboeuf, Sven Ruttkowski, Wolfgang Tieben.

Our research is being supported by the Deutsche Forschungsgemeinschaft DFG (G-Nr. Br 1556/2-3, G-Nr. Br1556/3-3) and the EU (MM1002).

# References

1. Brauer, V. (1994): Feature-basierte Erkennung dynamischer Gesten mit einem Datenhandschuh. *Diplomarbeit*, Universität Bremen
2. Brauer, V. (1996): Simulation Model Design in Physical Environments. ACM SIGGRAPH Computer Graphics, Vol. 30, No. 4, Nov.
3. Bruns, F. W. (1993). Zur Rückgewinnung von Sinnlichkeit – Eine neue Form des Umgangs mit Rechnern. *Technische Rundschau*, 29/30, 14-18
4. Bruns, F. W. (1998): Integrated Real and Virtual Prototyping. Proc. 24th Ann. Conf. IEEE Industrial Society, Aachen, Vol 4, 2137-2142
5. Fitzmaurice, G. W., Ishii, H., Buxton, W. (1995). Bricks: Laying the Foundations for Graspable User Interfaces. CHI'95 Mosaic of Creativity, 442-449.

6. Goldberg, A. Robson, D. (1983). Smalltalk-80: The language and its implementation. Addison-Wesley, Reading, Massachusetts

7. Grund, S. (1999): BREVIE Evaluation. Presentation at the Concertation Meeting of the EU, Brussels, 22. 1. 99 (soon to be published)

8. Ishii, H., Ullmer, B. (1997). Tangible Bits: Toward Seamless Interfaces between People, Bits and Atoms. CHI'97, Atlanta, Georgia. http://media.mit.edu/groups/tangible

9. Kang, S. B., Ikeuchi, K. (1994). Grasp Recognition and Manipulative Motion Characterization from Human Hand Motion Sequences. Proc. of IEEE Int. Conf. on Robotics and Automation, San Diego, Cal., Vol 2, 1759-1764.

10. Krauth, J. (1992): Comparison 2, Flexible Assembly System. EUROSIM Simulation News 2, May 1992.

11. Resnick, M. (1993): Behavior Construction Kits. Communications of the ACM. 36(7), 64-71

12. Rekimoto, J. (1998). Multiple-Computer User Interfaces: A Cooperative Environment Consisting of Multiple Digital Devices. In: Streitz, N., Konomi, S., Burkhardt, H.-J. (Eds.) see next. 42-52

13. Streitz, N., Konomi, S., Burkhardt, H.-J. (Eds.) (1998). *Cooperative Buildings - Integrating Information, Organization and Architecture.* Proceedings of the First International Workshop on Cooperative Buildings (CoBuild'98), Darmstadt, Germany (February 25-26, 1998). Lecture Notes in Computer Science, Vol. 1370. Springer - Verlag, Heidelberg.

14. Suzuki, H., Kato, H. (19195). Interaction-Level Support for Collaborative Learning: AlgoBlock – An Open Programming Language. *Proc. of the Computer Supported Collaborative Learning (CSCL) Conf.*, University of Indiana

15. Weiser, M. (1991). The Computer for the Twenty-first Century. Scientific American, vol 256, (3), 94-104.

16. Wellner, P., Mackay, W., Gold, R. (1993). Computer-Augmented Environments: Back to the Real World. Communications of the ACM, 36, 7, pp. 24ff.

# Bringing the Marks on a Whiteboard to Electronic Life

Eric Saund

Xerox Palo Alto Research Center
3333 Coyote Hill Road
Palo Alto, CA 94304
saund@parc.xerox.com

**Abstract.** This paper discusses our implementation and experience with a camera-based whiteboard scanner. The ZombieBoard system (so called because it brings to electronic life the marks on a whiteboard) is built into both the physical environment and the information space, while augmenting and linking the two. Computer vision underlies two key technology components. First, *image mosaicing* is used to obtain high-resolution images of large surfaces using relatively low-resolution cameras. Second, real time activity analysis and line drawing analysis enable a *Diagrammatic User Interface* whereby commands are issued to the system by drawing on the whiteboard itself. The system has been in routine use at our research center for two years and has demonstrated the value of this approach to linking whiteboards with the electronic document world.

**Keywords.** whiteboard scanning, ZombieBoard, image mosaicing, Diagrammatic User Interface, digital office.

## 1 Motivation

Few creative workplaces lack a whiteboard or chalkboard. Whiteboard-scale surfaces afford pacing, gesticulating, sharing with large and small groups, and stepping back to get a look at the big picture. Small office whiteboards support conversations, lists, and notes. Medium size conference room whiteboards participate in presentations and group collaborations. Large whiteboard walls maintain organizational reference material including schedules, timetables, and assignment postings.

For example, Figure 1 shows the latter stages of a meeting in which a group of eight people has used a conference room whiteboard to work out a series of steps required to introduce a new device to the local network. The discussion has raised many issues that filled two whiteboards. To document the deliberations and decisions reached, this information needs to be posted to a web site of meeting minutes.

**Figure 1.** User issuing a "Scan Whiteboard" command.

To facilitate this kind of work process in our research center, the Figure shows the group leader using the system described in this paper to capture the whiteboard contents as an electronic document. A pan/tilt camera in the ceiling has (with the help of some computation) constructed a high-resolution picture of the left whiteboard. The group leader has drawn a symbol (the box with an arrow pointing to the right) that commands the camera to now point at the right whiteboard, and she is in the process of placing a pre-printed command button on this board, which the camera will interpret as the command to next scan this surface. A print of this whiteboard image is delivered a few minutes later by the printer on the table behind her. An electronic image is also placed in a temporary file directory associated with this conference room. Later in the afternoon, when the group leader summarizes the meeting's accomplishments on a web page, she can type while referencing the whiteboard image printout, or she can directly include the electronic image. Before this technology was introduced, she would write a big "Do Not Erase" message on the whiteboard until she got around to transcribing the contents (often hastily and incompletely). Of course this practice disrupted use of the whiteboard for later meetings.

Several commercial devices exist today for whiteboard image capture (e.g. SMARTBoard, Softboard, Tegrity, Mimeo, VideoBrush). These are dominated by online, or stylus-tracking approaches which provide a record of the time course of strokes added to the whiteboard. Stylus-tracking approaches offer advantages in speed, but often involve specially-fitted whiteboards of limited size, bothersome apparatus and procedures for dealing with the pen, unreliability in detecting when the pen is touching the board, and a requirement to fidget with technology in order to turn the system on, connect it to a computer, etc.

By contrast, optical, or camera-based whiteboard scanning offers to transparently retrofit any existing whiteboard of any size. It provides "what you see is what you get" data acquisition: not only are pen strokes captured, but also posters, documents, and post-it notes---anything on the board. Even people present at the meeting are "photographed" if present in front of the whiteboard surface. For these reasons, we have explored the camera-based approach to instrumenting buildings for whiteboard capture.

This project is part of a larger effort to build office appliances that bring computationally-enabled functionality out into the physical world, but in a "calm" setting (Weiser and Brown, 1996, Black et al, 1998). By mounting a pan/tilt camera in the ceiling, the physical machinery for whiteboard capture is moved out of the way, to a place where it can double as a user interface input device. To obtain sufficient resolution, multiple zoomed-in snapshots are assembled into a larger composite or mosaic image. This is done using a serial port connection to a commercial camera (e.g. a Sony EVI-D30) allowing computer control of pan, tilt, zoom, and focus. Capture and processing of the needed zoomed-in frames is fully automated; a "photograph" of the whiteboard appears on a nearby printer a few minutes after a scan command is issued.

The primary mode for initiating the whiteboard scan function is through a *Diagrammatic User Interface* (DUI). A computer vision system continually monitors activity in front of the whiteboard and watches for users to draw and annotate "buttons" indicating commands and their associated parameters. Whereas a physical button is the most straightforward mechanism for getting a machine to do something, a diagram is often the most effective way of indicating spatial symbolic data. Stafford-Fraser described an initial exploration of this idea (Stafford-Fraser, 1996).

Our system, called "ZombieBoard" (because it brings to electronic life the lifeless ink marks on a whiteboard), has successfully been in routine use at our research center since the spring of 1997, and during that time has delivered over one thousand images to everyday users. Section 2 of the paper provides a brief technical overview of the system and motivations for the design choices made. Section 3 offers observations on the use of the system and its effectiveness in integrating the whiteboard component of the physical and electronic document worlds.

## 2 System Overview

As a device intended to augment physical space by connecting it to the computational world, a whiteboard scanner system faces the following issues: (1) getting the computational system to perform the desired function; (2) providing a user interface appropriate to the physical setting; and (3) integrating with the computational world.

### 2.1 Image Capture

The automatic construction of image mosaics from multiple overlapping images has recently become a popular outgrowth of computer vision research (e.g. Szeliski, 1994; Irani, et al, 1995; Capel and Zisserman, 1998) . The basic mosaicing problem is to determine image transformation parameters (e.g. pure translation, affine, true perspective) for all component snapshots that will align snapshots' overlapping regions without showing seams.

Existing approaches to this problem can be classified by a handful of properties. ZombieBoard was designed with its specific instrumented whiteboard application in mind. Accordingly, its place in the design space is as follows:

*Still frame vs. Video*: Several image mosaicing systems take as input video sequences characterized by a large number of image frames possessing large frame-to-frame overlap. To mitigate burden on computing resources, ZombieBoard uses instead a still-frame approach where snapshots overlap one another by about 30%. A typical 72" by 45" whiteboard will use about 18 snapshots.

*Signal or Feature*: Most image mosaicing systems search for image-to-image transformations that will minimize some pixelwise, or signal-level, cost function. For efficiency of computation in the sparsely-textured domain of whiteboard images, ZombieBoard uses a feature-matching approach whereby salient image features occurring in the whiteboard's contents are automatically detected and used to align overlapping snapshots.

*Painting versus Global Alignment*: The most straightforward image mosaicing methods treat the destination image as a "canvas". Each source image is "painted" in one at a time by registering with the existing destination image as it has been painted in thus far. This technique is prone to severely distorted resulting images because small errors in registrations tend to build up and compound one another as more frames are added. ZombieBoard is among the approaches that perform "batch" registration whereby all snapshots are aligned with each of its neighbors in an iterative global optimization process.

*One dimensional versus two-dimensional mosaics.* "Painting" methods work best in constructing one-dimensional mosaics where the set of images is a simple pan of the target scene. ZombieBoard is among the mosaicing methods that assemble composites representing up-and-down motion of the camera as well as right-to-left.

*General versus controlled camera positioning*: At the time a ZombieBoard installation is created, the pan/tilt camera's location and orientation with respect to the whiteboard is calibrated. This information is used to advantage when the whiteboard is scanned. The calibration information is used to bootstrap an initial "dead-reckoning" estimate of the image transform parameters required to construct a seamless mosaic.

*Blending versus color normalization.* Most image mosaicing systems hide seams by blending overlapping images. Because ZombieBoard is tailored to whiteboard scenes, we are able to simplify the blending step by applying a color normalization algorithm to each snapshot before combining them into the final mosaic. This color normalization involves segmenting "white" (whiteboard) regions and using these to estimate illumination which is then used to normalize intensities of ink regions.

A result image is shown in Figure 2. We typically provide whiteboard scans at a resolution of 30 dots/inch, but obviously this is controlled by the zoom factors of the snapshot layout.

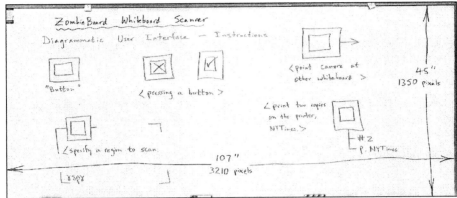

**Figure 2.** Whiteboard image obtained by automatic mosaicing of 19 snapshots from a computer-controlled pan/tilt video camera. Contents of this whiteboard represent the diagrammatic protocol designed for the Diagrammatic User Interface.

## 2.2 Diagrammatic User Interface

The simplest user interface to a whiteboard scanner would be a big "Print" button on the wall above a printer where the output would appear. One and only one function would be readily apparent to the user: scan and print the output on that printer. In any sophisticated cooperative environment however, one would want a more complex array of functionality. What if several copies were desired, one for each participant in the meeting? Or how would one specify an arbitrary electronic destination such as an email address or file directory? Could one command that only a subregion of the whiteboard be scanned?

While the simplicity of a big Print button remains attractive, the push-button as a command modality is severely limited. We seek to expand the interaction space and enable an open-ended set of commands.

Alternatives include keyboards, speech, and gesture interfaces. We perceive each as potentially viable but possessing serious impediments as well. Keyboards allow entry of arbitrary text by those who are inclined to type, but they require an accompanying console display that is expensive and ungainly in many whiteboard settings. More seriously, whiteboard work inherently occurs not through intricate finger movements, but at a physical scale of human arm and body movements, often in a social setting. To turn away from the other participants and attend to a keyboard/console interface in order to operate a piece of technology breaks the rhythm and dynamic of a meeting session. Speech recognition has reached commercial viability for some applications, but strongly favors high quality acoustic input which is difficult to achieve in an average whiteboard setting. Gestural input with a stylus is appropriate for whiteboard-scale interactive display surfaces, but not for the lower-tech ordinary whiteboard.

The ZombieBoard project has chosen to explore the notion of a Diagrammatic User Interface for several reasons. First, a diagrammatic interface befits the medium. Diagrams or drawings are one of the principal representation types people put on whiteboards. Second, a diagrammatic interface presents a calm mode of interaction.

The technology is hidden and unobtrusive to the user. A statically available drawing can be created at the user's own pace, and edited to their satisfaction. Third, diagrammatic interfaces can be expressive and flexible. Whiteboard marks can represent both symbolic information and spatial references. Finally, when a camera is already present as with an optical whiteboard scanner, a diagrammatic UI leverages the existing imaging and computing infrastructure.

The space of Diagrammatic User Interface command and interaction protocols is vast and ripe for exploration. The underlying technology of line drawing analysis is immature, especially where hand-drawn diagrams are concerned, so for any given application a protocol must be designed under constraints of both the needs and accessibility to users and the algorithmic capacities of machine vision systems.

Figure 2 shows the diagrammatic command conventions we have chosen; of course others are possible. The ZombieBoard Diagrammatic User Interface (or DUI, pronounced "dew-we"), is designed around the conceptual notion of a "button" which the user draws to gain the system's attention that a command is being issued. A button consists of a pair of nested squares. This pattern is easy to draw, rare to occur among common whiteboard material in most domains, and relatively easy to recognize by our line drawing analysis module. The button can be "pushed" by drawing an X or check mark inside. This amounts to issuing a "GO" or "SCAN" command.

Also, a button can be annotated to elaborate and parameterize the command. In our testbench prototype, button annotations include: (1) drawing an arrow to cause the camera to point at another whiteboard in the room; (2) encircling a region of the board to scan; (3) indicating symbolic information such as the number of copies to be printed, file directory, fax, and email destinations for the electronic image, and ink colors to be omitted from the output image. Of these, only the first has been included in the deployed system to date.

When not engaged in collecting zoomed-in snapshots of the whiteboard, the camera is zoomed back to view the entire whiteboard area. Detection and interpretation of diagrammatic commands is performed using images captured at this relatively low resolution.

Technically, the ZombieBoard DUI consists of two main functional modules. First a real-time Activity Analysis module filters an image stream to extract subimages that could possibly represent a diagrammatic command. In general, to analyze in detail the markings on a whiteboard is a compute-expensive job, even when the system is looking only for a stereotypical pattern such at the key Nested Box Button. Relatively little of the raw input stream is new material drawn on the whiteboard though; most of the time, most of the input images contain whiteboard material previously seen and analyzed, or else people engaged in whiteboard work. The system design therefore employs an activity analysis filter whose function is to pass to the next stage images only of newly modified persistent image content exemplified by material newly written on the whiteboard.

The second functional module of the DUI performs line drawing analysis to interpret any visible commands by extracting and analyzing the spatial pattern of whiteboard markings. Due to unconstrained imaging geometry and tremendous variability by people in drawing even simple figures such as the Nested Box Button, line drawing analysis must be extremely tolerant to deviations from the prototypical geometrical shapes. Our approach is based on perceptual grouping (Saund, 1990; Saund and Moran, 1994). The incoming line drawing image is subjected to center-surround filtering, thresholding, and thinning. Curvilinear lines are collected by tracing, and perceptually salient corners are found by a multiscale corner detection algorithm (see Saund, 1993). The result is a set of primitive curve element tokens representing relatively straight curvilinear contour segments. These tokens in turn undergo a series of grouping operations designed to make explicit spatial structure such as extended curvilinear arcs, corners, parallels, nested corners, and finally, the nested box.

In operation, when running on a Sparc 20 the DUI normally responds to hand-drawn commands within 5 to 10 seconds. This amount of delay is very significant and understandably annoying to users and we anticipate improving response time through the use of faster computing and frame-grabbing hardware.

## 2.3  Connection to the Electronic World

Increasingly, knowledge work is done online in the context of electronic document representations which may or may not exist on paper. Hardcopy prints of a whiteboard's contents are extremely useful because they may be carried away, copied, filed, and so forth. But it is equally important to provide access to whiteboard documents from the online world. We therefore provide a web-based user interface to ZombieBoard in addition to the Diagrammatic User Interface. A few clicks at a web browser takes the user to a page from which they can select among the nineteen or so ZombieBoard installations in the building.

An installation's web page provides two basic functions. Users can perform a whiteboard scan remotely, and they can access a gallery of images previously scanned in that conference room or office.

Images in the gallery can be cropped, copied to files, and sent to printers. At present, conversion from bitmap form to digital ink that be edited by sketch editing programs such as Tivoli (Pedersen, et al, 1993) is something we have technology for but not as yet attached to the deployed ZombieBoard system.

The ZombieBoard system is built with with a client/server architecture using the ILU distributed object system (ILU, 1991). Whiteboard scanning command and image processing operations are published services which could be accessed from other networked devices such as laptop computers and PDAs, although this capability has not yet been exploited.

## 3 Use and Effectiveness

*Deployment:* ZombieBoard  has been deployed in our research center among approximately 150 scientists and support personnel for over two years.  In that time the number of installations has grown to twelve in conference rooms, four in group working spaces, one in an open area, and two in private offices,  for a current total of nineteen.  The system is used on average 10-20 times per week, sometimes at the conclusion of a meeting, sometimes several times during a meeting or work session.  Many of these uses involve multiple scans.

*Use:* Several groups conduct weekly meetings or study groups in which the whiteboard is the focal point of the work and ZombieBoard scanning is performed religiously.  Some of the most ardent users are not researchers but technical support personnel whose whiteboard work includes planning meetings, to-do assignments, and schedules that must be consulted and distributed for days and weeks after the meeting.  Two of the conference rooms have very large whiteboards that on occasion get entirely filled with material.  Our observation is that the system is used more rarely in these rooms, but its value when needed is proportionately greater.

*Electronic images:*    A subset of users whose document work practices occur primarily online do not use the printed output at all,  but rely on the electronic image of their scan that is automatically stored in a public file directory.  Images are stored in jpeg format and typically consume 300 KBytes of memory to store the full-resolution color image plus two thumbnail images for browsing.  On account of file space, older scans in the public file space are expunged after four months. Some groups maintain online shared repositories to organize and provide access to their project's documents.  In these cases, ZombieBoard scans are typically copied from the shared public directory to the group's own file directories where they can be kept indefinitely.

*Privacy:* To assure privacy for meetings held behind closed doors, every ZombieBoard installed in a conference room is equipped with a simple pull-down shade that blocks the whiteboard from camera view.    These are indeed used on occasion, indicating that the presence of a camera can raise people's awareness and privacy concerns.

*User interface:* Feedback to the user is an important component of any user interface, and the deployed ZombieBoard does not as yet adequately address this issue.  After issuing a diagrammatic "GO" command by drawing a button, users can tell that a whiteboard scan has begun by observing the camera panning and tilting.  But to divert one's attention to notice this camera activity is distracting and inappropriate in a meeting situation.  Furthermore, the 5-10 second delay in response while the DUI processes the image is so slow as to be disruptive.  The delay problem can be eliminated through improvements to the algorithm and faster computers, but a better feedback mechanism is required to indicate the system's status.

In some installations, we have therefore experimented with audio feedback in the form of audio icons and background sounds played at an unobtrusive volume level. Sounds indicate that the command has been recognized, that image snapshots are being collected (and therefore people may want to stand clear of the board), when snapshot collection is complete, and finally when processing is done and the image has been sent to the printer.

Another issue arises with the mechanics of drawing a "GO" button. Due to the imaging conditions, reliable line drawing recognition depends on dark marks . Half–dried out markers under poor lighting conditions are virtually invisible to the DUI. Users, who are unfamiliar with the fact that their eyes are a lot better than the cameras', rapidly but justifiably become impatient when the system fails to recognize a weakly-drawn button. For this reason, we provide a card pre-printed with the "GO" symbol that sticks magnetically to a metal whiteboard. Slapping this button on the board is truly as easy and in most cases nearly as reliable as pushing a physical button.

*Reliability:* In our experience, the principle form of system-level failure occurs when, after a meeting, a user goes to the printer room and does not find his or her printout *not* because the whiteboard was not scanned, but because the printer is jammed or out of paper. Another failure mode occurs when users from across the building know how to use ZombieBoard but don't know where the printer is to find the output. This information is printed on an instruction sheet posted on the wall, but few users are prone to read instructions. No matter what the cause, *any* form of failure reduces users' confidence that their whiteboard work will be saved and they can safely erase the board. For this reason, we have recently begun deploying low-cost inkjet printers in each conference room equipped with a ZombieBoard so users will have their output on the spot.

# 4 Conclusion

The notion of Ubiquitous Computing opens a vista of alternative visions for augmented environments that support individual and group work. In this spirit, the ZombieBoard whiteboard scanner places cameras unobtrusively in front of whiteboards in order to link these physical document media with the computational world. Two component technologies borrowed from the field of computer vision---high-resolution scanning through image mosaicing, and Diagrammatic User Interfaces---have demonstrated their effectiveness through two years of routine use in a real-user setting. Many system-level and design options present themselves for exploration, and many opportunities remain for improvement. But we believe that this example demonstrates a powerful and realistically viable approach by which computationally-enhanced cooperative environments are beginning to come into fruition.

## Acknowledgements

Many people deserve thanks for their contributions to the ZombieBoard project. Dietmar Aust, Bikram Bakshi, Ron Frederick, David Goldberg, Josh Kesselman, and Dan Larner contributed to the working programs. For valuable suggestions, feedback and technical support I thank Andy Berlin, Michael Black, Becky Burwell, Todd Cass, David Fleet, Bill Janssen, John Lamping, Jim Mahoney, Tom Moran, David Marimont, Karin Petersen, Ken Pier, Dan Swinehart, and many early adopters who offered helpful encouragement.

# References

1. Black, M., Berard, F., Jepson, A., Newman, W. Saund, E., Socher, G, Taylor, M. (1998) The Digital Office: Overview *AAAI Spring Symposium on Intelligent Environments* Stanford University (March, 1998), 1-6.
2. Capel, D., and Zisserman, A. (1998). Automated Mosaicing with Super-resolution and Zoom. *(Proc. IEEE Conf. on Computer Vision and Pattern Recognition (CVPR '98).* Santa Barbara, CA (June 23-25). 885-891.
3. ILU: Inter-Language Unification (1991-1999) http://www.parc.xerox.com/pub/ilu/ilu.html.
4. Irani, M., Anandan, P., Hsu, S. (1995). Mosaic-Based Representations of Video Sequences and Their Applications. *Proc. 5$^{th}$ Int. Conference on Computer Vision,* Cambridge, MA (June 20-23, 1995). IEEE Press. 605-611.
5. Mimeo, *Virtual Ink, Inc.* http://www.virtual-ink.com.
6. Pedersen, E., McCall, K., Moran, T., Halasz, F. (1993) Tivoli: An ElectronicWhiteboard for Informal Workgroup Meetings. *Proceedings of the InterCHI93 Conference on Human Factors in Computer Systems.* ACM, New York.
7. Saund, E. (1990). Symbolic Construction of a 2D Scale-Space Image. *IEEE TPAMI,* 12:8, 817-830.
8. Saund, E. (1993). Identifying Salient Circular Arcs on Curves. *CVGIP: Image Understanding,* 58:3, 327-337.
9. Saund, E., and Moran, T. (1994). A Perceptually-Supported Sketch Editor. *Proc. ACM Symposium on User Interface and Software Technology (UIST '94).* 175-184.
10. SMARTBoard, *SMART Technologies, Inc.* http://www.smarttech.com.
11. Softboard, *Microfield Graphics*, http://ww.micg.com.
12. Stafford-Fraser, Q. (1996). BrightBoard: A Video-Augmented Environment, *Proc. ACM Conf. on Human-Computer Interaction (CHI '96).*
13. Szeliski, R. (1994). Image Mosaicing for Tele-Reality Applications. *Second IEEE Workshop on Applications of Computer Vision (WACV '94).* Sarasota, FL.
14. Tegrity, Inc. http://www.tegrity.com.
15. VideoBrush, *PictureWorks Technology, Inc.* http://www.pictureworks.com.
16. Weiser, M., and Brown, J.S. (1996). Designing Calm Technology, *PowerGrid Journal* v. 1.01. http://www.powergrid.electriciti.com/1.01.

# Meeting Capture in a Media Enriched Conference Room

Patrick Chiu, Ashutosh Kapuskar, Lynn Wilcox

FX Palo Alto Laboratory
3400 Hillview Ave, Bldg 4, Palo Alto CA 94304, USA
{*lastname*}@pal.xerox.com

Sarah Reitmeier

University of Michigan
School of Information
Ann Arbor, MI 48109, USA
sreitmei@umich.edu

**Abstract.** We describe a media enriched conference room designed for capturing meetings. Our goal is to do this in a flexible, seamless, and unobtrusive manner in a public conference room that is used for everyday work. Room activity is captured by computer controllable video cameras, video conference cameras, and ceiling microphones. Presentation material displayed on a large screen rear video projector is captured by a smart video source management component that automatically locates the highest fidelity image source. Wireless pen-based notebook computers are used to take notes, which provide indexes to the captured meeting. Images can be interactively and automatically incorporated into the notes. Captured meetings may be browsed on the Web with links to recorded video.

**Keywords.** meeting capture, note taking, roomware, cooperative buildings, multimedia applications, video applications

## 1 Introduction

Public conference rooms are sites of meetings and organizational activities that contain a wealth of visual and verbal information. Meetings span a broad spectrum of informational and collaborative activities; examples are staff meetings, design discussions, project reviews, video conferences, presentations and classes. It is often important to have a record of the meeting. This is usually done with handwritten notes, augmented with presentation material that is either hand copied or obtained from the speaker. In some cases, more detail is needed and the meeting is recorded on audio or video. A meeting record allows people who were at the meeting along with those who were absent to review the meeting. The tasks performed during review can be simple retrieval of facts and details, or more involved activities such as studying, preparing reports, and creating meeting summaries.

Multimedia is a promising technology for supporting meeting capture and note taking. It can capture activity in the meeting room as well as the presentation material. Digital video has been used for meeting capture in systems such as STREAMS (Cruz and Hill, 1994), but it uses a room camera to take images of the presentation material and is subject to poor image quality and interference when people or objects obscure the display. Other systems like Tivoli (Moran et al., 1996, 1997) and Classroom 2000 (Abowd et al., 1996, 1998) uses LiveBoard electronic whiteboards (Elrod et al.,1992, Pedersen et al., 1993) to capture visual material indexed to an audio recording. Classroom 2000 supports note taking on PDA devices with pre-loaded presentation slides and lacks the flexibility of real time slide capture. The Coral system (Minneman et al. 1995) is a confederation of tools that support multimedia recording of meetings. Coral also provides infrastructure for synchronization of video to digital ink notes taken with Marquee (Weber and Poon, 1994). With Marquee, images cannot be incorporated into the notes. Forum (Isaacs et al., 1994) is a workstation-based system that uses video for distributing live presentations and allows users to annotate slides with keyboard and mouse.

At the FX Palo Alto Laboratory, we have a media enriched conference room equipped for meeting capture with room cameras and microphones, video conference cameras, and a large display rear video projector. A variety of *roomware* (Streitz et al., 1998) facilitates the capture, display, and transfer of multimedia information. Meeting capture at its most basic level is supported by recording the video and audio streams, and by taking notes on wireless pen notebook computers. The images of the room activity and the presentation material can be interactively incorporated into the meeting notes. High quality images of the presentation material are captured by a smart video source management component. Captured meetings and notes with links to recorded video may be reviewed on the Web.

This paper is organized as follows: Section 2 describes the media enriched conference room, Section 3 discusses how meeting capture and note taking is performed, Section 4 shows accessing and browsing a captured meeting, Section 5 explains the media management and system architecture, and Section 6 is on user experience.

## 2 A Media Enriched Conference Room

The conference room at our lab is designed to support multimedia meeting capture and note taking in a flexible, seamless, and unobtrusive manner in a public conference room that is used for everyday work. A blueprint of the room is shown in Fig. 1, and a photo in Fig. 2. The center area of the room has the typical and familiar conference room furniture with standard tables and chairs in a U-shaped arrangement. As encountered in a field study by Covi et al. (1998), most shared meeting rooms have only tables and chairs, and it is useful to be able to work in our conference room in this familiar setting. For interacting with the digital world, wireless pen-based notebook computers, which may be freely positioned and moved around the room, serve as unobtrusive devices for meeting capture.

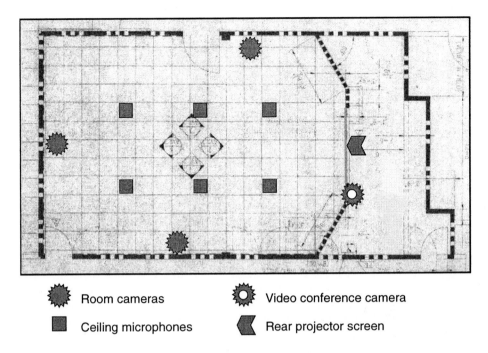

**Fig. 1.** Blueprint of conference room.

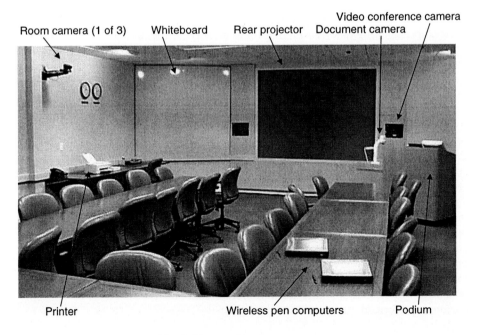

**Fig. 2.** Picture of conference room.

PC display, keyboard     Media selection
and mouse             and controls

**Fig. 3.** Podium and room viewed from the front.

On the front wall of the room is a flush-mounted large 120-inch screen rear video projector for displaying presentation material. Video of presentation material is fed into the rear projector from any of the following: a PC workstation, a document camera, a VCR, or a DVD player. A control room houses all of this hardware out of sight, and is walled off from the conference room with its own entrance in the hallway (see the right of Fig. 1). The document camera folds up and retracts into a podium drawer. A user may bring a laptop and plug it into a connector at the podium. The podium has controls that allow the presenter to select a source for the rear projector (see Fig. 3). It also has a thin LCD display, a keyboard and mouse hooked up to the PC in the control room.

There are three computer controllable cameras in the room plus a video conference camera for capturing and transmitting room activity. A room camera can be used to obtain an image of the whiteboard. Audio is handled by six ceiling microphones, combined into a single audio stream and mixed together with the video. Network connectivity is provided by a 1Mb wireless system. A small ink jet printer is available to produce hardcopies of notes or presentation material.

The room cameras may be tilted, panned, and zoomed from the control room. We have presets programmed for different types of meetings. For example, in a presentation meeting, one of the side cameras is aimed at the speaker at the podium, the other side camera at the participants around the table, and the back wall camera is set for a wide-angle shot of the whole room. When higher quality production is required, a person sits in the control room and directs the cameras.

With this setup, the underlying medium for capturing all types of visual images is video. The room video cameras provide images of the room activity and the scribbles on the whiteboard, the video conferencing system provides images of a remotely connected room, and the rear video projector provides images of the presentation material. Thus, video gives a seamless and flexible way to capture a variety of visual information from a meeting. There is a tradeoff between versatility and fidelity, which we will discuss in a later section. Before doing that, we describe how meeting capture is performed.

## 3 Meeting Capture

A meeting in the conference room is captured by recording the video streams from the room cameras, video conference sources, and rear video projector. The audio is captured by the ceiling microphones and mixed into the video streams from the room cameras. For later browsing and access, indexes for the video recordings are extremely helpful. A natural way to obtain indexes is to make use of notes taken by meeting participants. For this purpose, we have designed and built a client-server application called NoteLook. The standard technique of time-stamping notes and correlating them to multimedia data for retrieval was pioneered by Lamming and Newman (1991), and may be found in systems such as We-Met (Wolf et al., 1992), Filochat (Whittaker et al., 1994), Tivoli (Moran et al., 1997), Classroom 2000 (Abowd et al., 1996), Dynomite (Wilcox et al., 1997), and Audio Notebook (Stifelman, 1997).

NoteLook allows the user to take handwritten notes and interactively incorporate images from the room cameras, video conference cameras, and rear projector into the note pages. The client application runs on wireless pen-based notebook computers in the room (see Fig. 2). Users can write annotations and freeform notes with digital ink. A screen shot is shown in Fig. 4.

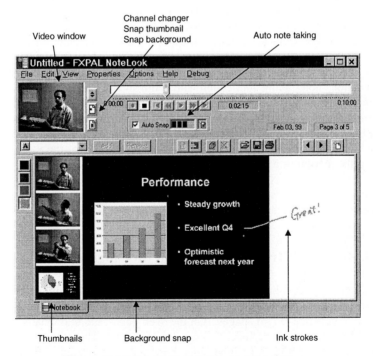

**Fig. 4.** NoteLook client application screen shot.

The user can view live video in the small window on the upper left corner. Next to the video window are three buttons for interacting with the video. The top button changes the video channels. We currently support two channels: one for the room activity from a pre-selected room or video conference camera, and one for presentation material shown on the rear projector. Usually, the pre-selected camera is a room camera pointed at the speaker at the podium. The middle button snaps the image in the video window as a thumbnail into the margin of the note page. When a sequence of thumbnails is snapped, they are automatically placed one below another. The bottom button snaps in a large background image. A newly snapped background image overwrites an existing background image on a page.

The interaction technique in NoteLook is *YCAGWYS (You Can Always Get What You See)*. Images of the room activity and the presentation material can be captured in real time as the user sees them. By using video as the underlying medium, this is accomplished by NoteLook in a seamless manner. To transfer information at a finer granularity between the shared display and pen-based notebooks, it is possible to employ techniques such as Pick-and-Drop (Rekimoto, 1998).

NoteLook has a set of standard VCR-type controls for recording and playback. Pressing the RECORD button makes a connection to the NoteLook server and initiates video recording and transmission to the clients. The video window displays the live video during note taking and the recorded video during playback. Above the VCR controls is a timeline with a pointer indicating the current video time position.

At the top right corner of the note page are buttons for previous page, next page, and new page. On the left is a palette of four pen colors for writing notes and annotations. Underneath the video window is a list box for entering keywords, and adjacent to the right is a set of four buttons for query and retrieval. The query and retrieval features are inherited from its predecessor Dynomite (Wilcox, 1997), which is a stand-alone note-taking application with audio and ink.

Furthermore, NoteLook has a facility for automatic note taking. In this mode, when the presenter puts up a new slide on the rear projector, it is automatically detected and snapped in as a background of a new page, and this page is appended to the stack of note pages. Also, a sequence of thumbnails from the room cameras is placed in the margin of that page. When the user turns to that page, she can annotate the images with ink. This feature relieves the user of the repetitive task of snapping in many slides during a presentation. In our experience, it is common to see 20 slides in a presentation and we occasionally have talks with over 50 slides.

## 4 Accessing and Browsing Captured Meetings

Captured meetings that have been indexed with NoteLook notes may be browsed on the Web. A sample is shown in Fig. 5. The NoteLook application has a menu command to generate HTML pages. On the Web pages, the thumbnails, background snaps, and ink strokes have links to the recorded video. These objects are all time-stamped during note taking, and the video playback is correlated to those times. The video is played back in a separate application window. We have integrated NoteLook Web pages with a video playback application developed at our lab called the Metadata Media Player (Girgensohn et al., 1999).

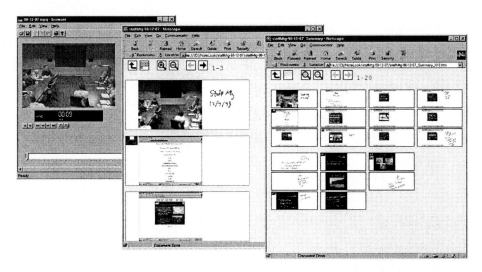

**Fig. 5.** Web access to captured meetings and notes. On the right is a table of contents page, in the center is a NoteLook Web page, and on the left is the Metadata Media Player.

Additionally, there are several standard navigational features on the Web pages. These are straightforward and we will only give a brief description. A top level page lists available NoteLook notes. For each session, a single table of contents page shows reduced images of all the pages. Clicking on a reduced image of a page brings up that page. Each page may be zoomed in or out with a range of five different magnification levels.

For private notes, users can store and playback NoteLook files on pen computers like the ones used in the conference room for meeting capture. The thumbnails, backgrounds, and ink strokes can be "played" by selecting them and pressing the PLAY button on the VCR controls. The video plays back in the NoteLook video window (see Fig. 4).

## 5   Media Management and System Architecture

The NoteLook client application is designed to be lightweight and flexible. However, digital video is a heavyweight medium because a substantial infrastructure is required to obtain adequate quality images of the room activity and presentation material. To deal with this tradeoff, we off-load most of the video processing and media management to the NoteLook servers and switchers. While the space in the conference room is relatively clutter free (as shown in Fig. 2), there are many pieces of the system outside the room hidden away from the users. The various components of the system are shown in Fig. 6. The key pieces are the NoteLook clients, servers, and switchers for video source management. We describe the interplay of these along with other components in more detail below.

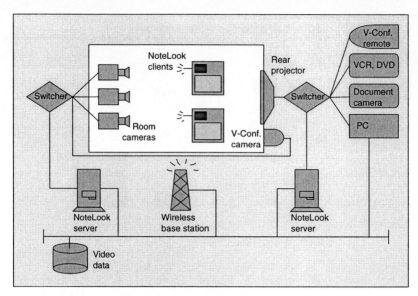

**Fig. 6.** NoteLook system architecture.

The NoteLook system is auto-configurable, extensible, and scalable. The clients and servers configure themselves automatically using resource discovery techniques. Adding and removing servers or channels does not require modifying existing clients, and multiple clients are supported by multicasting.

Each video channel corresponds to a server, which is associated to a set of sources. Currently, we support two channels: one for the room activity given by the room cameras and video conference cameras, and one for the presentation material given by the set of sources that feed into the rear video projector. The switchers are used to manually and automatically select the desired source.

A smart source management component addresses the *versatility/fidelity* tradeoff. Video provides a versatile way to capture room activity and presentation material. The images of the presentation material can come in a variety of forms: PowerPoint slides or Web pages from a computer, paper or plastic transparency overhead slides via the document camera, whiteboard via a room camera, video clips from VCR or DVD, etc. While the rear projector video feed is versatile enough to capture images of any type of presentation material, it does not always provide the highest quality images. For example, by the time an image of a PowerPoint slide travels from a PC's video output through the plumbing (which may contain various splitters and scan converters) and reaches the rear projector, the captured image is degraded to a level that sometimes makes it difficult to read the text on the slide.

The source management component deals with this problem by identifying the highest fidelity source available for capturing images. In the previous example, when the rear projector displays PowerPoint slides running from the PC workstation, the source management component directs the server to get the images from the PC by screen snap (i.e. the PC's screen bitmap, not the PC monitor video signal, not the rear projector video signal). In the case when a speaker supplies her own laptop, the server must gets its images further downstream from the video signal of the rear projector with some unavoidable degradation in fidelity. The source management component operates automatically in real time and interfaces with the switchers and a commercial AMX room control system. The result is that the best obtainable images are always captured while video source management is hidden from the user.

The NoteLook servers take video and audio inputs, process them, transmit the output to the NoteLook clients, and store the data for later retrieval. When a user initiates a session by pressing the RECORD button on the client application, it broadcasts a request for service, the servers respond and identify themselves, and connections are established. The video is transmitted to the clients at a highly reduced frame rate (1 per 2 seconds) to conserve wireless bandwidth. Meeting participants do not necessarily need full motion video for note taking since they are present in the room watching the live action. Automatic note taking is handled by a software component that runs on the servers and analyzes the video data. When the speaker puts up a fresh slide, it is detected and packaged along with a sequence of thumbnails of room images, and these are sent to the client for creating a new note page.

## 6   User Experience

We have conducted a user study over a six-week period with 13 meetings (Reitmeier et al., 1998). These meetings were presentations, staff meetings, and Japanese classes. We found that the system performed successfully for meeting capture and note taking. It supported seamless capture of room activity and a variety of presentation material. From interviews, we found the system to be minimally intrusive to the speaker and the participants in the room. The user study provided insights that resulted in several refinements to the system, notably it led us to develop the video source management component and automatic note taking feature.

We are currently using the meeting capture capabilities of our media enriched conference room in many of our meetings. Over the long term, we plan to gain more usage experience, continue to refine the system design, and observe how it co-evolves with the meeting work practice.

**Acknowlegements**

We thank Sara Bly, John Boreczky, John Doherty, and Andreas Girgensohn for all of their valuable help on this project.

## References

1. Abowd, G. D., Atkeson, C. G., Brotherton, J., Enqvist, T., Gulley, P., and LeMon, J. (1998). Investigating the capture, integration and access problem of ubiquitous computing in an educational setting. *Proceedings of the CHI '98 Conference*. ACM Press, pp. 440-447.

2. Abowd, G. D., Atkeson, C. G., Feinstein, A., Hmelo, C., Kooper, R., Long, S., Sawhney, N., and Tani, M. (1996). Teaching and learning as multimedia authoring: the classroom 2000 project. *Proceedings of the ACM Multimedia '96 Conference*. ACM Press, pp. 187-198.
3. Covi, L., Olson, J., Rocco, E., Miller, W., Allie, P. (1998). A room of your own: What do we learn about support of teamwork from assessing teams in dedicated project rooms? *Proceedings of CoBuild '98*. LNCS 1370. Springer - Verlag, Heidelberg, pp. 53-65.
4. Cruz, G. and Hill, R. (1994). Capturing and playing multimedia events with STREAMS. *Proceedings of the ACM Multimedia '94 Conference*. ACM Press, pp. 193-200.
5. Elrod, S., Bruce, R., Gold, R., Goldberg, D., Halasz, F., Janssen, W., Lee, D., McCall, K., Pedersen, E., Pier, K., Tang, J., Welch, B. (1992). LiveBoard: A large interactive display supporting group meetings, presentations and remote collaboration. *Proceedings of the CHI '92 Conference*. ACM Press, pp. 599-607.
6. Girgensohn, A., Boreczky, J., Wilcox, L., Foote J. (1999). Facilitating video access by visualizing automatic analysis. *Proceedings of Interact '99, to appear*.
7. Isaacs, E. A., Morris, T., and Rodriguez, T.K. (1994). A forum for supporting interactive presentations to distributed audiences. *Proceedings of CSCW '94*. ACM Press, pp. 405-416.
8. Lamming, M. and Newman, W. (1991). Activity-based information technology in support of personal memory. Technical Report EPC-1991-103, Rank Xerox, EuroPARC, 1991.
9. Minneman, S., Harrison, S., Janssen, B., Kurtenbach, G., Moran, T., Smith, I., and van Melle, B. (1995). A confederation of tools for capturing and accessing collaborative activity. *Proceedings of the ACM Multimedia '95 Conference*. ACM Press, pp.523-534.
10. Moran, T. P., Chiu, P., Harrison, S., Kurtenbach, G., Minneman, S., and van Melle, W. (1996). Evolutionary engagement in an ongoing collaborative work process: a case study. *Proceedings of CSCW '96*. ACM Press, pp. 150-159.
11. Moran, T. P., Palen, L., Harrison, S., Chiu, P., Kimber, D., Minneman, S., van Melle, W., and Zellweger, P. (1997). "I'll get that off the audio": a case study of salvaging multimedia meeting records. *Proceedings of CHI '97*. ACM Press, pp. 202-209.
12. Pedersen, E. R., McCall, K., Moran, T. P., and Halasz, F. G. (1993). Tivoli: An electronic whiteboard for informal workgroup meetings. *Proceedings of INTERCHI '93*. ACM Press, pp. 391-398.
13. Reitmeier, S., Chiu, P., Bly, S., Kapuskar, A., Wilcox, L. (1998). NoteLook User Study. FXPAL Technical Report TR98-039, FX Palo Alto Laboratory.
14. Rekimoto, J. (1998). Multiple-Computer Interfaces: A cooperative environment consisting of multiple digital devices. *Proceedings of CoBuild'98*. LNCS 1370. Springer - Verlag, Heidelberg, pp. 33-40.
15. Stifelman, L. (1997). *The Audio Notebook: Paper and Pen Interaction with Structured Speech*. PhD Thesis. MIT, 1997.
16. Streitz, N., Geißler, J., Holmer, T. (1998). Roomware for cooperative buildings: Integrated design of architectural spaces and information spaces. *Proceedings of CoBuild '98*. LNCS 1370. Springer - Verlag, Heidelberg, pp. 4-21.
17. Weber, K. and Poon, A. (1994). Marquee: A tool for real-time video logging. *Proceedings of CHI '94*. ACM Press, pp.58-64.
18. Whittaker, S., Hyland, P., and Wiley, M. (1994). Filochat: handwritten notes provide access to recorded conversations. *Proceedings of CHI '94*. ACM Press, pp. 271-276.
19. Wilcox, L. D., Schilit, B. N., and Sawhney, N. (1997). Dynomite: A Dynamically Organized Ink and Audio Notebook. *Proceedings of CHI '97*. ACM Press, pp. 186-193.
20. Wolf, C., Rhyne, J., and Briggs, L. (1992). Communication and information retrieval with a pen-based meeting support tool. *Proceedings of CSCW '92*. ACM Press, pp. 322-329.

# Going Public:
# Collaborative Systems Design for Multidisciplinary Conversations

Cheryl Geisler, Edwin H. Rogers, John Tobin

Rensselaer Polytechnic Institute
Troy, New York USA 12180
geislc@rpi.edu

**Abstract.** The driving idea behind our work has been the concept of *going public* with the goal of supporting the emerging work practices of multidisciplinary teams. In this chapter, we outline the theoretical basis for going public, describe the underlying architecture of a public collaborative system and introduce two embodiments, the Design Conference Room™ and the Collaborative Classroom™. The underlying architecture of a public collaborative system, overlaid with lines of view, sight, and control, provides system-sharing functionality via the Reconfigurable Collaboration Network™, supporting fully collaborative conversations, with their trajectory of work processes from private, to public, and back again. Innovations are described in the disciplinary domains of architecture, computer science, and communication.

**Keywords.** Public, private, system sharing, teamwork, collaboration, multidisciplinary, conversation, Design Conference Room™, Collaborative Classroom™, Reconfigurable Collaboration Network™

## 1 Background

The driving idea behind our work has been the concept of *going public* with the goal of supporting the emerging work practices of multidisciplinary teams. We suggest that multidisciplinary collaborations involve crossing and recrossing the boundaries between public and private work. The public collaborative systems which we have designed link together interactions over physical and virtual space through innovations in spatial arrangements, system sharing, and collaborative protocols — all centered around the concept of public space. In this chapter, we outline the theoretical basis for going public, describe the underlying structure of public collaborative systems and introduce its embodiments, the Design Conference Room™ and the Collaborative Classroom™.

## 1.1 Collaboration as Conversation

In environments that are increasingly distributed and asynchronous, team work is often understood as *coordinated work*, work done by individuals, often in different times and in different places, which produces information intended to be used as a shared resource by all (Bardram, 1998; Engeström *et al.*, 1997; Muller, 1997; Johnson, 1989). In such coordinated contexts, work is predominantly private. It produces artifacts, both real and virtual, that belong to the team and must be shared with the team, but the actual work processes which produce these artifacts are usually kept behind the closed doors of private workspaces. Successful coordination in these team contexts requires information-sharing, adequate updates, timely notification, and occasional interactions to adjust plans or discuss unexpected issues, but the need for going public is limited. Computer print-outs, projected slide shows, output "played" on any variety of players — all of these methods are sufficient for public space designed to support coordinated work.

*Collaborative work* goes one step further than the coordination of work to include the co-construction of team decisions and artifacts (Bardram, 1998; Olson *et al.*, 1993; DeSantis & Monge, 1998). In fully collaborative contexts, work processes come out from behind closed doors into team workspaces, supporting not simply the sharing of information, but also co-construction. In these contexts, sharing information is not synonymous with collaborating. Sharing is only preliminary, the first step in a communicative process that may eventually lead to the agreements that take the collaborative work forward

Successful collaboration, in fact, requires the creation and maintenance of what Clark (1996) has called "common ground." According to Clark, participants solve the coordination problems inherent in collaboration using conversation. Participants use their conversational turns to display their understanding of the current state of the collaborative work, an understanding that other participants may, in subsequent conversational turns, either ratify or correct. Through sequences of such conversational pairs, participants accumulate the common ground necessary to support collaborative work.

Underlying Clark's model of joint activity is the premise that conversation is essential to collaboration, a premise which we share. Conversational turns, whether direct and unmediated as in face-to-face meetings, or diffuse and highly mediated as in email and other asynchronous settings, form the language-based backbone of collaborative work. Going beyond simple information sharing, successful collaboration requires continually and seamlessly going public. In making, exploring, justifying, and ratifying the proposals which, taken together, constitute the co-constructed work, team members routinely call on a wide range of work processes. Public space designed to support such collaborative work must, therefore, provide a broad range of application-based resources.

## 1.2 The Special Requirements of Multidisciplinary Teaming

Teamwork which is multidisciplinary poses additional complications for the finely-tuned coordination of collaborative work. As we have become increasingly aware, different disciplines often work in distinct object worlds (Bucciarelli, 1994; Medway, 1996), worlds with objects and processes which are nearly opaque to those outside the disciplines. Although these objects have become increasingly virtual in the information age, they have not become easier to manipulate. In fact, highly-specialized applications, loaded with features, have made disciplinary objects more rather than less arcane.

When the need is only for the coordination of work, the opacity of disciplinary objects creates limited requirements for public space. Others outside the discipline need to view the object and understand enough about it to coordinate their own work with it, but technologies for viewing objects such as we noted earlier — print-outs, slide shows, and players, all under the control of the disciplinary specialist — suffice. When public space must support collaboration across disciplines, however, new requirements emerge (Jaryenpaa & Leidner 1998; Van House *et al.,* 1998). Others outside the discipline need not only view disciplinary objects, but also share control of them: to suggest changes, to make changes, and to evaluate the impact of those changes. Shared control of applications thus becomes important.

In addition to shared control, public spaces must also support a more complex ratification process in multidisciplinary conversations. Once participants have used a conversational turn to display their current understanding of the collaborative work, often embodied, as we have noted, in virtual objects created through specialized applications, they then seek ratification from team members for that understanding. Here is where the collaborating team moves beyond simple sharing to creating common ground in Clark's sense.

In multidisciplinary contexts, ratification can be complex because it cannot rely exclusively upon the ground of shared understanding. In simple collaborations, that is, participants can ratify one another's proposals for how to take the collaborative work forward because they understand those proposals and, fully understanding them, they approve of them. In multidisciplinary collaborations, such full understanding is not always possible. What seems to happen instead is that each disciplinary specialist must explore the implications of a proposal from the viewpoint of their own private object-world and then, once that exploration is complete, return to the public space to ratify or decline to ratify as the case may be. Ratification in multidisciplinary collaborations thus requires repeated movements between public and private space, necessitating a permeable membrane between the two.

## 1.3 The Concept of Public

The concept of public we have been using here deserves comment. Commonsense understandings of "public" as opposed to or complement to "private" space quickly yield on analysis to more fuzzy concepts. In a modern or post-modern society, little of what we call "private" work is actually done in complete isolation from others.

Instead, individuals work under a variety of conditions of copresence in the sense first analyzed by the sociologist Erving Goffman (1981)

Face-to-face conversations between what Goffman calls the ratified authorized participants — the people who are supposed to be there and who are authorized to contribute — serve as our paradigm of what conversation in public is supposed to be about. Such conversations actually represent only a subset of the situations of copresence. In many work situations, individuals find themselves under a variety of conditions of physical copresence — viewable, overhearable, even touchable — most of the time. True physical privacy is scarce and at a premium. In virtual space, privacy may be even rarer. Arrangements for networking, storage, and interaction may indeed make most of what we assume to be private space quite public under some circumstances. When we refer to "public" space, then, we need to acknowledge that the term is relative. Relative to the individual working in a cubicle, the team meeting may be considered public. Relative to broadcast via the World Wide Web, the team meeting may be considered relatively private.

Designers working to develop collaborative systems that go public need to consider the intellectual heritage of the concept of public and well as the deeply ingrained cultural attitudes toward public space. Public space is widely recognized as the pre-condition for equitable interaction (Bitzer, 1978; Halloran, 1978), but is also acknowledged to be difficult to maintain in our highly specialized culture (Clark & Halloran, 1993; Phillips, 1996). In our work, we aimed to support collaboration in public spaces, spaces in which others are copresent, ratified, and authorized to contribute. We have explored how the design of space, both physical and virtual, signals to its inhabitants to expect such public interactions and how such interactions may be made either harder or easier to sustain.

## 1.4 The Scenario of Fully Collaborative Conversations

Our goal has been to design public collaborative systems that support fully collaborative conversations. In our paradigmatic scenario of fully collaborative conversations, participants move through six stages in collaboration:

| | |
|---|---|
| SHARING | Participants introduce and review the results of their private work. |
| PROPOSING | Participants make proposals and counterproposals about how to take the work forward. |
| DISCUSSING | Participants explore the implications of proposals, bringing forward issues and arguments for and against adopting specific proposals. |
| RATIFYING | Participants together ratify, or adopt, a proposal. |
| UPDATING | Participants update their current understanding of their work given newly ratified proposals. |
| DISSEMINATING | Participants disseminate back to private individuals the results of the collaborative conversation in the form of a revised current understanding of the work. |

The overall trajectory of work in a fully collaborative conversation is from private to public and back again: From private space, where it is developed using disciplinary tools, to public space where it is shared, proposed, discussed, ratified, and updated, and back to private space where it is available for another cycle of work. Public collaborative systems should support this trajectory.

## 2 Public Collaborative Systems

We began our work[1] on public collaborative systems in 1992 with the design of the Design Conference Room™ which has been in continuous use at Rensselaer Polytechnic Institute since it opened in the fall of 1995. A second, educational facility was brought on-line in 1997 when the Collaborative Classroom™ became available to the community for teaching classes using teamwork. It has been fully scheduled since it opened. Though different in embodiment, both facilities share the common underlying architecture we call a public collaborative system. In this section, we begin by delineating this underlying architecture and then, in the next section, describe the two individual embodiments.

The basic architecture underlying a public collaborative system supports a collaborative conversation by interweaving conversational exchange in the physical space with information exchange in the virtual space using (a) lines of view, (b) lines of sight, and (c) lines of control.

To begin with, as diagrammed in Figure 1, a public collaborative system provides each participant in a conversation with lines of view to two kinds of systems, one public and one private. Private systems, located to the left or right of each participant in the unshaded area in the diagram, provide participants with a view of their private work which may be stored directly on the local private machine or accessed indirectly through a network. A single public system, displayed through multiple monitors shown in the shaded area of the diagram, provides a line of view to common or public work being co-constructed during the collaborative conversation. With lines of view to both systems, participants can repeatedly shift between public and private space during a team meeting, evaluating proposals in the public space against their implications for work in their private spaces.

[1] Our work has been supported by the National Science Foundation under CISE grants CDA-9214892 and CDA-9634485.

94

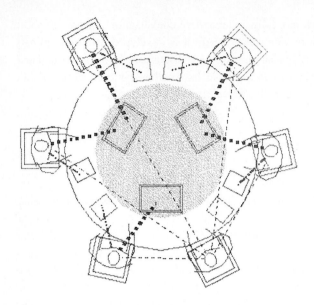

**Fig. 1.** The underlying architecture of a public collaborative system.

Next, a public collaborative system provides each participant with clear lines of sight to each of the other participants in the collaborative conversation as well as to the public and private systems. Lines of sight to participants are shown with single dashed lines in Figure 1; lines of sight to public and private systems are shown with multiple dashed lines. This integration of lines of sight to physically copresent colleagues as well as to the virtual objects which are the subject of their work allows participants to shift attention between the two as required as well as to maintain gaze awareness (Ishii *et al.,* 1993). At times, participants lean back and focus attention exclusively on each other; at times they lean forward, hunched over public or private systems, concentrating on the virtual object at hand; and at times, they move their attention back and forth between virtual and physical space.

Finally, a public collaborative system provides each participant with lines of control between their private system and the public system using the Reconfigurable Collaboration Network™[2] (RCN). RCN is system-sharing software designed to provide turn-taking control of the public system, allowing users, linked through multiple private systems, to create and modify common work. In addition, the RCN provides each participant in a session full access to all software which the public system can run and to all of its network services from the participant's private machine. The RCN is platform independent so that a mixture of Windows, Unix systems (of various flavors), and MacOS may be used in this full system collaboration. With access to the full panoply of professional applications,

---

[2] The Reconfigurable Collaboration Network™ is owned by Rensselaer Polytechnic Institute and licensed to shareDesign, LLC.

participants can make, explore, and finally ratify proposals during the co-construction of common work.

Increasing recognition is being paid to support object-centered collaborations (Van House *et al.*, 1998; Hindmarsh *et al.*, 1998; Gay *et al.*, 1999). Objects can serve as boundary objects (Star & Griesemer, 1989), linking together disparate communities and providing a level of collaboration deeper than unmediated conversations (Henderson, 1991). A variety of strategies are being explored for supporting such collaborations from shared editors and whiteboards (Olson *et al.*, 1993) to collaboratories (Finholt & Olson, 1997), shared surface representations (Olsen *et al.*, 1998), and coordinated PDAs (Myers *et al.*, 1998). Our approach has been to develop the Reconfigurable Collaboration Network™ to build upon rather than replace the disciplinary tools collaborators use in private, minimizing the barriers to entry in multidisciplinary work. In addition, our focus is on creating distinct virtual space for public computing — rather than simply bring up a public window on an otherwise private desktop — in order to more closely mirror the distinction we make between public and private in the deployment of physical space.

By overlaying lines of view, sight, and control, a public collaborative system supports the trajectory of collaborative work from private to public and back again. Private work, available either locally or over a network, is accessible on individual private systems throughout the collaborative conversation. By taking control of the public system, a participant can move information from private to public system, thereby *sharing* private work and possibly *proposing* a course of action for the team. Once viewable in the public space, colleagues take turns controlling the public space *discussing* the proposal, making changes, exploring implications, and even generating counterproposals. Participants eventually *ratify* a set of proposals which all can view and agree to, and then *update* the work in the public space. Finally, participants make arrangements for *disseminating* this updated information back to private systems.

## 3  Embodiments

Public collaborative systems have been embodied in two separate facilities at Rensselaer Polytechnic Institute, the Design Conference Room™, a team meeting facility supporting the work of one team at a time, and the Collaborative Classroom™, a working classroom supporting the work of multiple teams and their integration in an educational setting.

### 3.1  Design Conference Room™

The Design Conference Room™ provides seating for up to six participants around the custom-built conference table shown in Figure 2. Here, the public system is viewable through buried and angled monitors on three sides of a central modified hexagon. Private systems, here in desktop form, are similarly buried in extensions to the three remaining sides of the hexagon.  In the photograph to the left in Figure 2, the participants at the front are viewing one of the three public monitors; their private systems are to the right and left outside of view. Four of the participants at the rear are looking at two other private systems located across from each other at one of the hexagon's extensions. Their public monitors are located to their sides, shown closer in view. A fifth participant stands at an electronic whiteboard creating a sketch which can also be viewed on the public system. In this facility, public and private systems are Macintoshes. Shared control of the public system is through the mice and keyboards attached to each private system using the Reconfigurable Collaboration Network™.

**Fig. 2.** The Design Conference Room™ in photo (left) and layout (right).

The design of the spatial arrangement in the Design Conference Room™ emerged gradually. A series of early design studies using sketches, models and full-size mock-ups examined how various spatial configurations affect the relationship between participants and their work. These initial design studies temporarily put aside hardware requirements so that concepts centered on human interaction would take precedence, with technical resources supporting that initiative rather than leading it. Two major designs immediately presented themselves: The first option, sitting around a space, can be likened to pulling up chairs for a chat with team members. It is an informal interaction process that literally - and psychologically - places no barriers between the team members. However the second option, sitting around a table, is closer to the kind of interaction normally found in meetings, because it acknowledges that in any team process - even a computer-mediated one - there are artifacts to be viewed. Because of its familiarity and improved utility for group processes, we chose to develop this second option.

One major concern about placing large monitors under a sheet of glass was that veiling reflections could render the screen invisible. To more fully understand potential problems that might arise, we tested various lighting strategies in-situ as soon as the space became available. The approach used kept ambient light low, especially over the table itself, and to place indirect uplighting torchiere lamps along the perimeter walls. Tinted glass darkened the ceiling reflections but also allowed the screen to be viewed through it. The results are quite acceptable, and the screens are visible while viewing documents.

A second issue concerned the angle at which the table extensions would meet the central hexagon. Each pair of participants shared a single public monitor but also required lines of sight to their private screens. The simple solution, a table extension with parallel sides, did not work. Using a full-scale mock-up, we experimented until an angle was found that afforded the lines of sight as well as provided a comfortable position and adequate space for participants. In tandem, we experimented with the shape of the glass over the public monitors to insure that the full screen was viewable from the position being created by the angle. Together, the extension angles and glass shape shown to the right in Figure 2 work to create a comfortable and functional space for each team member.

## 3.2  Collaborative Classroom™

The Collaborative Classroom™ was developed to extend insights in public systems design to an educational context. Because teamwork is an emerging work practice in industry (Katzenback & Smith, 1993), more and more educators are employing teamwork in classrooms (Barrett, 1993). On our campus, classrooms designed a half-century ago supported team work by spacing team tables for up to six students around large halls. Instructors mentored team by moving through the hall for team consultations. When the building in which these classrooms existed was slated for renovation, we set a goal to develop a team-based classroom that would provide technological support through an integration of physical and virtual space, allowing students and instructors to go public in their collaborative work.

The Collaborative Classroom™ provides team tables for seven teams of four to six students. At each table, as shown to the left in Figure 3, a public system serves students via two monitors buried in the table wings. Laptops ports along the top edge of each wing provide connectivity for laptops that serve as private systems. In addition, two sets of keyboards and mice directly connected to the public system allow for direct control for students without laptops. At the front of the room, as show to the right in Figure 3, a podium system, linked to the team publics across the network, controls a high-end projection system. In this facility the public and podium systems run the Windows NT operating system. Private laptop systems may run any variety of operating systems: Windows, Macintosh, or UNIX.

Based on our observations of instructors at Rensselaer, courses requiring collaborative work use five major kinds of activity. The first three employ communication patterns similar to those used by the teams for which we designed the Design Conference Room:

TEAM MEETING  Students engage in team meetings both during regularly scheduled class time and after hours.

CONSULTATION  Instructors and clients move through the classroom, consulting on developing projects.

| PRACTICE | Students practice new techniques while fellow team members provide help. |
|---|---|

Two other activities, however, required communication in a unit larger than the team:

| LECTURE & DEMONSTRATION | Students attend to a lecture or view a demonstration done by the instructor at the front of the room |
|---|---|

| PRESENTATION & CRITIQUE | Students present their work to the entire the class for critique and suggestion. |
|---|---|

The key innovation in moving the concept of a public collaborative to accommodate this more complex pattern of communication in classrooms involved the addition of the concept of a *super-public* in both physical and virtual space. In addition to lines of sight to each other and to their public and private systems, students in classrooms need to attend regularly to a common, whole-class, focal point. In the Collaborative Classroom™, this whole-class focal point is provided through a podium computer known as the super-public.

Integrating the super-public into this public collaborative system involved changes in both physical and virtual space. Physically, lines of sight to the front of the room were created by changing table shape to a set of wings forming a tulip-shape, the V's of which are all oriented toward the super-public. As a result, as shown in Figure 3, lines of sight are simultaneously maintained to team colleagues, to the public and private systems at the table, and to the super-public at the front of the room. Virtually, the super-public was created in the Reconfigurable Collaboration Network™ by nesting the turn-taking control of the team publics within a turn-taking control of the super-public. Each team's public system can take turns controlling the super-public, showing team work or contributing to a whole-class exercise.

**Fig. 3.** The Collaborative Classroom in photo (left) and layout (right).

# 5 Conclusion

The concept of going public as described here has evolved through multidisciplinary interactions among the authors, one of whom is an communication specialist, one a computer scientist, and one an architect. Innovations were required in the disciplinary domains of all three: the underlying architecture of a public collaborative system with overlaid lines of view, sight, and control; the Reconfigurable Collaboration Network™ with its system-sharing functionality; and the concept of fully collaborative conversations, with its trajectory from private, to public, and back again. Like the teams we design for, we have brought our disciplinary insights from behind closed doors, unified our work through the common goal of supporting of multidisciplinary conversations, and developed a common commitment to going public in the design of physical and virtual space.

# References

1. Bardram, J. (1998). Designing for the dynamics of cooperative work activities. In *CSCW '98* (pp. 89-98). Seattle: ACM.
2. Engeström, Y., Brown, K., Christopher, L., Gregory, J. (1997). Coordination, cooperation, and communication in the courts. In Y.E. M. Cole, and O. Vasquez, (Eds), *Mind, culture, and activity.* Cambridge: Cambridge University Press.
3. Muller, R. (1997). Coordination in Organizations. In S. Kirn, and G. O'Hare, (Eds.), *Cooperative Knowledge Processing: The key technology for intelligent organizations* (pp. 26-42). Springer: London.
4. Johnson, B. (1989). How is work coordinated? Implications for computer-based support. In M. Olson (Ed.), *Technological support for workgroup collaboration.* Hillsdale, NJ: Erlbaum.
5. Olson, G.M., Olson, J. S., Carter, M. R., Storrosten, M. (1993). Small Group Design Meetings: An Analysis of Collaboration. *Human-Computer Interaction*, 7(4): p. 347-374.
6. DeSantis, G., and Monge, M. (1998). Communication processes for virtual organizations. *Journal of Computer-Mediated Communication, 3,* http://www.ascusc.org/jcmc/vol3/issue4/desanctis.html.
7. Clark, H.H. (1996). *Using language.* Cambridge: Cambridge University Press.
8. Bucciarelli, L.L. (1994). *Designing engineers.* Cambridge, MA: MIT Press.
9. Medway, P. (1996). Virtual and material buildings: Construction and constructivism in architecture and writing. *Written Communication*, 13(4): pp. 473-514.
10. Jaryenpaa, S. L., and Leidner, D. E. (1998). Communication and trust in global virtual teams. *Journal of Computer-Mediated Communication*, 3(4), http://www.ascusc.org/jcmc/vol3/issue4/jarvenpaa.html.
11. Van House, N., Butler, M. K., and Schiff, L. R. (1998). Cooperative knowledge work and practices of trust: Sharing environmental planning sets. In *Proceedings of CSCW '98*. New York: ACM, pp. 335-343.
12. Goffman, E. (1981). *Forms of talk.* Philadelphia: University of Pennsylvania Press.
13. Bitzer, L. (1978). Rhetoric and public knowledge. In. I. D. M. Burkes (Ed.), *Rhetoric, philosophy, and literature: An exploration.* W. Lafayette: Purdue University Press.
14. Halloran, S. M. (1978). Doing public business in public. In K. Kohrs Campbell and K. Hall Jamieson (Eds.), *Form and genre: Shaping rhetorical action.* Washington, D. C.: Speech Communication Association.

15. Clark, G., and Halloran, S. M. (1993). *Oratorical culture in nineteenth-century America: Transformation in theory and practice.* Carbondale, ILL: Southern Illinois University Press.
16. Phillips, K. (1996). The space of public dissension: Reconsidering the public sphere. *Communication Monographs*, 63, pp. 231-248.
17. Ishii, H., Kobayashi, M., and Grundin, J. (1993). Integration of interpersonal space and shared workspace: ClearBoard design and experiments. *ACM Transactions on Information Systems*, 11(4): pp. 349-375.
18. Hindmarsh, J., Fraser, M., Heath, C., Benford, S., and Greenhalgh, C. (1998). Fragmented interaction: Establishing mutual orientation in virtual environments, *In Proceedings of CSCW '98*, New York: ACM, pp. 217-226.
19. Gay, G., Sturgill, A., Martin, W., and Huttenlocher, D. (1999). Document-centered peer collaborations: An exploration of the educational uses of networked communication technologies. *Journal of Computer-Mediated Communication.* 4 (3), http://www.ascusc.org/jcmc/vol4/issue3/gay.html.
20. Star, S. L. and Griesemer, J. R. (1989). Institutional ecology, 'translations' and boundary objects: Amateurs and professionals in Berkeley's museum of vertebrate zoology, 1907-39. *Social studies of Science*, 19 (3), p. 387.
21. Henderson, K. (1991). Flexible sketches and inflexible data bases: Visual communication, conscription devices, and boundary objects in engineering. *Science, Technology, and Human Valuesw*, 16 (4), pp. 448-473.
22. Olson, J. S., Olson, G. M., Storrosten, M, and Carter, M. (1993). Groupwork close up: A comparison of the group design process with and without a simple group editor. *ACM Transactions on Information Systems*, 11 (4), p. 321-348.
23. Finholt, T., and Olson, G. M. (1997). From laboratories to collaboratories: A new organizational form for scientific collaboration. *Psychological Science*, 8 (1), pp. 28-36.
24. Olsen, D. R., Hudson, S., Phelps, M., Heiner, J., and Verratti, T. (1998). *In Proceedings of CSCW '98*, New York: ACM, pp. 129-138.
25. Myers, B., Steil, H., and Gargiulo, R. (1998). Collaboration using multiple PDAs connected to a PC. *In Proceedings of CSCW '98*, New York: ACM, pp. 285-294.
26. Katzenback, J. R., and Smith, D. K. (1993). The discipline of teams. *Harvard Business Review*, pp. 111-120.
27. Barrett, E. (1993). Collaboration in the electronic classroom. *Technology Review*, pp. 51-55.

# The Studio: Reflections and Issues Arising

Mike Robinson & Samuli Pekkola

Department of Computer Science and Information Systems
University of Jyväskylä
P.O. Box 35 (MaE), 40351 Jyväskylä, FINLAND
`mike@cs.jyu.fi, samuli@cc.jyu.fi`

**Abstract.** An advanced Telematic Studio was built at the University of Jyväskylä to combine the latest technologies for local and distributed work and/or meetings. The objectives were to combine leading edge technologies with ethnographic design principles derived from CSCW and HCI to support a broad range of activities. We informed the design by studies of similar facilities on other sites. The Studio is popular, and it is easy to give glowing accounts of its use. Nevertheless, over three years a significant number of problems have arisen with both technologies and uses. Some of these are local. Others may be generalisable to any 'cooperative building'. For example: problems with videoconferencing; incompatibilities between Office and Theatre design metaphors.

**Keywords**. cooperative building, telematic studio, design, theatre, CSCW

## 1  Introduction

An Advanced Telematic Studio was built at the University of Jyväskylä, Finland, to combine the latest technologies for local and distributed work and/or meetings. The technologies include meeting support, groupware, and CSCW software, running on 15 built-in Pentium PC's and Silicon Graphics workstations (SGI); 4 videoconferencing systems; simulation programs; Virtual Reality applications; document cameras; local and distributed monitors and large screen projections; electronic whiteboard; local and wide area networking via Internet (TCP-IP), ISDN and ATM.

The objective was to combine leading edge technologies with ethnographic design principles derived from the last decade of work in CSCW and HCI. We were concerned to create a worksite beyond "real" studios and offices. We supported our design by CSCW studies of workplaces, and our own practice (small and large offices in different European countries, papermills, oil refineries, telecom companies, remote teaching, etc.) and by looking carefully at 'electronic meeting rooms' (e.g. Mantei 1988; Nunamaker et al. 1988; Streitz et al. 1997) . We attempted to overcome known problems with 'meeting rooms' and with videoconferencing (a major feature of the Studio). The latter usually do not offer remote adequate camera control, or multiple cameras — both of which are helpful for understanding contextual aspects of other physical sites, and for accessing material being worked on in a flexible, timely, and appropriate way.

The first part of the paper will describe the functions and design background of the Studio. The second part will look at successful and problematic uses, with a view to drawing lessons for the design of cooperative buildings (Streitz et al. 1998).

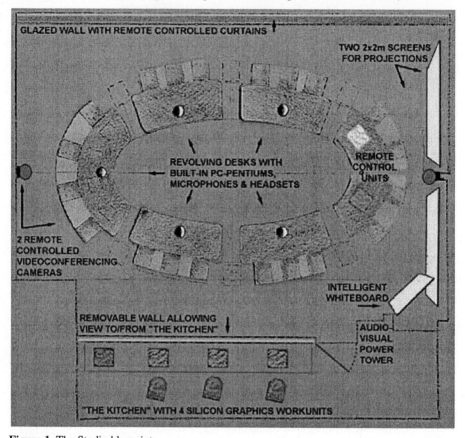

**Figure 1.** The Studio blueprint.


## 2 The Studio

"The Studio" was opened in May 1996. The physical environment measures 15 x 10m., with an annex that can be opened for additional space, specialised equipment, or supportive activities. The Studio is equipped with full audio-visual and teleconferencing facilities. These include: 3 large (2m x 2m) presentation screens; video (multiple format); dual large screen TV monitors; overhead, desk & transparency projectors; document camera/projector; 4 video conference systems (PictureTel & Intel ProShare are both available with ISDN, and Internet/ATM programs CUSeeMe and NetMeeting). Pentium PC's are set into the desks, laptops and SGI's are in the Annex. Software includes NT, Microsoft Office, Netscape

Navigator, Lotus Notes, cAme, Groupsystems, Meta Edit+, TeamWare, Simprocess, Intra Builder among others. The original intelligent whiteboard (IMCO) has now been replaced by a Smartboard. High quality audio (stereo, surroundsound) can draw on PC's, tapes, CD, CD-I, and microphones, including wireless.

The desks each contain 3 consoles, and can seat from 3 to 9 people. Unusually for meeting rooms, they can be repositioned as required. A large bearing in the centre base takes cables and air ducting, while allowing the desk to rotate through 360°. The consequence is that the Studio can be arranged in an oval as in Figure 1 (which is actually the architect's drawing), or as Theatre (facing front), semi Theatre (facing front centre), or Café (each desk facing a random direction for separate small groups work). All configurations are used by different groups. The Studio can be used for work, meetings, or playful activities[1]. It is comfortable for up to 40 people, but not over-solemn for a few (See Figure 2).

**Figure 2.** A mobile camera design session in the Studio.

Various commercial and external organisations in addition to the University use the Studio. It is interesting to contrast the different usages, and different configurations of technology and communication arrangements both local and remote. For instance, one group of executives were concerned to define formal arrangements for Finnish European Union programs. They used a circular seating arrangement (usually

---

[1] It makes a rather good Disco in the evenings.

considered "informal"); a facilitated and strongly proceduralised set of discussion conventions; and GroupSystems text based software with desktop input and large screen projection. Some local Graphic Designers needed to make frequent comparisons of developing work and techniques with a similar group in Helsinki. They used a theatre seating arrangement (usually considered "formal"); free discussion; and the PictureTel videoconferencing system with large screen projection. Other groups use e.g. Lotus Notes or TeamWare.

# 3 Design, Social & Work Practice Issues

## 3.1 Studio Design Principles

Three main qualitative principles inform the design of the Telematic Studio: Flexibility, Shared Material, and "Beyond Being There" (BBT).

**Flexibility** is due to Robinson's (1993) Design for Unanticipated Use. Put briefly, this means that *each and every* feature, facility, and configuration of CSCW artefacts *should* be flexible. A good example of this is the desk rotation already illustrated. The initial question was whether the desks should be in Theatre or Circular formation (the classic configurations in DSS rooms). The principle of Flexibility dictated that they should be both, and maybe other things besides. There was considerable initial opposition to rotating desks from the planner and the builders. The 3x1m wooden desks with 3 built in system units, monitors, and associated items were extremely heavy. The complex of cabling went directly into the floor. Nevertheless, with the help of the architect, it proved possible to design and implement a bearing that allowed stable egress for ducting and cables, while enabling 360° desk rotation.

**Shared Material** reflects our belief that the key to understanding and supporting group processes is not only dialogue, discussion, conversation, or interaction. Equally important is the sharing, in various ways, of the material being worked on (Sørgaard 1988; Star and Griesemer 1989; Robinson 1993). We believe that applications that only support dialogue, or only support shared material will be of limited usefulness. Users may get round this deficiency for well-liked applications by using another tool in parallel (sharing a screen document, and simultaneously talking on the phone, for instance). This is especially important for video conferencing, where, with Nardi (1993) and Saffo (1997) we believe the design and development path should concentrate on appropriate representations of objects and processes rather than improved images of dialogue partners.

**"Beyond Being There"** (BBT) is a *quality principle* theoretically identified by (Hollan and Stornetta 1992). It argued that simulating face-to-face co-presence was the objective of most tele-application designers: environments should be as close as possible to "being there". This does not parallel experience. A phone call or an email is often more effective or appropriate than a visit to another's office or a conversation. The authors argue that each medium has its own affordances. Mere approximation to face-to-face is a bad design objective, and does not mirror experience. We take the point further, and believe BBT is a *quality principle* for CSCW applications. *If and only if* there are circumstances in which people prefer to use a virtual medium to being physically copresent, then that application has quality. As Fitzpatrick et al. (1998) point out, this is extremely hard to achieve.

A number of issues from CSCW provided further design background.

**Direct awareness and interaction** cover such phenomena as eye contact, facial expressions, and gesture. We note that facial expression and especially gaze direction (Ishii and Kobayashi 1993) are technically difficult and cumbersome to reproduce in video or VR. Gesture is an area where videoconferences differ significantly from normal conversations. Heath and Luff (1993) for instance show that body movements and small gestures are hard or even impossible to transmit between participants.

> A speaker will attempt to produce a description and during the course of its production use gesture to gain a visually attentive recipient. The gesture becomes increasingly exaggerated and meets with no response, the description reveals linguistic difficulties and it may even be abandoned. (Heath & Luff,1993. p.839)

We have observed similar troubles. Some are due to self-consciousness, some to technical issues such as delays, desynchronisation of video and audio, and quality of service. Much is undoubtedly due to the nature of the medium, as for instance when pointing fails because the object is out of camera, or a person in a different "place" to different participants (Buxton 1993).

**"Peripheral awareness"** has been extensively explored by (Heath and Luff 1991; Heath et al. 1993). They show that environments as diverse as a London Underground Control Room, and a Stock Exchange Dealing Floor depend for their competences, coordinations, and effectiveness on "overhearing" and "out of the corner of the eye" awareness of others. Video, per se, does not seem good at supporting this since it does not provide wide or background awareness.

There are also many occasions when direct work on documents needs to be done. Video is rarely the best medium for this work hence we try to allow for simultaneous use of text, graphics, and document handling software. Thus our Studio design attempted to compensate for known problems with videoconferencing. In particular we provided remote camera control, camera for documents and small objects, and parallel document handling.

### 3.2 Successful Uses

The following have been popular and frequent uses. We will only note that all have a theatrical flavour; that all except one are fundamentally local; and that none require access to own files outside the Studio.

- Presentations
- Visiting Lectures
- Open Days
- Demonstrations
- Special Meetings
- Some types of lecture (where computers are required)
- Very limited teleconferencing (where display of objects was carefully set up)

### 3.3 Problematic Uses

In this paper more stress will be laid on problematic uses, since these are likely to have implications for cooperative building design.

**Most videoconferencing**. We have found that our videoconferencing is deficient in many respects, despite our efforts: it does not offer adequate remote camera control, or multiple cameras for accessing working materials or context. There are also technical problems with architecture, management, and disproportionate bandwidth requirements. The videoconferencing is well used (and well advertised), but most users do not return. The exception (graphic designers mentioned earlier) spend up to 6 hours preparing camera angles, appropriate objects for discussion, etc. It other words, their work on remote presentation is very close to a TV performance.

**Work**. We initially hoped for 24 hour uses of the Studio. Part of this, we surmised, might be students working together on embryonic commercial software products, special projects, and the like. There were some difficulties with University permissions for 24 hour access. The main discouraging factor was the inability to configure a computer as *my* computer, maintain paper files, or even leave anything around. There are no cupboards and no physical or aesthetic space for them.

**Lectures where computers are not required**. Students surf the net, read email, and do not pay much attention to the topic. The (computer friendly) physical layout also poses problems. Students are much more widely spaced than is usual. This can result in a feeling that the lecturer is only speaking to a few people at the front, missing the majority at the back. The computer friendly layout also more or less forces the lecturer to stay at the front — onstage, and in control of the technology — which is sometimes inappropriate for ordinary lectures. The tables cannot be moved to new places to avoid this, since they are anchored by the rotation mechanism. Also the tables (if the computers are not in use) are far too big, thus increasing the feeling of isolation, and the temptation to dream into the net. Further features that are demanded by the technology (over-powerful air conditioning when the computers are off, noise from the ceiling projector fan) are often a simple nuisance when the technology is not being used.[2]

**Managing demand (and jealously)** Something that it is easy to forget in planning an advance technical facility is demand and jealousy management. If the facility is successful, demand will outstrip capacity; if not, there will be political pressures against the group. We attempted to regulate high demand by price — but this was appealed and the University prohibited internal charging. We now have a simple solution: paper. Studio bookings are made by writing with a *pencil* in a *book* in our secretary's office. This effectively gives priority to those in the adjoining offices: ourselves. We are not aware of any electronic booking system with a similar affordance.

---

[2] Against this one lecturer noted that students use computers to make notes during his lectures, and this works quite nicely. During one course, visiting lecturers and the students wrote commented summaries in small groups which were then distributed to the class.

### 3.4 Some Things That Worked Technically or Physically

Here we found that many features, for example lighting, curtains, and large screen projection worked well, and contributed to the popularity of the Studio. These are not specially hi-tech or advanced. But if they are not given considerable design attention, then their lack or faults will likely undermine cooperative technologies provided.

**Technical support** It was originally thought that the Studio design would be so user-friendly that anything other than part-time or occasional technical support from our existing technicians would be unnecessary. This was a mistake. There is too much to explain to new users: an introductory session for up to 20 people takes about 40 minutes. Maintaining and updating the hardware and software, and understanding all the wiring is more than an occasional task. We employed graduate students (one year contracts) on a half-time basis, and this was successful. Nevertheless, it adds considerably to running costs. We now believe that any advanced facility needs to plan for ongoing technical support. This would be generalisable to cooperative buildings.

**Figure 3.** The heart of the Studio – the front and back of the equipment tower.

The nature of tasks now performed by the technician can be seen from one Minute, which listed 29 items from the trivial (cups, coffee machine, CD racks) to maintenance (stronger catches on flaps under desks which were dropping open with a blast of hot air in the users faces) to security (codes for international phone lines) to technical (projector sound and picture to be independent allowing CD with TV, SGI, PictureTel cameras, etc.). This (and Figure 3, which shows the equipment tower) give an idea of the mix of items needing attention in a facility like the Studio.

**Window between SGI workarea and studio** The Studio was built in a reconstructed restaurant area — the only available space large enough for our requirements. By luck, we also inherited the former kitchen at the back of the Studio, which we were able to utilize first as a technical control area, and later as a workspace for the SGI's which we did not wish to open for public access in the Studio. We now regard adjacency of the technical control area and the Studio as essential. Without adjacency, the technician could not know what is happening in the Studio, and could not give technical or other support to presentations. We later refined this by creating a 1.5 x 4 m window between the two that could be open (especially useful in setting up equipment); closed by glass (visual but not audio access — although if someone speaks loudly in the workarea, you can hear it in the Studio); closed (the window disappears and becomes a noticeboard).

This looks like a mundane, local, practical issue. It seems likely to us that any cooperative building constructed in the next couple of years is going to have a similar high profile to the Studio, have important uses for presentations and demonstrations, and be, at least in part, theatre. The issue of the back-stage and its relation to front-stage is mundane, but we suggest it is perilous to ignore it.

**PictureTel** The only one of four videoconferencing systems that never gave us problems was PictureTel. It is professional and full featured (e.g. local and remote camera control, zoom) if connected to identical remote system. It is also expensive.

**Large screen projection** The versatility of large screen projection from PC's, document camera, TV[3], video, was a key ingredient in the success of the Studio. This is a modern variant on the older and equally successful overhead projection. The ability to have a common display space and private spaces (paper or computer) seem essential ingredients of presentations, demos, and teaching. There is significant evidence — e.g. (Nardi et al. 1993; Heath and Luff 1996) — that cooperative buildings also need this feature, and some provide it handsomely (Streitz et al. 1998)

The only complaints we have are: powerful projectors cooling fans are too noisy, and the document camera was disappointing. Its luminosity is not high enough for slides, or for text. It works well for small 3D objects, though (apart from demos) there is not much demand for this.

---

[3] The ski competitions in the Winter Olympics and other sport activities were especially popular. Such informal uses are not be underestimated as contributions to the success of technically advanced facilities.

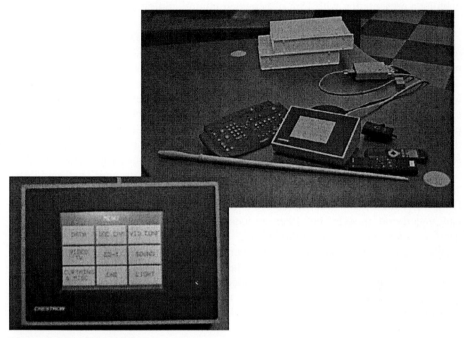

**Figure 4.** Central control box.

**Central control box** This unit (see Figure 4), about 1/3 the size of a laptop, is used by presenters to control audio, video, lighting, curtains, and projectors. It provides simple hierarchical menus on a touch screen, and is quick to learn. In fact we have had guest lecturers arrive late, and use it immediately with no instruction. We regard this single, simple control point as essential for presentations[4]. The only complaint we have is the difficulty of re-programming — so we usually leave it to the company that installed it.

**High quality audio systems** include the option of surround sound. These work well, and are appreciated. We now take it for granted that high quality audio is essential for presentations — as any theatre person could have told us. As a small caveat, we note that wireless microphones will always be left on after performances, and will need new batteries each time.

**Lighting and curtains** were designed on a quasi-theatrical model, and are controlled from the control box. The following sets can be used singly or in all combinations. Central (over the basic oval of tables), over each table, left side, window side, front, back. Any combination can be dimmed or brightened from the control box. One entire side of the Studio is a window giving panoramic views towards the lake. As a practical matter, heavy curtains are necessary for any presentation using projectors. There is also a certain style and drama involved in

---

[4] This can be compared with the 7 remote control units we also have. Their functions (even which machine they control) are obscure, and, worse, they are always getting lost.

opening a presentation with 15m of heavy curtaining gliding over the windows as the lights dim on the audience and brighten on the speaker.

**Silicon Graphics Technical Work Area** The technical area, or back room (the old restaurant kitchen) adjacent to, and looking into the Studio, is essential for on-line technical support, and for locating bulky or expensive equipment. It was here that the Silicon Graphics (SGI) Workstations were placed for Studio related VR development, Mbone connections, and high quality graphics support for presentations. It is the only part of the Studio that has been used consistently for work. Apart from special projects, the SGI's attracted a highly talented group of developers, known locally as the Dead Poets. Their work was possible because, unlike the main Studio, access was severely limited, machines could be configured as *my* machine, paper files could be maintained, items could be pinned to the wall, and things left around. The Dead Poets work was consistent with, sometimes used, and sometimes enhanced the special facilities of the Studio. Our experience is that the two space have different functions and underlying models, but their co-location is highly symbiotic. This may be generalisable to cooperative buildings.

**When you go the Theatre, you expect a Programme.** Another easy to neglect item in planning a cooperative facility is the glossy programme, and the work needed to create it and update it. Such a leaflet exhibits the Studio technical facilities (essentially it is a Quick-Start manual), is a PR document for our group, thanks our sponsors, and provides contact addresses.

### 3.5  Some Difficulties with the Technical and Physical

**Built in workstations** Now we need to upgrade the boxes (not just the cards or the memory) the spaces inside the desks are too small for new generation PC's (see Figure 5.). Although our configuration looks smart, we have doubts about the real usefulness of built-in PC's as opposed to laptops. These reservations extend to cooperative buildings.

**Figure 5.** A desk, few computers and a lot of wires.

**Wiring** is so complicated that (on many occasions) we cannot change/repair it ourselves, but have to call in the firm that installed it. Unbelievably, this was also true when a fault developed on the main projector (a crucial facility). Adding new devices to control rack is currently impossible, since there are not enough input/output plugs.

If we want to add something new, we have to change the multiplexer, and that is very expensive. ISDN connections were expensive, need book-keeping and use-accounts, sometimes disappeared (disconnected apparently at random by the University) and dedicated cards soon outdated.

**Interconnections can be problematic** The image quality from PC to TV monitor is unacceptable due to a bad converter and inadequate wire quality. Showing a screen from one PC on any of the others proved problematic. We were unable to afford the cost (and did not like the idea) of extra wiring between all computers. The software solution is not as useful as we had hoped, since it is complicated to use.

**Limited access to files.** A severe limitation on the use of the Studio for work was that own files (on other machines) were only accessible with difficulty, and often not at all. Since upgrading to NT, user profile-centric stuff is stored on a server, and accessible from computers in- and outside the Studio. NT has also been configured to prevent customisation (destandardisation) of the PC's. In the first couple of years of use there were considerable problems when one group would come in, only to find the carefully set up configuration had been changed, even deleted by the group before. This machine constancy is important for presentations etc, but mitigates against use of the Studio for ongoing work.

**Cost** A capital cost of Euro 300K and annual running costs of at least E50K were justified by an experimental facility with multiple purposes whose idea gained wide political support. The pressures from the financing to be 'high profile' inevitably pushed the Studio in the direction of Theatre and Performance, and away from the model of Office and Work.

# 4 Some Issues and Conclusions

Videoconferencing, despite our efforts to provide camera control and document handling, proved problematic except when staged as a TV performance. There are, we believe, some generic difficulties with videoconferencing that may (or may not!) be addressed by multiple monitors, or by the addition of VR, or of haptic interfaces (Brave et al. 1998). We think it probable that cooperative buildings will face similar demands to support videoconference-like remote collaborations (in part to justify cost). We believe it is relatively easy to support performance (local or remote) but harder to support collaboration in workspaces that are not dedicated to one function. Which brings us to our main conclusion.

No single space is likely to support all types of activity. This is an obvious point, but easy to forget in designing the space and justifying the cost to different audiences needed for political and financial support. In our case, the Studio was intended as a Workspace *and* a Presentation Space. These appeal to, and the design drew on two different paradigms that are not easily reconciled: the office/factory model and the theatre model. In retrospect, we recognise that the theatre model was implemented at the expense of an office model. The lighting, curtains, acoustics, ongoing technical support, and front-stage space for presentation were pure theatre. Essential features for office work were neglected. The computers cannot be *my* computer. There is no storage space for paper, and things cannot be left around. These were not a failure of design but an incompatibility between the models. Paper storage, open cupboards, *my* computer, and things left around are disallowed when a work session is two hours, followed, for example, by a session in which the Rector of the University has scheduled a presentation to Members of Parliament and EU Officials.

It seems likely to us that any cooperative building/space is going to face this dilemma. Work is ad hoc, and needs to configure its own spaces (computational and physical) in an enduring way. Presentation tends to Theatre, and needs aesthetic and disciplined spaces. Goffman pointed out a long time ago the radical differences between front-stage and back-stage. Cooperative building designers need to make a choice. This is harder than it sounds. The sources of finance are likely to what to see a highly visible facility for their money: Theatre. As CSCW researchers, we are more interested in understanding and supporting ongoing work processes. It *is* tempting to promise both.

# References

1. Brave, S., H. Ishii and A. Dahley (1998). Tangible Interfaces for Remote Collaboration and Communication. *In Proceedings of the Conference on Computer-Supported Cooperative Work (CSCW'98)* Seattle, ACM.
2. Buxton, W., A.S. (1993). Telepresence: Integrating Shared Task and Person Spaces. In *Readings in Groupware and Computer Supported Cooperative Work: Assisting human-human collaboration.* Baecker, R.M (Ed.) San Mateo, CA, Morgan Kaufmann. 1993. 816-822.
3. Fitzpatrick, G., S. Kaplan and S. Parsowith (1998) Experience in Building a Cooperative Distributed Organization: Lessons for Cooperative Buildings. In *Cooperative Buildings - Integrating Information, Organization, and Architecture. Proceedings of CoBuild'98.* N. Streitz, Konomi, S., Burkhardt, H.-J. (Eds.). GMD, Darmstadt, Springer. Lecture Notes in Computer Science 1370.
4. Heath, C., M. Jirotka, P. Luff and J. Hindmarsh (1993). Unpacking Collaboration: The Interactional Organisation of Trading in a City Dealing Room. In *the Proceedings of the European Conference on Computer-Supported Cooperative Work (ECSCW'93).* G. de Michelis et al (Eds.) 13-17 Sept. Milan, Italy. Dordrecht, Kluwer Academic Publishers.
5. Heath, C. and P. Luff (1991). Collaborative Activity and Technological Design: Task Coordination in London Underground Control Rooms. In *the Proceedings of the European Conference on Computer-Supported Cooperative Work (ECSCW'91)* L. Bannon et al. Amsterdam, Kluwer Academic Publishers: 65-80.
6. Heath, C. and P. Luff (1993). Disembodied Contact: Communication through Video in a Multi-Media Office Environment In *Readings in Groupware and Computer Supported Cooperative Work: Assisting human-human collaboration.* Baecker, R.M (Ed.) San Mateo, CA, Morgan Kaufmann. 1993.
7. Heath, C. and P. Luff (1996). Convergent activities: Line control and passenger information on the London Underground. *Communication and Cognition at Work.* Y. Engestrom, & Middleton, D. N.Y., Cambridge University Press: 96-129.
8. Hollan, J. and S. Stornetta (1992). Beyond being there. In *the Proceedings of Conference on Computer-Human Interaction (CHI '92)* Monteray, CA., ACM.
9. Ishii, H. and M. Kobayashi (1993). ClearBoard: A Seamless Medium for Shared Drawing and Conversation with Eye Contact. In *Readings in Groupware and Computer Supported Cooperative Work: Assisting human-human collaboration.* Baecker, R.M (Ed.) San Mateo, CA, Morgan Kaufmann. 1993. 829-836.

10. Mantei, M. (1988). Capturing the Capture Lab Concepts: A Case Study in the Design of Computer Supported Meeting Environments. In *the Proceedings of the Conference on Computer-Supported Cooperative Work (CSCW '88)* Portland, Oregon. Sept.26-28 ACM.

11. .Nardi, B., H. Schwartz, A. Kuchinsky, R. Leichner, S. Whittaker and R. Sclabassi (1993). Turning Away from Talking Heads: The Use of Video-as-Data in Neurosurgery. In *the Proceedings of INTERCHI '93*, Amsterdam, 22-29 April, ACM.

12. Nunamaker, J. F., B. R. Konsynski and L. M. Applegate (1988). "Computer Aided Deliberation: Model Management and Group Decision Support." *Operational Research* Nov/Dec '88

13. Robinson, M. (1993). Design for unanticipated use .... In *the Proceedings of the European Conference on Computer-Supported Cooperative Work (ECSCW'93)*. G. de Michelis et al (Eds.) 13-17 Sept. Milan, Italy. Dordrecht, Kluwer Academic Publishers.

14. Saffo, P. (1997). CACM *CACM "The Next 50 Years"* **40**(2 (Feb.97)): 93-97.

15. Sørgaard, P. (1988). Object Oriented Programming and Computerised Shared Material. In *the Proceedings of the European Conference on Object-Oriented Programming (ECOOP '88)* Springer Verlag, Heidelberg.

16. Star, S. L. and J. R. Griesemer (1989). Institutional Ecology, 'Translations' and Boundary Objects: Amateurs and Professionals in Berkeley's Museum of Vertebrate Zoology, 1907-39. *Social Studies of Science* **19**: 387-420.

17. Streitz, N. A., J. Geißler and T. Holmer (1998). Roomware for Cooperative Buildings: Integrated Design of Architectural Spaces and Information Spaces. In Streitz, N., Konomi, S., Burkhardt, H.-J. (Eds.), *Cooperative Buildings - Integrating Information, Organization, and Architecture. Proceedings of CoBuild'98.* LNCS 1370. Springer, Heidelberg. pp.4-21.

18. Streitz, N. A., P. Rexroth and T. Holmer (1997). Does "roomware" matter? Investigating the use of personal and public information devices and their combination in meeting room collaboration In *the Proceedings of the European Conference on Computer-Supported Cooperative Work (ECSCW'97)*. J. Hughes et al. (Eds.) 9-11 Sept. Lancaster, UK. Dordrecht, Kluwer: 297-312.

# OWL: An Object-Oriented Framework for Intelligent Home and Office Applications

Bernd Brügge, Ralf Pfleghar, Thomas Reicher

Technische Universität München
Lehrstuhl für angewandte Softwaretechnik
Arcisstraße 21, München D-80290 München, Germany
{bruegge,pfleghar,reicher}@in.tum.de

**Abstract.** The goal of OWL (Object-Oriented Workplace Laboratory) is to provide an object-oriented and component-based framework that supports the engineering of applications for the design, simulation, construction, and operation of buildings with more efficient use of building facilities. OWL is based on a software architecture using a combination of web and object technology. It offers location transparent and manufacturer independent access to a variety of facility control systems, and allows users to define "scenes" to adapt their work environment.

In this paper, we describe the requirements, system design and a conceptual prototype of the OWL framework. We discuss how the application of design patterns and component technology impacts the framework to support the maintenance of corporate sites globally distributed across the world. A conceptual prototype of OWL written in Java is operational, managing distributed facilities at the Intelligent Workplace at Carnegie Mellon University and at Technische Universität München.

**Keywords.** intelligent workplace, object-oriented workplace, control system, facility management, design patterns, framework, component-based software engineering, jini

## 1 Introduction

The health, well-being, motivation and productivity of office workers (over half of the U.S. work force of 120 million people) depend significantly on the pleasant personalized arrangement of their office interior. Examples would be quantity and quality of lighting, including daylighting systems. Glare (reflected or indirect), illuminance and contrast values are critical (Loftness, 1994).

OWL attempts to deal with some of these problems, and provides users with a high degree of control over their work space in a cooperative building. From their user interface, they can request changes in the temperature, light level, and other aspects of the environment. These changes are then effected through adjustments in exterior louvres, internal lighting systems, and the HVAC system. Through a network of environmental sensors located in each work area, an energy-efficient adjustment of building climate systems can also be formulated and executed by OWL.

Today there are several different control system solutions available for facility management, such as the European Installation Bus EIB (EIB Association, 1999) developed by Siemens, Luxmate from Zumtobel AG (Zumtobel AG, 1999) or Metasys from Johnson Controls. One problem is that these solutions cannot cooperate. A company might start with a homogenous control system but due to evolution and mergers with other companies, it soon faces the problem of heterogeneous control systems globally distributed over several locations. Another shortcoming with the current solutions is that the level of control is coarse. For example, a facility manager can group several lamps, adjust the lightness, and map them to a specific switch. But each switch can only be mapped to a single group. Multiple users cannot allocate switches to different groups.

OWL is independent from proprietary control systems and allows a flexible customization of the office interior by the user.

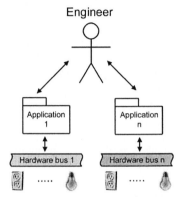

Fig. 1. Solution without OWL

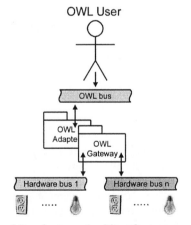

**Fig.2.** Solution with OWL

We introduce a layer of abstraction that is built on top of the control systems which are hidden from the users unless they need to see them, like a Luxmate engineer that has to check Luxmate controlled facilities. Controlled objects can form a scene, that is a group of devices and commands that can change the settings. Scenes can be changed dynamically and are user-specific. Users can adapt their scenes, starting with a default scene set up by a facility manager.

The paper is organized as follows. In the next section we represent the requirements and models of an adaptable framework for intelligent home and office applications, such as a facility management system. In section three we give an overview of the framework and describe the system components. A major design goal was the use of design patterns (see Gamma et al.,1996) to create a reusable and extendable framework. For our models we use the Unified Modeling Language from Booch et. al (1998). In section 4 we describe the communication within OWL. We describe the status of our work in section 5 and related work in the next section. We conclude with a summary and a description of future work.

## 2 Requirements Analysis

For the requirements analysis we define some typical scenarios that OWL based applications should support. From the scenarios we derive the functional and non-functional requirements for the OWL framework.

*Scenario 1: Control.* Office worker Ralf enters his office. He launches the OWL based facility management application, and changes the view appropriately to display the floorplan of the office and the controls for all the devices associated with it. He adjusts the lights for better comfort. A moment later, the lights and the louvres in the room are set to a new level that satisfies his preferences. The display warns him that one lightbulb is inoperative. Ralf replaces it and the display indicates that the lightbulb is working again.

*Scenario 2: Directing.* The facility user Jane wants to make her office more comfortable. She logs into the system, defines a new group of office facilities, and assigns new settings and behaviors to them, such as starting the air conditioning after she entered the office building, and closing the louver of the upper windows. She saves this scene under the name "Jane's summer settings", and attaches it to her user profile.

*Scenario 3: Getting Status.* The facility manager Joe takes inventory of the equipment in a particular room. After launching the OWL based facility management system, a display comes up with a view of the entire site. Joe selects the appropriate building and views its 2-dimensional layout. He requests "Show me conference room B," and a moment later the display shows the room and its contents. The temperature sensor for the room shows that the temperature is currently fluctuating between 76 and 77 degrees Fahrenheit.

*Scenario 4: Diagnosis.* The facility manager Jack receives an alarm on his personal digital assistant indicating that an air-conditioner is malfunctioning in a certain room. Visiting the room in 3-dimensional mode, the facility manager selects the hot spot associated with the air-conditioner which contains information such as model, make, last date of maintenance, serial number, manufacturer and an error code for the failure.

*Scenario 5: Repair.* As the damage is only minor the facility manager orders the janitor Wilma to repair the malfunctioning air-conditioner. As the site is quite large the janitor uses a wearable computer with head mounted display where she is shown the shortest way to the room. Vendor specific on-line repair instructions have already been transmitted together with the provision of the appropriate replacement part for the air-conditioner. After Wilma repairs the air-conditioner, OWL automatically reports to the facility manager that it has successfully been restarted.

The functional requirements for the OWL framework are:

- navigate remotely through a corporate site at varying levels of granularity, where a corporate site is defined as a set of one or more globally distributed company sites.
- visualize critical information such as ownership of workspaces and distribution of resources such as computers, printers, or video beamers.
- dynamically reconfigure building resources.
- control sensors for the environment and climate such as light fixtures, blinds, HVAC systems, heaters and thermostats.
- allow a user to set up and run a simulation to compare different architectural solutions.
- visualize sensor information and the effects of controls.
- remotely manage the facilities of a site that includes several distributed buildings.
- allow a user to define custom configurations for one or more facilities and save them as a scene.

To provide a truly usable application that competes with the simple operation of traditional building controls such as a light switch, it is important to note, that users will simply not accept a system that would require the operation of these controls via a desktop computer. Turning on the lights of an office should be as simple as using the physical light switch in that room. This has important ramifications for the non-functional requirements of the OWL framework. First, the control system must be accessible via standard switch interfaces. Second, the user interface must be provided with a meaningful display of the information obtained from the system sensors, as well as a mechanism that allows easy manipulation of sensors. The framework therefore should support different types of inputs, for example speech-based input, pen-based input, mouse/keyboard based input and other modalities such as gesturing, clapping, face tracking, and motion sensing. Moreover, the applications using the OWL framework should not expect users to have their hands free when interacting with the system. For security reasons the framework has to be able to safely authenticate the user that wants to manipulate a device. Third, the system must be platform independent, and interact with control systems from different manufacturers. To provide manufacturer independence, the OWL system has to be flexible and

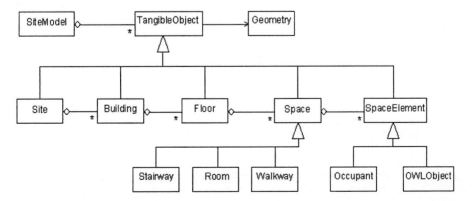

**Fig.3.** Class Diagram of the SiteModel

modular to support hardware from different vendors with various degrees of computer interaction and a variety of input/output controls. In particular OWL must be able to simultaneously control a variety of sensors provided by different manufacturers. Finally, the OWL system must provide location transparent access to sensors and actuators of the whole site, independent from their physical locations.

The site model shown in figure 3 is an abstraction of corporate sites as they can be found in reality. The site model is similar to the SEMPER model (Mahdavi, 1996) and can be instantiated using a CAD system such as MicroStation from Bentley Systems (Bentley Systems, 1999).

OWL distinguishes five types of users with different needs and rights. A *User* represents a person physically located in the site or building, has a location and a user profile, and may move within the site, and change the position. An *Occupant* is a User object that can control and observe resources in the building. An Occupant must be properly identified and can have different access rights for different resources. Occupants can specify a variable number of user-specific preferences as scenes to customize their environment, and have a specified workplace position. Occupants can display site models in 2D or 3D.

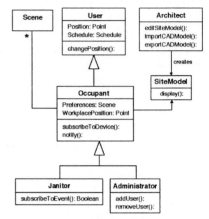

**Fig.4.** User Class Diagram

*Administrators* manipulate devices, manage users and groups, can define OWL events and formulate default settings for user profiles. The Administrator can also define specific access rights to rooms or devices. A synonym for Administrator is facility manager. *Janitors* are Occupants with additional rights in controlling OWL. They can manipulate user profiles and can release policies, for example to prevent waste of energy. *Architects* create and edit the site model. They have the right to import/export complete site models from CAD systems and they can also modify the models.

OWLObject is the super class of all objects that represent tangible objects in the site model and that may be contained in a Scene. The subclass Sensor contains all

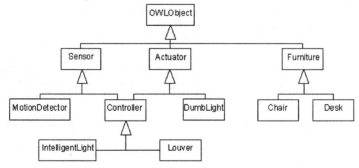

**Fig.5.** OWLObject Class Diagram

devices of the real world that are capable of generating events, for example a motion sensor can generate a motion event. Actuators are devices that can react on commands. Controllers are able to do both. For example, a lightbulb that "knows" its condition would be a controller. Furniture is an OWL object that does not react on electronic signals. Note that in our classification, a simple Edison-type lightbulb is a Furniture object. Furniture objects can be included in scenes, for example an OWL scene might require a video beamer and a table for a slideshow presentation. Inclusion of Furniture objects is important to support mobile users who frequently change their offices but require the same OWL scene to work effectively in different parts of the building or at different sites.

Scenes are an important feature of the OWL system. An OWL scene is either a single OWLObject or a composite object (Grouping object) that in turn may consist of several OWL scenes. Scenes are modeled as a composite pattern (Gamma et. al, 1996). The composite pattern allows users to change the members of a scene dynamically. Scenes are linked to user profiles which allows users to modify existing scenes or create their own user-specific scenes.

Scenes can subscribe to events and allow users to provide OWL objects with commands to be executed. Assume, for example, a scene from user Jim that contains the three OWL objects Heater, Light, and Timer. The scene includes commands for starting the Heater half an hour before Jim enters his office. The Timer issues a timer event and Jim's scene executes the commands to start up the heating device and turn on the lights.

In the simplest case, a scene acts like a batch file that is started by the occurrence of an event and publishes its own events. This way, users can link the setting of an OWL object with the adjustment of a user defined parameter such as a lighting level. In a further step there should be the possibility to check scenes

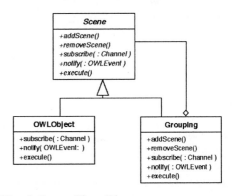

**Fig. 6.** Scene Class Diagram

for consistency and completeness and a way for handling exceptions. For example, if a command cannot be executed, the decision is needed whether the execution of the scene should proceed or be canceled, or if a roll back of an executed action should be performed. Moreover there should be rules to resolve conflicts with other scenes from other users. For example, there is a conflict if an occupant wants a temperature of 70 degrees Fahrenheit in his office whereas the company's policy says 50 degrees are enough. We suggest the use of agents for the execution of the scenes. If an agent identifies a conflict or an inconsistency it has to try to resolve the conflict. In the above example an agent for the user specified temperature would negotiate with the janitor agent that released the temperature policy.

# 3 System Design

The OWL framework consists of three major subsystems operating on a site which is modeled as set of OWL objects: User Applications, System Applications, and System Services.

User Applications provide the basic functionality for the management of a Site. The *Facility Management* application helps the administrator to control a Building by providing him with different views of the Site. For example, one view might be a navigatable map of all OWL objects, another one might be a list of all malfunctioning controllers. The *Scene Creator* allows the creation of user defined scenes. OWL presents a list of the available OWL objects to the OWL user who can select and group some of them, define user-specific settings and save it as a scene. Scenes can be attached to OWL events, so they can be

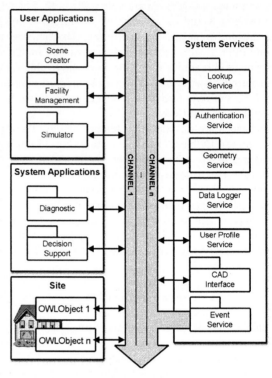

**Fig. 7.** OWL Subsystem Decomposition

triggered automatically when the event occurs. An example would be the start of the HVAC system and the closing of all the blinds in a set of offices, when a certain temperature has been reached. *Simulations* can be run on a Site or on a Building object. Administrators are able to manipulate the Site attributes without affecting the real environment. A typical use case is the simulation of the energy consumption of the building with different window sizes.

System Applications are core applications provided with the framework. They can be used by any User Application. The *Decision Support* subsystem analyzes user behavior and generates models about the behavior. That way inefficient behavior (waste of energy) might be detected by comparing the actual behavior with an optimal model. The *Diagnostics* subsystem detects system failures and changing device behavior. For example the addition of new sensors or actuators to the site might cause a change in the behavior of the building, such as an increase in energy consumption in a particular set of offices.

System Services support the operation of User and System Applications. All subsystems are location independent, therefore a mechanism for locating a subsystem is necessary. The Lookup Service keeps track of all subsystems, which register with the Lookup Service at startup time. The *Authentication Service* provides the means of user authentication with a range of methods ranging from fingerprint scanners and smartcards to iButtons (Dallas Semiconductor Corp,1999). The *CADInterface* subsystem provides the interface and import/export filters for different CAD formats and tools. The interfaces can be used for dynamic updates of the building by importing updated CAD models of the Site. 3-dimensional views of the Site cannot be generated on the fly without any preprocessing, especially on devices with small compute power like wearable devices. The Geometry Service connects to the CADInterface and calculates a 3D model of the site or building. This model can then be used a User Application to provide, for example, a VRML model of the site. The *Data Logger Service* logs OWL events when OWL based applications are running. For example, the data can be used in field service applications for error tracing as well as by the Diagnostics subsystem. A user profile stores a range of user specific information such as the name of the user, and scenes associated with the user. User profiles can be stored on a smart card or in a local database, accessible via a local area network. The *Event Service* implements the communication mechanism within the OWL framework. It provides a set of event channels on which events are exchanged between subsystems.

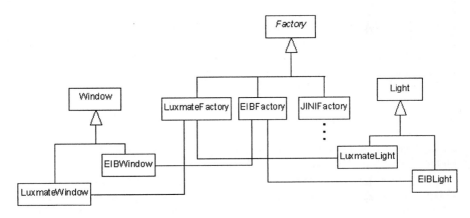

**Fig. 8.** Use of the Abstract Factory Pattern

OWL objects from the same vendor specific control system are modeled as a family. As shown in Figure 8, the European Installation Bus Family (EIBFactory) creates a family of EIB controlled lights (EIBLight) and windows (EIBWindows) whereas the Luxmate factory does the same for Luxmate controlled devices (LuxmateLight, LuxmateWindow). Using the abstract factory pattern the OWL application developer does not have to know how vendor specific lights are controlled. OWL based applications simply access OWL objects.

The bridge pattern shown in Figure 9 provides a way for vendors of control systems to offer different implementations that can be changed at runtime. For example, when the EIBFactory creates a

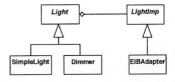

**Fig. 9.** Use of the Bridge Pattern

new object that implements the Light interface, such as SimpleLight or Dimmer, it provides the Light object with a separate delegate object. The delegate object (in the example in Figure 9 the LightImp object) is responsible for the connection to the control system. As the access to a control system is vendor specific, subclasses of LightImp are used to do vendor specific tasks. For example, EIBAdapter implements the connection to the EIB system. The EIBAdapter can easily be exchanged at runtime, for example the default EIBAdapter can easily exchanged with EIBViaPowerlineAdapter.

# 4 Communication

The OWL framework provides two major abstractions: applications and services on one side and OWL objects on the other. Applications and services, such as the Facility Management application or the Authentication Service can be controlled by the administrator and are rarely added or removed after startup. OWL objects on the other hand can be and removed from the system at any time, in the worst case without a warning.

To support the cooperation of spontaneous networks is the underlying idea of Jini (Javasoft, 1999). Jini offers service providers and consumers to discover each other at runtime. Jini enabled devices send a description of the services they provide together with some attributes. The Lookup Service which makes an entry in its service list. Other devices send a description of the service they look for. The Lookup Service then attempts to find a matching service in its database and returns a reference to the service consumer. Once consumer and provider have found each other they build a federation (a so-called djinn). The OWL framework uses Jini for the subsystems to discover each other. For example the Facility Management application uses Jini to find the Data Logger Service or the Diagnostics Service.

Communication between OWL subsystems can be done via direct communication or the Event Service. The Event Service itself is implemented as a Jini service that can be found by the OWL objects and OWL services via the Jini Lookup Service. Once an OWL object connects to the Event Service, it can ask for information about existing event channels and connect to any event channel either as a publisher or a subscriber. Messages are sent by publishers to all the subscribers of a particular OWL channel. An example of an OWL publisher could be a lightbulb, which notifies two subscribers of its current status: facility management and data logger.

There are three types of OWL events. Sensor events allow OWL objects to issue interesting occurrences such as a change in the temperature or light, a motion, a vibration, smoke or something similar. The second type of OWL events are Control events that enable users and OWL subsystems to send commands to other OWL objects. Simple examples are "Start of OWLObject" and "Stop Operation of OWLObject". Response events allow OWL objects to respond to Control events and user actions such as turning on a light. Examples of Response events are "OWLObject has started", "OWLObject has stopped". If OWL objects receive a Control event not from another object but from a user, for example by pressing a switch, they publish an event to the connected channels.

# 5  Prototype

A prototype demonstrating some of the capabilities of OWL has been developed for two distributed locations: the Intelligent Workplace located at Carnegie Mellon University, and the Intelligent Home lab located at the Technische Universität München. The prototype provides access to two Luxmate lighting control systems via a Web based user interface.

The prototype was developed with JDK 1.1. For the implementation of the OWL bus we used remote method invocations which we tested with CORBA 2.0 and RMI from Javasoft, respectively. A comparison between the approaches with CORBA and RMI can be found in Fernandes (1997).

A demonstration of scenario 1 is available on the OWL homepage at http://atbruegge13.Informatik.tu-muenchen.de/OWL/. Two movies show the scenario 1 "Control" where the OWL user Ralf is working on his computer. One movie shows the user interface (see Figure 10) of the prototype, and the responses of the Luxmate lighting box (Figure 11) in parallel. The second movie shows Ralf with his laptop in the lab. With his OWL based facility management application he controls each light of a Luxmate lighting system. The user interface shows a detailed 2D floor plan of the OWL controlled building with the lights symbolized as boxes in the upper left corner. The upper right corner contains the control buttons for the lightbulb that is actually selected. The lower left corner contains control output, and the lower right corner is for 2D navigation through the building.

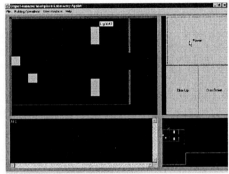

**Fig. 10.** OWL User Interface

**Fig. 11.** Luxmate Lighting box

The movies show how Ralf turns several lights on and off. When a light is turned off the color of the light icon becomes gray, when it is turned on it changes to green. When a lightbulb is out of order (demonstrated by Ralf removing the lightbulb) OWL announces it to the user by turning the light icon red. OWL also knows the location of the lightbulb from the CAD drawing, and moves the focus of the detailed map to that location. When Ralf replaces the lightbulb the light icon turns green.

# 6 Related Work

Control bus systems such as EIB or Luxmate are not designed for openness and collaboration. They enable the control of building facilities but do not incorporate any intelligence into the devices. Instead a centralized control unit controls the devices.

Other approaches handle electronic devices as objects, and establish communication between them. The objects are accessible over an object oriented API. Examples are the Jini technology from Sun Microsystems (Javasoft, 1999) for Java capable devices, or the HAVi homepage (1999) for Java capable home entertainment devices. Another effort is the Open Service Gateway Initiative (OSGI, 1999) that aims at specifying an open standard for connecting the coming generation of smart consumer and small business appliances with commercial Internet services on top of Jini. Related efforts are also persued in the Things That Think consortium of the MIT Media Lab (see the TTT homepage,1999), for example in the Personal Information Architecture group (see PIA homepage, 1999), or the Hive project (see Hive homepage, 1999).

Schulz and Schütze (1996) modeled a facility control system and facility simulation with the casetool Statemate. This model could be used for a refinement of the site model used in OWL.

The Adaptive House project of Mozer et al. (see Mozer, 1999) uses neuronal networks to learn the user's behavior. The goal is to anticipate user needs and to conserve energy. The system is called ACHE (AdaptiveControl of Home Environments), and uses low-voltage conductors for collecting sensor data and a power-line communication system for controlling lightings, fans, and electric outlets. Applications like the Adaptive House could be built on top of the OWL framework.

# 7 Summary and Future Work

In this paper we presented an object-oriented framework for a family of collaborative building applications, such as distributed facility management. First we developed the requirements for a facility management system that is general enough to adapt to the needs of different user types ranging from the facility manager to normal user such as an office worker. With these requirements we designed a framework that consists of subsystems communicating via the OWL bus. We then described the subsystems in detail and showed where the use of design patterns lead us to manufacturer independence and reusability. Finally we described an existing conceptual prototype and the relation to other research efforts.

We continue to work on the OWL architecture in two directions. First, we would like to improve the software architecture with respect to building management. Our future efforts will aim at a stronger user integration into OWL controlled environments. This includes several aspects such as mobile users equipped with augmented reality systems, various authentication methods, and agents for negotiations of competing user needs.

Second, we would like to extend the OWL architecture to a general-purpose framework for a wider class of applications. We hypothesize that applications such as train maintenance, aircraft inspection, remote health care and car diagnostics can be addressed with an architecture very similar to the one described in this paper and in Bruegge et al., 1996.

## Acknowledgments

This work was partially supported by the Bayerische Forschungsstiftung, Zumtobel AG and Staff, Siemens Corporation, and the ABSIC consortium and is based on the work of Prof. Hartkopf and his colleagues who built the Intelligent Workplace at Carnegie Mellon University, Pittsburgh.

# References

1. Bentley Systems (1999): MicroStation Academic Edition, http://www.bentley.com/academic/products.
2. G. Booch, J. Rumbaugh, I. Jacobson (1998), The Unified Modeling Language User Guide, Addison-Wesley.
3. B. Bruegge, B. Bennington. (1995). Applications of Mobile Computing and Communication, IEEE Journal on Personal Communications, Special Issue on Mobile Computing, pp. 64-71, February 1996.
4. B. Bruegge, T. Fenton, K. Tae Wook, R. Pravia, A. Sharma, B. Fernandes, S. Chang, V. Hartkopf (1997): Turning lightbulbs into Objects, OOPSLA 97, Addendum to the Conference Proceedings, Atlanta, October 1997.
5. Carnegie Mellon Unversity (1996a): OWL I Homepage, http://cascade1.se.cs.cmu.edu/15-413/default.html.
6. Carnegie Mellon University (1996b): The Intelligent Workplace, http://www.arc.cmu.edu/cbpd/iw_press.htm.
7. Carnegie Mellon University (1997): OWL II Homepage, http://cascade1.se.cs.cmu.edu/15-499/default.html.
8. Dallas Semiconductor Corp (1999): www.iButton.com, http://www.ibutton.com.
9. European Installation Bus Association (1999): EIBA, http://www.eiba.com.
10. B. Fernandes (1997). An Experimental Evaluation of A Component-Based Distributed Application: The OWL System, Master's Thesis, Carnegie Mellon University.
11. E. Gamma, R. Helm, R. Johnson, J. Vlissides (1996): Design Patterns, Addison-Wesley.
12. HAVi Consortium (1999): HAVi - home, http://www.havi.org.
13. Hive project (1999): Hive - a TTT Toolkit, http://hive.www.media.mit.edu/projects/hive.
14. Javasoft (1999): Jini Technology Architectural Overview (1999), http://www.sun.com/jini/whitepapars/architecture.pdf.
15. Johnson Controls (1999): Metasys(R) Facility Management System, http://www.johnsoncontrols.com/Metasys
16. V. Loftness, V. Hartkopf, A. Mahdavi, S. Lee, A. Aziz, and P. Mathew (1994): "Environmental Consciousness in the Intelligent Workplace," Paper presented at NEOCON 1994, held in Chicago, Illinois, June, 1994.
17. S. Schulz, M. Schütze (1996): Modellierung einer Gebäudesteuerung und -simulation mit Statemate, 4. Deutsches Anwenderforum für STATEMATE/ExpressV-HDL, Systemtechnik Berner & Mattner GmbH, Munich (D), June 1996.
18. TTT (1999): Things That Think, http://www.media.mit.edu/ttt.

19. Mahdavi (1996): SEMPER: A New Computational Environment for Simulation-based Building Design Assistance. Proceedings of the 1996 International Symposium of CIB W67 (Energy and Mass Flows in the Life Cycle of Buildings).Vienna, Austria. pp. 467 - 472.
20. Mozer, M. C. (1999): An intelligent environment must be adaptive, IEEE Intelligent Systems, in press.
21. MIT PIA-Group (1999): Personal Information Architecture Group - PIA, http://www.media.mit.edu/pia/index.html.
22. OSGI Consortium (1999): OSGI Homepage, http://www.osgi.org/osgi_html/osgi.html.
23. Zumtobel AG (1999): Zumtobel STAFF The Light, http://www.zumtobelstaff.co.at/luxmate.

# Predator : A Distributed Location Service and Example Applications

## J.N.Weatherall[+], A.Hopper[+*]

[+]Laboratory for Communications Engineering
Cambridge University Engineering Department
Cambridge, England
{jnw22, hopper}@eng.cam.ac.uk
http://www-lce.eng.cam.ac.uk/~jnw22
http://www.eng.cam.ac.uk/~hopper

[*]AT&T Laboratories Cambridge
24a Trumpington Street
Cambridge, England
ahopper@eng.cam.ac.uk
http://www.uk.research.att.com/~hopper

**Abstract.** This paper introduces a simple distributed location service, suitable for deployment on a wide variety of heterogeneous platforms and which is scalable to cope with location forwarding on a global scale. Also described are two existing applications of the Predator location service, in particular to support of a wireless-via-wired routing service for low-power mobile devices, suitable for deployment both in-building and over a wide area.

**Keywords.** cooperative buildings, ubiquitous computing, piconet, wireless routing, distributed location service, CORBA

## 1 Introduction

Recent work in distributed computing has focused on the problems of mobility both of software components of systems and of the devices on which they operate.

There are desirable features of conventional distributed middleware architectures such as CORBA (OMG, 1998) which we would like to be able to integrate seamlessly with the more stringent requirements of mobile systems.

One of the primary difficulties in such integration is that of location, both of distributed services and of mobile devices by clients. Common approaches to device location, for example IP Routing (Baker, 1995) and DNS (Mockapetris, 1987), require that the name of a machine reflects its physical location to some degree.

Similarly, distributed architectures built on IP and DNS usually require that programs exporting services not migrate between devices, if clients are to be able to access those services. Mobile services will therefore be considered as equivalent as regards location to mobile devices for the purposes of this report.

## 2 Existing Mobile Location Schemes—Pure vs Impure Names

The issue of transparent location is tackled by a number of different schemes, which can be divided, for the most part, into three general categories;

1.  Schemes such as the Globe Object Model's location service (Hauck et al, 1997), that use *pure* names (Needham, 1993) which convey no information to the client as to how the corresponding entity should be located. These systems are seldom as scalable as we might like, since most implementations require that some central node is aware of every object in existence.

2.  Schemes such as Mobile-IP (Perkins, 1996) and the CORBA LifeCycle service (OMG, 1996), that use *impure* or *composite* names, most often comprising a home agent location and a key. These systems can fail when the home agent is unavailable for some reason and can suffer from performance degradation when the mobile entity is far away from its home.

3.  Hybrid schemes such as ALICE (Cunningham, 1998), in which the mobile entity's home is effectively mobile itself and the composite name of the entity is transparently munged to reflect its current home, older names of the entity being forwarded to it's current location transparently. This approach is more efficient than 1 and more manageable than 2 but suffers similar robustness problems to the latter. It is also unclear as to how long these surrogate homes should hold forwarding information for.

## 3 The Predator Model of the World

The Predator system assumes a world of roaming mobile devices with intermittent connectivity, via *contact-point*, to a backbone of static, wired network infrastructure.

Mobile services can be modelled in the same way, since their contact-points are effectively the devices on which they operate (which may in themselves be mobile).

The core of the Predator system is its location service, on which the Predator IIOP-Forwarding service and PicoNet (Bennett, 1997) Routing service are built as applications. For convenience, this is constructed as a CORBA service and deals only with CORBA Object references. In order to track other mobile entities, such as mobile devices, a wrapper layer must be constructed to abstract the mobile devices into CORBA objects, which can then be registered with the Predator Location service on their behalf.

CORBA was chosen as the base middleware for Predator because of its platform and language interoperability and its popularity as an open standard for component software operation. In choosing CORBA, very little restriction was placed on how wrapper layers must be constructed for mobile entities. Although in principle the same techniques could be applied to, for example, a Java RMI environment, it was felt that this might prejudice the system by polluting it with platform-specific optimisations.

# 4 The Predator Location Service

The Predator Location service (from here on referred to as the Location service) is run on all machines wishing to export or import mobile objects. Location service nodes are arranged in a simple, hierarchical tree structure representing the *global domain*, with similar, hierarchically structured trees representing the *sub-domains* implemented as *distributed objects* over the global or *base* tree.

## 4.1 Search Tree Structure

Each node of the Location service has a concept of a parent node, which it may query for locations of devices which cannot be found locally, and may be aware of its peers and/or its ancestors in order to allow for failure recovery features.

Nodes in the base tree are grouped according to physical locality. For example, all the Location service nodes running on the PCs in a room may be grouped under a single parent node which represents that room. The parent nodes for each room will then in turn be grouped under a node responsible for the building containing those rooms and so on.

Fig 1 shows a simple search tree structure that might be used to handle mobile devices in a small building.

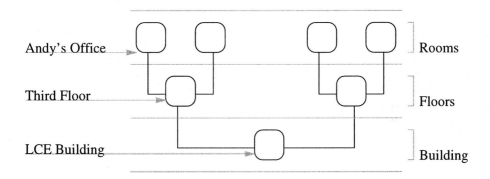

**Fig. 1.** Hierarchical Tree Structure for a Small Building

## 4.2 Sub-trees as Distributed Objects

In the Globe object model, the top-level entities are known as *distributed objects*.

A distributed object consists of multiple *implementation objects* running in separate address spaces on a number of machines and communicating with each other via the network in order to behave as a single entity.

130

Distributed objects *expand* and *contract* as implementation objects are added and removed. How the objects cooperate to achieve the desired behaviour is up to the objects themselves and may be tailored to the specific task.

Using the Predator Location service, mobile objects are accessed via a *logical* hierarchical naming scheme. The key difference between Predator and DNS-style systems is that this logical hierarchy is in no way tied down to the physical hierarchy of the system.

Instead, the Predator service is implemented as several layers of search trees, one for each domain in the hierarchical namespace. At the base layer, there is a single tree to represent the global domain. At the next layer up, the search trees implement different sub-domains, which may represent different tasks running on the system. For example, there may be trees implementing "Paging", "IIOP-Forwarding" and "Email" domains. Tree nodes implementing these domains will exist at any particular point in the network *if and only if* mobile objects belonging to them exist at that point.

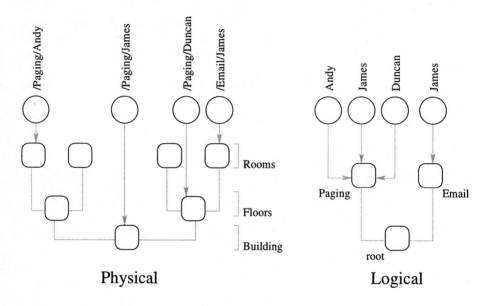

**Fig. 2.** Physical and Logical Layouts of an Example Network

Fig. 2 shows example physical and logical layouts of a backbone network and some mobile objects. Fig. 3 shows the structure of the search tree corresponding to the "Paging" domain, overlayed on the physical network layout.

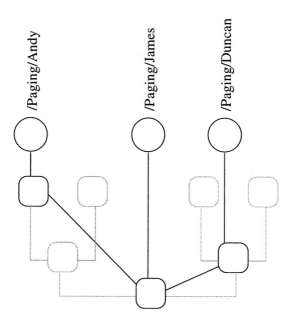

**Fig. 3.** Layout of the Paging Domain Search Tree

The "Paging" domain can be considered as a distributed object, since it is made up of a number of distributed nodes working to provide a single, unified function—that of locating objects used for the task of "Paging". The "Email" domain can be considered, similarly, as a distributed object, even though it is only implemented in one place. The root domain is special in that it exists everywhere and its structure reflects the underlying geographical structure of the wired network.

## 4.3 Using the Predator Location Service

### 4.3.1 Locating a Mobile Object

When a client wishes to locate an object using the Location service, it passes the appropriate hierarchical name to the base Location service on the local machine. For convenience, our implementation runs on a well-known port number and uses a well-known CORBA object key.

The base Location service will attempt to resolve the first part of the name (if the desired name was "Paging/Andy", for example, the first part would be "Paging") in the global domain, either locally or by querying its parent node. If the attempt fails then an exception will be thrown to indicate that no object exists with the desired name.

If the attempt to resolve the first part of the name succeeds then the returned Location service node (which could be anywhere in the world) is queried to resolve the next part of the name. This continues until the entire name has been resolved, at which point the desired object will have been found.

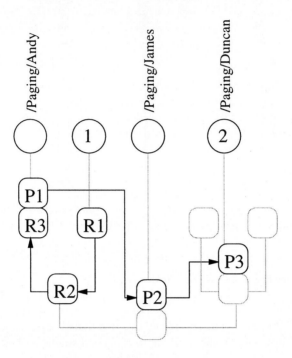

**Fig. 4.** An Example Search of a Layered Search Tree

Fig. 4 shows an example search in which client object (1) attempts to locate mobile object "Paging/Duncan". The "Paging" domain is implemented as a tree of co-operating nodes—those labelled P1, P2 and P3 in the diagram. Once a client can see *any* node which is part of the "Paging" domain, it can then locate *any* object that belongs to that domain, simply by searching the domain's tree in the same way as it would search the global tree.

- The client (1) asks the Location service at node "R1" to find the object "Paging/Duncan" (2).

- Node "R1" first tries to locate the nearest node in the "Paging" domain.

  - ♦ "R1" cannot see any nodes in the "Paging" domain locally, so it falls back to its parent, "R2".

  - ♦ "R2" has been told by "R3" that it knows of a node in the "Paging" domain, so "R2" forwards the request to "R3".

&#9830;   "R3" can now return a reference to "P1", direct to node "R1". Note that "P1" is not the base of the "Paging" domain's tree but the node in that tree that is closest to "R1". This helps us avoid long-distance searches throughout a tree when the desired mobile object is actually local to us.

- Node "R1" now asks "P1" to find the object called "Duncan" in the "Paging" domain. A similar search is then performed of the "Paging" domain to that performed on the global domain, returning "P3" as the current location of the object called "Duncan".

- The resulting object reference is returned to the client and may be used until it fails for some reason, at which point the client can fall back to another search for the name "Paging/Duncan". Caching schemes can help reduce the search path on subsequent attempts to relocate an object that has moved.

### 4.3.2 Registering a Mobile Object

Registering an object with the Location service under a particular name follows the same basic pattern to locating an object. The primary difference is that nodes of all the required domain trees will be created local to the object being registered, if they don't already exist there.

For example, consider the case in which a new object is to be registered under the name "Email/Andy", as in Fig. 5a

- The new object (1) calls down to its local Location service node and asks the Location service to register it as "Email/Andy".

- The Location service performs a normal search, to locate the nearest node in the "Email" domain and finds node "E1" [Fig. 5b].

- If the nearest node is not local then a new "Email" domain node is created locally and linked to the existing one.

- If there are no existing "Email" domain nodes then one is created locally.

- The object is now registered with the local "Email" domain node, "E2", under the name "Andy" [Fig. 5c].

134

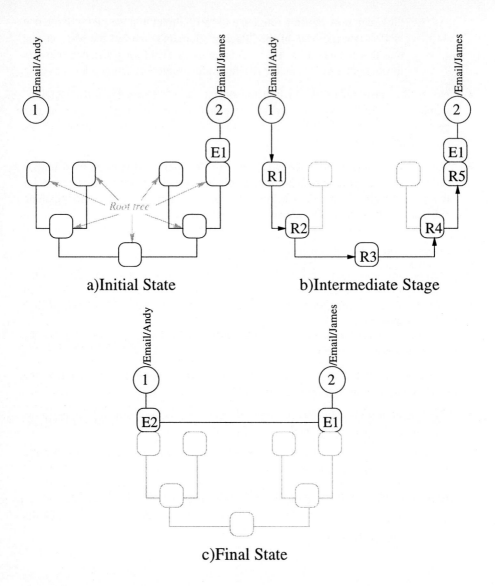

a)Initial State  b)Intermediate Stage

c)Final State

**Fig. 5.** An Example Registration of a Mobile Object

## 5 Location Service Implementation

The present implementation of the Location service is a minimal one, with the following limitations:

1. Automatic failure recovery and configuration of nodes in the base tree is not currently implemented since, on the prototype's present scale, such features are neither required nor easily tested.

2. All key names are currently flat. For example, the hierarchical name "PicoNet/ORL/64" is implemented as the flat, munged name "pNET00000064". Work is in progress to implement hierarchical keys and to automate redistribution of domain trees.

3. No security is currently available. Some way of limiting who is allowed to bind particular names is required, in order to avoid namespace clashes and denial-of-service attacks, for example. Use of the CORBA Security Service may go some way towards providing this security.

# 6 The Predator IOR-Forwarding Service

The Predator IOR-Forwarding service, allows applications to generate *global object references* and to pass these to clients in place of the actual object references involved.

When a CORBA service wishes to export a mobile object, it calls into the Forwarding service local to it and requests that the object's reference be bound to a global object reference in the Location service. The service can then pass the global object reference to client applications, in place of the object's real reference. An instance of the Forwarding service must be running on all client and server machines in this model, although it is possible to get round this requirement to support legacy systems at the cost of scalability.

Migration of an implementation to a new site becomes straightforward using the Forwarding service, since the new implementation can be created, initialised and bound to the underlying Location service and the old instance, if required, can simply be torn down. Clients using compliant ORB implementations will detect the failure of the original object and automatically revert to using the global IOR, thus implicitly accessing the Location service to obtain the new instance's IOR. The client process can remain completely unaware that anything has changed.

# 7 The Predator PicoNet Routing Service

## 7.1 PicoNet

PicoNet is a lightweight, low-power wireless communications system for embedded and mobile devices. The low-power requirement, needed in order to allow PicoNet to be embedded in even the tiniest devices and therefore be truly ubiquitous, imposes consequent bandwidth and latency penalties on the system. As a result, PicoNet is a technology aimed primarily at low-bandwidth control and negotiation situations, rather than mass data transfer situations as are catered for by systems such as BlueTooth (BlueTooth, 1999) and HomeRF (HomeRF, 1999).

In its current incarnation, PicoNet allows short range point-to-point communication between devices. While this is ideal for many location-sensitive tasks, it restricts the available applications somewhat—if the recipient of a message is not within about 5 metres of the sender then the message cannot be sent.

## 7.2 The PicoNet Routing Architecture (RLink)

The Predator PicoNet Routing architecture (RLink) assumes a backbone of wired machines (in our case desktop PCs), with a PicoNet gateway node attached to at least one machine in each room, or more if the room is particularly large. The mobile PicoNet nodes then traverse this backbone as they are carried around by their owners and, while they are still able to communicate directly with each other over short distances without requiring any backbone infrastructure, they can usually fall back to routing via the wired network if the device they wish to contact is not locally available.

Location of PicoNet nodes in this system is, once again, performed by the Predator Location service. It is used to retrieve the IOR of a CORBA object which is willing to act as a gateway to the desired node. If the node has moved away by the time the message is passed to a gateway by a client then the gateway will try to re-locate the client and pass the message on to the new gateway. This avoids repeated traversal of the search tree, since the receiving node is unlikely to have moved very far from the original gateway.

Several assumptions are necessary in the implementation of this scheme;

- Firstly, it is assumed that *only* messages with a specific destination address should be routed through the wired network. The PicoNet system also allows broadcast requests for services to be made but in general such requests implicitly expect that only local instances of the desired service will respond.
- Secondly, it as assumed that *all* messages with a specific destination address may be routed through the wired network.

One useful result of these two assumptions is that although a PicoNet device can make a plea for any nearby instance of a desired service, it may continue to refer to that service instance specifically, by its address, until the transaction is complete, whereupon it may fall back to requesting any local instance again. This session-based mode of operation allows transactions to continue to completion even when the nodes involved are no longer co-located, provided they are both near a Routing gateway.

## 7.3 Experiences Using RLink

The RLink wireless-through-wired router has been used as the basis for several prototype applications. Two simple examples are discussed briefly below.

### 7.3.1 Active Door Badges

For some years the AT&T Labs in Cambridge have had an infrastructure of sensors for the Active Badge system (Want et al, 1992). Various automated applications have been constructed using this technology such as Teleporting (Richardson et al, 1994) but the major use remains simply that of finding out where people are so that they can be contacted.

In particular, users visiting a coworker's office will often find that that person is busy or absent and in the latter case they will resort to the Active Badge system to find them. In the former case, it would be desirable for there to be some indication on the door into a worker's room that they are busy, and perhaps some way for people to register the fact that they would like to talk to them when they're done.

To this end some PicoNet devices with small LCD displays and a few buttons have been constructed and used as door signs. In normal operation, such signs will display static information on the room and its usual occupants, and the display hardware is optimised power-wise for this case. However, since the door signs have access to Rlink gateways local to them, when one of their buttons is pressed they can fetch current location data for the usual occupants of the room and display it, avoiding the need for the visitor to go to a PC terminal to find the person they wish to visit.

Similarly, it is possible to send pieces of text to be displayed on a door sign in addition to the other information, providing for indications such as "This Room is Busy" or "Wet Paint", for example.

In this case, wireless PicoNet devices were able to transparently access wired backbone services without regard for the location of either party, through use of the Predator and RLink services.

### 7.3.2 Generic Remote Controller

As part of a demo for a separate project, a CORBA-based mobile streaming architecture was built in our lab. Among other control methods experimented with, a door sign PicoNet node was reprogrammed to instead support a simple audio-player interface, with Play, Pause, Stop, Fast Forward and Rewind buttons.

In addition to supporting the control operations normally associated with an infra-red remote, the PicoNet controller was also capable of retrieving information from the audio player, such as the name of the track currently being played.

For the purposes of our demo, the audio player had actually been a standard PC with an archive of MPEG files stored on it. Because we used the RLink architecture to connect the two, users could roam between rooms and continue to control their audio player from the new location, seamlessly.

In addition, the controller could, without modification, control a real CD player or similar device, provided the device had a PicoNet node attached and was exporting a simple audio-player interface. Control of such a device could either be local or transparently remote, via the Rlink service. This feature was especially important, since in using the Predator and RLink services to provide access between remote devices and to backbone services, we hadn't sacrificed the ability to operate in an ad-hoc manner.

# 8  Conclusion

The Predator Location Service aims to tackle the shortcomings of pure-name, impure-name and current hybrid-name approaches to addressing large numbers of highly mobile objects or devices over a static, wired network infrastructure. It improves on these approaches in the following ways:

- By partitioning the overwhelmingly large global search domain into more manageable logical domains we avoid the scalability issues associated with flat name space systems such as the Globe Object Model.

- By allowing logical domains to themselves be mobile we avoid imposing artificial constraints on the mobility of objects while at the same time providing a means to optimise the search space for related objects. This gives clear advantages over schemes such as DNS, by allowing the topography of the search tree to alter to match the requirements of its clients.

- By the use of two orthogonal trees—the hierarchical logical namespace and the hierarchical physical search space—we allow searches to be optimised to avoid traversing large distances unnecessarily when locating nearby nodes. In addition to supporting far greater scalability, this approach avoids the problems often associated with impure-name and hybrid-name schemes. In particular, there is no single point of failure as in home-agent systems like Mobile-IP, nor is there a need to maintain forwarding addresses for mobile objects indefinitely as in systems such as ALICE.

- By constructing the search trees for sub-domains as we do, we avoid some of the worse pathological cases possible with a more general tree structured architecture. While pathological cases still exist, they are rare and introduce only minimal extra cost into the system. In general the locality heuristic inherent in the Predator system is appropriate for the target application domains we are interested in.

The transparent IIOP forwarding features of Predator may be applied to distributed systems such as DAWS (Grisby, 1999) to simplify the tasks of component migration and failure recovery. This service's co-existence with the RLink routing service illustrates the generic nature of the Predator service. The Predator service could equally well be used to enhance the mobility capabilities of other architectures such as Jini (Jini, 1999).

Some work using the Predator service as a basis for enhancing the usefulness of a wireless ad-hoc technology in an office environment has been briefly described. Research continues into aspects of interoperation between PicoNet devices, in particular for purposes of control, both of backbone services and of local devices.

## Acknowledgements

The authors wish to thank Ant Rowstron, Duncan Grisby, Sai-Lai Lo and Alan Jones for their patience in proof-reading the many drafts of this paper. Thanks are also due to Paul Osborn and Gray Girling of the AT&T Laboratories Cambridge, for their help and advice in building the PicoNet side of the system.

# References

1. Baker, F. (editor), (1995). Requirements for IP Version 4 Routers. *RFC 1812* (June 1995).
2. Bennett, F., Clarke, D., Evans, J.B., Hopper, A., Jones, A., Leaske, D., (1997). PicoNet - Embedded Mobile Networking. *IEEE Personal Communications* (October 1997), No. 5, Vol. 4, pp 8-15.
3. BlueTooth, (1999). BlueTooth Website. *Http://www.bluetooth.com*.
4. Cunningham, R., (1998). *Architecture for Location Independent CORBA Environments (ALICE).* Dissertation for MSc in Computer Science (September 1998), Trinity College, Dublin.
5. Grisby, D.P., (1999). *A Distributed Adaptive Window System (DAWS).* PhD. Dissertation: Computer Laboratory, University of Cambridge.
6. Hauck, F.J., Steen, M., Tanenbaum, A.S., (1997*). A Location Service for Worldwide Distributed Objects.* Technical report: Dept. of Math. And Computer Science, Vrije Universiteit, Amsterdam, The Netherlands.
7. HomeRF, (1999). HomeRF Website. *Http://www.homerf.org*.
8. Jini, (1999). Jini Connection Technology. *Http://www.sun.com/jini/overview*.
9. Mockapetris, P.V., (1987). Domain names - Concepts and Facilities. *RFC 1034, RFC 1034* (November 1987).
10. Needham, R.M., (1993). Names. In: *Distributed Systems* (editor Mullender, S.J.), Addison-Wesley Publishing Co., Chapter 12.
11. (OMG) Object Management Group, (1998). The Common Object Request Broker: Architecture and Specification (February 1998), Revision 2.2.
12. (OMG) Object Management Group, (1998). LifeCycle Service Specification. In: *CORBAServices: Common Object Services Specification* (December 1998), Chapter 6.
13. (OMG) Object Management Group, (1998). Security Service Specification. In: *CORBAServices: Common Object Services Specification* (December 1998), Chapter 15.
14. Perkins, C. (editor), (1996). IP Mobility Support. *RFC 2002* (October 1996).
15. Richardson, T., Bennett, F., Mapp, G., Hopper, A., (1994). Teleporting in an X Window System Environment. In: *IEEE Personal Communications Magazine* (Fourth Quarter 1994), No. 3, Vol. 1, pp 6-12.
16. Want, R., Hopper, A., Falcao, V., Gibbons, J., (1992). The Active Badge Location System. In: *ACM Transactions on Information Systems* (January 1992), No.1, Vol. 10, pp 91-102.

# Matching Information and Ambient Media

Albrecht Schmidt, Hans-W. Gellersen and Michael Beigl

Telecooperation Office, University of Karlsruhe
Vincenz-Prießnitz-Str. 1, 76131 Karlsruhe, Germany
{albrecht, hwg, michael}@teco.edu
http://www.teco.edu/

**Abstract.** Ambient media have recently been introduced as a means to present information in our surrounding space in subtle and unmonopolizing ways, promoting peripheral awareness. This paper explores the issue of matching virtual information to ambient media, investigating *ambient counterparts* as natural matches and *ambient links* as user controlled matches. Ambient counterparts are media in our surroundings that have an intuitive and strong relationship with the virtual information they present, and we report on an application of such counterparts for comparative web site awareness employed for group motivation in their workplace. Ambient links are relation between ambient media and events in the virtual world actively assigned by the user for ambient notification. We describe two tools for creating ambient links, the first one for marking web pages for ambient notification much in the style of bookmarking, and the second one extending an email filter to create ambient links for email events. Finally we effects of our experiments in the workplace.

**Keywords.** ambient media, calm technology, world-wide web, linking virtual and physical world, ubiquitous computing

## 1  Introduction

The amount of detailed information available to us is incredible. To reduce this information overload researchers from different areas are developing methods to condense the amount of information. This ranges from simple statistics (e.g. analyzing web access), over filtering mechanisms according to profile (Lieberman 1995) to more sophisticated agent technology using artificial intelligence methods as pointed out by Maes (1994 and 1997). Many of these approaches deliberately trade in the timely context of virtual and real events.

Calm technology and ambient media enable new ways to consume information. Calm technology advocates peripheral awareness of activity in the virtual world or mediated through the virtual world (Weiser and Brown 1995). Ambient media (or *ambient displays*, Wisneski et al 1998) are means for information presentation in our surroundings. Examples described in the above referenced papers include Jeremijenko's dangling string, and the ambientROOM with water ripples, active wallpaper and ambient sound, showing that ambient media are a rich concept for creation of interfaces between people and virtual worlds, engaging all of the human senses, and blending into our surroundings. Such seamless integration of our environment informational space is discussed in the Tangible Bits vision described by Ishii and Ulmer (1997). An interesting aspect of ambient media is to present information in largely abstracted and unmonopolizing ways while preserving the timely context, for example for subconscious awareness of information. Such awareness can for instance give a sense of being connected to others (Holmquist 1998), an important aspect in cooperative workplaces, or a sense of reward as reported by Liechti et al (1998) in their work on social awareness of web site visitors.

Assuming ambient media as highly suited for peripheral information awareness the question is which information to select for ambient presentation, and what kind of ambient medium to use for presentation. This is discussed in Wisneski et al (1998), basically concluding that the decision is not straightforward and that the matching of information and ambient media depends on a wide range of factors. Reported examples of ambient media tend to describe the relation between information and ambient medium in terms of metaphors, for instance for the dangling string presenting network traffic the metaphor of jumping bits is used to describe the meaning of string vibration. The reported examples generally suggest an importance of abstraction in the choice of ambient medium, as less abstract (i.e. more literal) media tend to be perceived as more intrusive.

In this paper we report on investigation of two concepts for matching of information and ambient media. The first one, *ambient counterparts,* is based on the assumption that much of the information that we handle in our virtual worlds has a natural counterpart in our physical environment, to which it can be related intuitively. In some sense this presents a slight departure from abstraction in the choice of ambient medium. One idea developed in exploration of ambient counterparts is that similar chunks of information will relate to a collection of similar ambient media, supporting an awareness of for instance comparative information. This idea was studied in an application of ambient media for comparative web site awareness employed for group motivation in their workplace.

The second concept for media matching that we report on is to let users themselves create and control *ambient links* to relate information to ambient media. This may be seen as drastic departure from the concept of calm technology as it requires the user to some extent to attend to technology they should not be consciously aware of. Yet we would argue that provided the creation of ambient links is easy to perform, it will empower users to create personal ambient spaces to handle their information. We describe two tools for user control over ambient links, the first one for marking web pages for ambient notification, and the second one extending an email filter to create ambient links for email events. Prior to the discussion of ambient counterparts in section 3, and ambient links in section 4, we briefly describe the underlying ambient media system.

## 2 Ambient Media System

**Web-based Architecture.** The architecture of the system we built for exploration of ambient counterparts and ambient links is depicted in figure 1 shaded in gray, with a standard web server and a media controller for each ambient medium available.

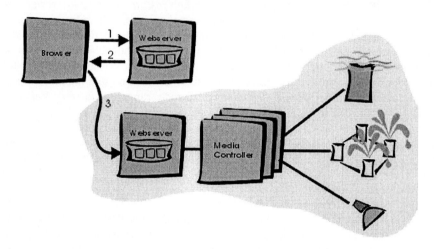

**Figure 1: Architecture**

A standard web server with CGI is used to receive the requests that control ambient media. The use of web server and CGI allows to write control applications that can be accessed from anywhere. In this architecture, new ambient media can be integrated by simply providing a CGI-script to control it. A media controller can be fully implemented in software as CGI program if the ambient medium is connected by a standard interface (e.g. laser unit connected via the serial port). If this is not the case, control hardware is required in addition to the CGI program (e.g. parallel interface switching power plugs). Depending on the control hardware a CGI program may be parameterized with supported control sequences. The CGI program determines how an ambient medium presents information, and hence the design of such programs is considered part of the design of ambient media rather than application design.

The media controllers are the system abstraction from ambient media, which means that any physical media can be integrated into the system, provided they can be controlled through a defined interface. In the simplest case, very basic devices may be controlled by switching power on and off; more advanced gadgets may be controlled by the power supply (e.g. motor, lights); and rather sophisticated appliances may actually be computer controlled (e.g. serial line controlled laser).

**Event Communication.** The web server in our architecture is accessed using the standard HTTP-protocol for communication. Virtual events such as web page access, incoming email, calendar events, and modification of web pages, are sent via HTTP-GET-request to the web server connected to the media controllers. For clients that access a media controller, based on virtual events, the HTTP-protocol is a reasonable choice as well. In the case of web page access this HTTP-request is automatically sent by the browser while loading the page, because in our approach *ambient links* are embedded as image in the HTML page (cf. section 4 for description of the ambient links concept). This scenario is illustrated in figure 1: a browser requests a page from a web server containing pages with ambient links (1), the page is sent back to the browser (2), containing an IMG-tag with a URL pointing to the media control web server. The browser analyzes the HTML-code and requests all images (3) including the CGI-script that controls the ambient media. The request of the CGI script triggers manipulation of the related ambient medium; it does not return any data to the client. The support for the HTTP-protocol is on most platforms and for major programming languages (Perl on Unix, Visual Basic on Windows, Java) very well what makes the creation of not browser-based clients easy.


## 3 Ambient Counterparts of Virtual Information

**Ambient Counterparts.** According to our experience much of the information in our virtual spaces has an intuitive and strong relationship to objects in our physical spaces. For instance, product information in a companies web pages can be related to products in a showroom; incoming email from close people can be related to a personal photo gallery; and papers downloaded from a research group's web can be related to posters in the group's office environment, in the case of our research group actually the hallway. We suggest that physical objects in such relationships lend themselves to ambient presentation of related virtual information as its ambient counterpart. For certain relationships between virtual events and real world objects this link may seem obvious, for others it may depend on individual associations, e.g. a postcard of Munich in the office may be associated with *home, a great holiday,* or *a friend living there.*

An interesting aspect of the examples stated above is multiplicity: a class of physical objects is related to a class of virtual information. This leads to the consideration that counterparts can be used collectively for an ambient presentation of class-based rather than instance-based information. Consider the email example, then notification of an individual email through, say, brief illumination of the related photo would constitute instance-based information. Use of illumination to show who was in touch over the last week can also be perceived as class-based information (e.g. density of light), providing an overview rather than detail on one instance. Overview is one example, others are comparison of information, and order of events; further information characterizations worth to be investigated is reported in literature on Intelligent Multimedia (e.g. Maybury, 1993).

To study ambient counterparts, we implemented a web site awareness system, in which parts of the web site were related to posters in our hallway. These posters were used to provide an ambient presentation of access to the related pages, to support comparison.

144

**Comparative Web Site Awareness.** In this experiment we explored the effect of giving users in a workspace the awareness of other people who are interested in their work. When we have visitors to our office we usually get an impression of what things they are more interested in and which things they do not pay much attention to, as they walk past posters in the hallway, look at different prototypes in the hardware lab, or pick paper copies from our handout material. We also have visitors to our web site and it is certainly of interest to get an impression of what these virtual visitors are intersted in. There is a wide range of tools to monitor web site visits, evaluating web server log-files, but only few people use them regularly, because it just enlarges the information overload.

Liechti et al (1998) report on work giving individual users awareness of visitors to their personal web space. In their study, ambient audio is used to notify access to user selected web pages, and they report that such simple notification can be highly motivating to keep web pages interesting and updated. In our study, we extended this concept of web site awareness from the individual to the group.

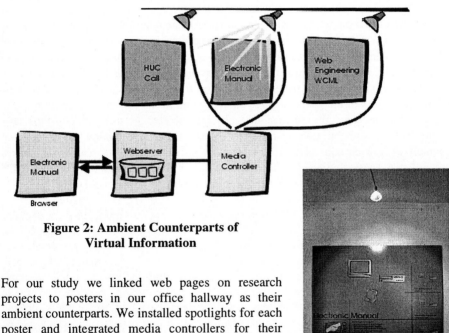

**Figure 2: Ambient Counterparts of Virtual Information**

For our study we linked web pages on research projects to posters in our office hallway as their ambient counterparts. We installed spotlights for each poster and integrated media controllers for their manipulation in our ambient media system described above. In the scenario shown in figure 2, the web page on project "Electronic Manual" is accessed through a browser. This leads to execution of the media controller script, turning the spotlight of the related poster on, to then slowly fade off over time. The photo in figure 2 is a snapshot of the "Electronic Manual" poster, illuminated after access to the project pages in the web. The choice of presentation in this study, slowly fading light, was somewhat arbitrary. Another way to display access activity would for instance be to accumulate hits over time and adjust the light level accordingly. This choice of mapping from data to ambient presentation, and also the choice of how transient or persistent an ambient effect is, remains to be studied.

The setup for ambient web site awareness provided staff and students involved in the respective projects with a good impression of what topics are of interest to our visitors. It also provided feedback on the effect of URL announcements in newsgroups. Most interesting is that the setup quickly gives an impression of how popular parts of the web site are in comparison, which may well stimulate competition among project groups to gain popularity for their web pages. Our small study was not suited to derive significant results on such effects but we feel confident to propose comparative web site awareness as a group motivation tool, for example for groups editing electronic journals or other highly dynamic web sites.

## 4   User Controlled Ambient Links

**User Controlled Ambient Media.** As another aspect of matching virtual information with ambient media we investigated the concept of user controlled ambient media, and developed end user tools for management of ambient links. To require users to decide about usage of ambient media is quite in contrast to the philosophy that users best not be aware at all of the technology that blends into their surroundings. Yet, to have ambient media at one's disposal to create highly individualized ambient spaces seems very intriguing. Also given that the decision on choice of ambient media is far from understood but clearly depends on users' tasks and preferences (cf. Wisneski et al, 1998), it may make sense to defer the decision from design time to run time.

**Figure 3: Patterns and Table Fountain**

A critical issue in giving the user control over ambient media is the effort required for creation, modification and deletion of ambient links. We describe two tools that we developed for managing ambient links, both concerned with provision of easy-to-use mechanisms to link virtual information to ambient media. The first tool is for relating web page access to ambient presentations, and the second one extends an email filter for ambient notification. Both examples uses a small table fountain as ambient medium.

146

**Table Fountain as Ambient Medium.** A simple but nevertheless useful and pleasant ambient media is a small fountain placed in our office. It has four pumps that can be switched on and off independently (see figure 3). A PC controls the power plugs over the parallel interface board. The same interface can be used to integrate other devices that are controlled by switching on and off the power, for instance we have also used ultrasonic humidifiers in other demonstrators. The media controller for the fountain is a CGI-program running on the control PC, and generating control information send to the interface board over the parallel port. This CGI program has memory of earlier events and of the current state of the fountain, and implements support for different patterns and control effects of the fountain, such as *flash, circle, all on, rotate*, and *add*. The effects *flash* and *circle* are transient and leave no trace an event has been presented. The effects *all on, rotate*, and *add* are less transient, with the effect of an event remaining visible for some time afterward because of the state change.

**Marking Web Pages with Ambient Links.** The first tool we developed had the goal to mark a web page with an ambient link in a way as easy as marking a web page with a bookmark. The tool allows to browse through a web site to select pages to link with an ambient medium which then is triggered by each access to that page. For instance, in the screenshot shown in figure 4, a workshop web page has been selected to get notification on virtual visits. The tool allows for selection of an ambient media effect, with *flash* chosen in this case so that access to the specified page will let the fountain bubble briefly. Obviously, the tool is geared to control of the table fountain described above but it is straightforward to envision a generalized management tool supporting selection among multiple ambient media, and media-specific selection of effects.

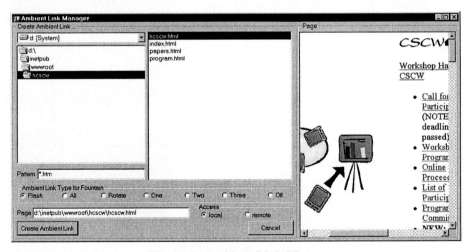

**Figure 4: Ambient Link Manager**

After selection of web page as information source and the ambient presentation effect, ambient links are established by pushing the create button. This actually leads to insertion of a line of HTML-code to the file. This line contains a call to the CGI-script on the web server controlling the ambient media:

```
<IMG SRC="http://teco154pc.teco.uni-karlsruhe.de/
cgi-bin/bm_flash.exe" width="1" height="1">
```

Note that insertion of this line in an arbitrary web page in the world-wide web would result in our table fountain bubbling for a moment whenever that page is accessed! The effect is not restricted to local web pages but of course the creation of ambient links is restricted to pages for which the user has modification rights.

It also has to be noted that of course different pages can be linked to the same ambient medium, and one and the same page can have links to different ambient media. The ambient link management tool also provides the functionality to remove ambient links from web pages, that is to remove the inserted image tag.

**Ambient Email Notification.** The tool for ambient email notification is based on the elm mail filter system. The tool allows the user to create rules that call a media controller (i.e. a CGI-script). In the condition part of the rule *subject* and *sender* can be selected to identify mails, and in the action part the user can specify the ambient effect to be triggered by an incoming email that meets the condition. The technical realization is done using a Perl-script that calls the CGI-program controlling the ambient medium. An example of a rule generated by this tool is:

```
if (subject "Urgent") then executec
"/users/albrecht/bin/cgicall.pl flash"
```

The effect of this rule is that email containing *Urgent* in the subject line causes the table fountain to bubble for a moment (*flash*).

**Further User Controls.** At the moment we a working on two further tools, one to map calendar events to ambient media and another one to monitor other web pages and give notification by physical output. The calendar editor is straightforward, additional to the time when the user should be notified it will be possible to select the system that is used to notify the user. The channel editor has enhanced functionality and can be used to monitor any web page. The user selects the URL to monitor the event they are interested in (e.g. change of page or certain keyword appearing on page), and the ambient effect that should be produced if the condition is true. Execution will be based on Unix system cron jobs.

## 5 Conclusion and Future Work

We have explored two ideas for matching of virtual information and ambient media, with a range of interesting findings. First, investigating ambient counterparts of virtual information we came to consider class-information rather than instance-information for ambient display, enabling for example overview and comparison. We applied the idea of ambient comparative information in a study that extended web site awareness from the individual to the group, a concept we believe has potential for group motivation in the workplace, and for better integrating web sites or other informational spaces as virtual extension of work environments. As second idea, we considered user control over links between virtual information and ambient media, and described tools that make ambient linking as simple as bookmarking. We would argue that with such tools users can be empowered to create personal ambient spaces to handle information in entirely new ways.

While designing the prototypes we realized that for various virtual events the link to real world objects is easily conceivable by users. But still for numerous virtual events links to real world objects are perceived differently by different people, for one it seams straightforward while for another one it is very artificial. Therefore we think letting the user decide were to place the ambient links is a good decision. The link management must be very easy to handle by the user to make it possible to change ambient media when changing the foreground task to avoid interference between foreground task and ambient display as discussed by Wisneski et al. (1998).

After getting used to the ambient media setup this becomes quickly valuable to us; the peripheral information space becomes part of the work environment. So far we have not carried out a formal user study but we will describe some observation we made while using the prototypical system. We found out that depending on the things we were working on, the focus and goals we had, and also the personal form we used the system differently. Firstly the mapping chosen depended very much on what we were interested in, e.g. after announcing a conference call to news groups we chose a transient mapping of this page to the fountain or when waiting for email from somebody while reading or doing some other work not at the computer this was mapped persistent to an output. Secondly the perception of the events depended mainly on the personal condition, when working under time pressure the ambient information was hardly realized whereas when bored an ambient indication led people to look at the log-file of the server to find out who it was.

In the setup of the first experiment we found out that the inclusion of ambient media control affects the design and structure of the information that is display on the web pages. For this approach it is certainly a reasonable decision to design ambient media together with the web pages.

The effect that virtual events become more real at the workplace has interesting implications. First the motivation can be increased by feeling every now and then that someone is interested in your work and in the thinks you a displaying on your website, this is also reported by Liechti et al. (1998). Virtual events become more a part of your work life, colleagues sharing the office asked once *your fountain didn't bubble the whole morning - is your server down?* A setup as described in the first experiment introduces implicit competition, by making access to certain web pages public. This can have positive effects and lead to discussion but in highly competitive environment this could be negative, too.

In the future we plan to create a dynamic mapping of media according to the preferences and context of the user. We are also looking for new application domains and working on the support of more general control system using power line control (e.g. X10). Furthermore we think there is need for a model that describes mappings of information to ambient media with respect to persistence and transience based on the communication goals.

# References

1. Holmquist, L. E., Wigström, J., Falk, J. (1998). The Hummingbird: Mobile Support for Group Awareness. *Demo at the Conference on CSCW'98*. Seattle, 14-16. November 1998. To appear in Handheld CSCW, *Personal Technologies* (special issue), vol. 3 no. 1, 1999.
2. Ishii, H. and Ullmer, B (1997). Tangible Bits: Towards Seamless Interfaces between People, Bits and Atoms, in *Proceedings of CHI '97* (Atlanta GA, March 1997), ACM Press, 234-241.
3. Lieberman, H. (1995). Letizia: An Agent That Assists Web Browsing, *Proceedings of the 1995 International Joint Conference on Artificial Intelligence*, Montreal, Canada, August 1995.
4. Liechti, O., Siefer, N., Ichikawa, T. (1998). A Non-obtrusive User Interface for Increasing Social Awareness on the World Wide Web. *Workshop on Handheld CSCW on the CSCW'98*, http://www.teco.edu/hcscw/papers.html. Seattle, USA (November 14, 1998). To appear in Handheld CSCW, *Personal Technologies* (special issue), vol. 3 no. 1, 1999.
5. Maes, P. Agents that Reduce Work and Information Overload, *Communications of the ACM*, Vol. 37, No. 7, (July 1994).
6. Maes, P. (1997). Interview: Pattie Maes on Software Agents: Humanizing the Global Computer. *IEEE Internet Computing*. July-August 1997.
7. Maybury, M. (1993). *Intelligent Multimedia Interfaces.* AAAI Press. Menlo Park, USA.
8. Weiser, M., Brown, J.S. (1996). Designing Clam Technology. *PowerGrid Journal*, v 1.01, http://powergrid.electriciti.com/1.01 (July 1996).
9. Wisneski, G., Ishii, H., Dahley, A., Gorbet, M., Brave, S., Ullmer, B., Yarin, P. (1998). Ambient Display: Turning Architectural Spache into an Interface between People and Digital Information. In: *Proceedings of the First International Workshop on Cooperative Buildings (CoBuild'98)*, Darmstadt, Germany (February 25-26, 1998). Lecture Notes in Computer Science, Vol. 1370. Springer - Verlag, Heidelberg.

# Observing Cognitive Work in Offices

Saadi Lahlou

EDF R&D Division
1, Ave du Gal. de Gaulle. 92141 Clamart Cedex FRANCE
saadi.lahlou@edf.fr

**Abstract.** The information revolution has a deep impact on office work. To create better environments for cognitive workers, we designed two observation tools recording office activity. The Subcam (subjective camera) is a miniature, wearable, wide angle video camera, clipped on a pair of glasses ; it records individual activity from a subjective point of view, wherever the user goes. The Offsat (office satellite) takes a picture every minute from the ceiling, showing long term evolution in the spatial distribution of information artifacts (piles, etc.), and measuring the distribution of gross activity (meetings, stand alone computing, etc.). We currently use these tool in a series of new furniture and information artifact design experiments.

**Keywords.** observation, specification, evaluation, cognitive work, video, furniture, design, office, white collar.

## 1   Context

The nature of work, its distribution between Humans and Artifacts, is deeply changing in connection with Information Technology. Work settings have to be redesigned for this new deal. More specifically, some offices are settings where important decisions are taken when navigating in a rich information world ; they should be designed with the same care as aircraft cockpits.

But while information production and flow increased, the human cognitive process of giving meaning to it and taking decisions hasn't yet been augmented. A simple visit in any office building will convince that the cockpit-office is not yet a reality. And indeed users complain of cognitive overflow: too much information to process, not enough time. Information overload [Hiltz & Turoff, 1985], Information Shock Syndrome [Lea, 1987] ; information overflow [Ljungberg, 1996], Information Fatigue Syndrome [Lewis, 1996], Cognitive Overflow Syndrome („ COS ") [Lahlou et al., 1997], infoglut etc. all are symptoms which stress the inadequacy of present work environment to actual cognitive work requirements.

Obviously, we need better information environments, to improve decision, provide users with clear overall vision of tasks and priorities. At EDF R&D Division, conscious that cognitive work is a critical issue for competitiveness, we started in 1993 a research program to improve cognitive workers' comfort and efficiency

[Lahlou, 1994, 1998b ; Fischler & Lahlou, 1995 ; Autissier et al, 1997 ; Lahlou 1999]. This means understanding the present problems encountered by users, their needs, specifying and testing new environments to empower and augment cognitive workers, and finally evaluating these environments. We consider here not only the „ knowledge workers ", but all those whose work mainly consists in processing information (e.g. secretaries).

For this we need a good description of cognitive workers' activity. This paper describes two tools we designed for that purpose, and which we are currently using.

## 2  Observation Problems

Various studies have shown how office work is a series of complex activities, involving many actors and objects in decision processes, relying on the context and setting, and specially on information artifacts [Simon, 1957, 1964 ; Mintzberg, 1973 ; Suchman, 1983 ; Malone, 1983 ; Norman, 1991, Heath & Luff, 1991 ; Sébillote, 1992].

Office activity seems harder to describe than physical work. Actions must be understood in the perspective of the actor's intentions, which are seldom openly observable in cognitive work. Also, cognitive workers perform many varied tasks, so systematic codification is difficult (which may explain the success of ethnographic approach). For example, first level managers perform an average of 68 tasks per person per day, 25% of which are interrupted [Autissier et al. 1997]. They are mobile and interact with small and transient „ details " (e.g.: alphabetic characters on a screen, colleagues' voice tone, and the like). Therefore, capturing fined grained behavioral data on office workers is necessary to understand what they do and why they do it.

One reason why it is so difficult to study office activity is merely technical: the lack of proper observation techniques. Fixed video yields insufficient results, because many office workers are very mobile, inside and outside their office. For example, engineers, managers or programmers we observed -and whose agendas we checked- were often a third of their time out of their office (for meetings, "on the field", or searching for information). With fixed video, one hardly sees what the subject does when he turns his back to the camera, and a lot of tape show empty office.

Office workers manipulate a wide range of artifacts (paper, etc.), so recording only their computer log, screen, or their telephone conversations is not enough. Monitoring all media turns out difficult, heavy, and multiplies the sources of observation failure ; also, subjects feel „ big-brotherized ".

Office workers are hardly aware of their own routines [Simonsen & Kensing, 1997], so, as we could test for ourselves, their reconstruction during interview are not reliable sources for understanding what they *actually* do. And asking them to record their own activity themselves, on the fly, is not realistic: at fine grain level, describing an action may be as long as performing it.

Finally, it is not a person alone who does the job, but a distributed system made of the user and his/her artifacts. White collars in their office are like crew members in an aircraft cockpit described by [Hutchins, 1994, 1995], they perform their job as part of a larger cognitive unit [Lahlou & Fischler, 1996]. It clearly appears (cf. infra) that the cognitive worker is highly environment driven, so observation should capture the setting (displays, affordances, messages etc.) which drives and frames activity.

To sum up, present observation tools, well designed for operators with a single activity in a fixed setting (e.g. on the assembly-line), fail to provide detailed and reliable record of the activity of mobile office workers in the course of their work. This is especially true for cooperation. They also fail to provide long term records (over months) of how the *setting* behaves. So, how can we test if new furniture will improve activity? Or if a new software improves overall information management?

The *Subcam* tries to overcome the first observation problem (following the user's activity at fine grained level) ; the *Offsat* the second (long term observation of office settings). Of course, they do not solve all the problems, but they may help cognitive scientists and designers who want to create better environments and artifacts for cooperative, distributed, cognitive work.

## 3  The Subcam (Subjective Camera)

The Subcam records data for fine grained analysis of the perception/action loop of users. We use it for exploratory analysis, problem spotting, design tests.

The Subcam is a miniaturized, wide angle, color video camera, with microphone, clipped on a pair of glasses worn by the user. It is a wearable video recorder, capturing the point of view at eye level. The subject wears the glasses, and a jacket or holster which includes a miniature VCR and a control unit. The system has up to 4 hours of autonomy, and provides a continuous record, on Hi-8 or DV tape [Lahlou, 1998a].

The Subcam gives a good account of what the user sees, hears, says and does, even if it doesn't track the eye gaze. It has been demonstrated in CSCW '98 ; a video [Fayard & Lahlou, 1998] is available. As wearable video progresses rapidly [e.g. Mann, 1997], we believe the Subcam or its equivalents will soon be used in many labs.

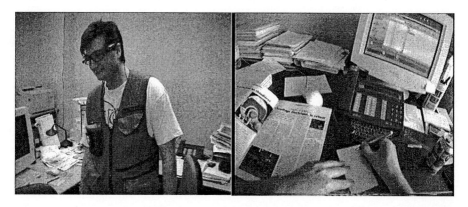

**Fig.1 a & b.** Left, the first version of the Subcam (1997), with which most observations described here were made. The jacket is convenient, but not very aesthetic and heavy ; the newer versions are nicer and lighter. Right, a picture extracted from a Subcam tape: the subcamer is writing a post-it. Present resolution of 400 lines is insufficient to read what is written in font smaller than 16 on paper or screen, although sufficient for subcamers to remember what they were doing, during debriefing.

The recordings provide an insight of the subjective experience of the wearer. It is quite different from the so-called „ subjective view " in cinema, because you see the subjects hand's moving, follow head movements, etc. It is a way of getting in the subject's shoes. The Subcam allows understanding better the user's perspective, his own perceived world, his „ Umwelt " [Uexküll, 1934] ; and capturing the affordances of the environment [Gibson, 1967, 1979].

On the field, after careful preparation of the social setting, volunteer users are given a Subcam, therefore becoming „ subcamers ". Subcamers are left alone by the researchers, and wear the Subcam while performing their usual activities, during half-day sessions. They quickly forget they are wearing the Subcam, which is completely silent[1]. In some cases, several co-workers may each wear a Subcam during the same sessions for collaboration study. Then, the tapes are collected by the research team, for analysis. The „ interesting " moments of the tapes are shown to the subcamers in debriefing sessions, where subcamers are invited to comment their subjective view of the situation (intentions, interpretation, feelings etc.). Debriefing is also videotaped.

Debriefing sessions enable better understanding and testing hypotheses [Lahlou & Fayard, 1998 ; Lahlou 1999]. When viewing their own tapes, subcamers seem to

---

[1] More precisely, subcamers report not to forget the Subcam "completely all the time", but say they act the same way they would without the Subcam, except in few occasions, like when a external visitor comes in and they must explain the experiment. And the tapes look realistic indeed. For this reason, ethical aspects of data collection protocols and analysis, and features of the Subcam itself, have been carefully designed and tested for the sake of subcamers and other colleagues. Because, here as in any video protocol, ethics is a key issue [Mackay, 1991]. See the section on ethics, infra.

remember quite well their intentions, even weeks after ; in contrast to difficult remembrance during interviews without „ subtape " support. Whether this is due to easier (but fallacious) reconstruction, or better remembering because of the availability of a large number of visual and auditory cues identical to lived experience remains to be tested. Anyway, these debriefing sessions are rich for understanding problems „ as seen by the user ".

The Subcam is presently used for getting a fine grained record of user's every day life, including „ problems ". It is specially useful to get a record of „ rare " events, and get a detailed cognitive analysis of it. For instance, our assistant Ms. Fayard extracted 101 „ interruption " clips (when the subcamer was interrupted by external event) from some 50 hours of Subcam tapes of 8 subjects. We coded those interruptions, for modeling and statistics which are now been used in a current study aiming at preventing and curing the bad effects of interruptions on cognitive work, in collaboration with David Kirsh and Aaron Cicourel (UCSD).

We also use the Subcam for demonstrating new tools or furniture, and in one occurrence a Subcam visit of a new building during its construction was used for showing the setting to future users, and collecting their opinion for installations. This spared the burden of the visit to many.

Another use, although the Subcam is basically a qualitative instrument, is *quantifying* the cost of various difficulties, an essential prerequisite for design and research funding decisions. Still, now, we only use „valued lost time " as a cost indicator.

Debriefing allows collecting the subcamer's subjective feeling and intentions, and expressing his/her needs. It also helps to understand how actors use or misuse new artifacts, e.g. prototypes under testing. E.g., several subjects became aware, when viewing the tape, that their telephone was not situated in the best place: they had to move a lot, several times a day, and/or could not access their file cabinet or other artifacts when on the phone because of the wire. This revealed they had left the telephone location on their desk (as placed by technician or themselves on their first day) as a „ default value " which was inappropriate.

Also, the Subcam made us aware that some tasks are in fact not done as common sense represents them (e.g. when searching for a document on a desk, one often actually uses vision prior to memory - „ scanning " the desktop before recalling where it is). This spares time in design by avoiding making misadapted prototypes.

Still, analysis is long, and we do not yet have a good catalog of activities which would enable fine statistical analysis. This is certainly the main limitation of the tool.

Subcam tapes analysis gave the feeling that the activity of subjects was heavily context driven, just as in other activities [Suchman, 1987 ; Lave, 1988]. Often, the context seemed to divert them from their initial intentions (e.g. post-its on their desks or agendas reminding them to do other things), or even forcing them into activities (telephone calls, incoming colleagues). More generally, the context appeared full of inscriptions which are action triggers, attractors [Lahlou, 1999], some of which have been set up by the subject himself to program his own activity in the future (agendas, post-its, piles etc.). Therefore the office appears as a control panel where decisions are taken and actions performed through inscriptions on information artifacts [Lahlou, 1996, 1998b]. This is coherent with interview studies conducted on similar fields [Malone, 1983 ; Fischler & Lahlou, 1995 ; Fischler & Therrien, 1998].

These findings orient our design directions to „ clarify " office setting ; transforming present scattered and disruptive stimuli, so that affordances and display of information artifacts provide users with synthetic views of activity.

# 4   The Offsat (Office Satellite)

As the office is an action unit, where the display of information artifacts is part of the cognitive processing, we wanted to study the office (room) as a behavioral unit. What happens in an office in ethologic terms? Are there specific zones for different activities? These questions have been investigated by Proxemics (Hall, 1966) ; but quantification and precise zoning are necessary for design. What are exactly the relevant zones and their limits? We also wanted a rough breakdown of activity ; in order to evaluate the impact of changes on office life, and artifact distribution. For instance: do new file cabinets change the organization of paper stacks on desktops : do new desks enhance collaboration?

The Office Satellite (Offsat), a video camera fixed on the ceiling upon the desk, offers us an aerial view on the office which can help us to understand the global organization and its evolution. Moreover, the Offsat provides middle term and long term information: at a rate of one picture every 2 seconds, the Offsat films clearly show the activity zones during a day. At a rate of one picture every 30 seconds, they show the life of piles and the drifts of large artifacts. Compared to the Subcam, the Offsat offers complementary views on the office spatial organization, on its evolution and on the subject interactions with it.

Technically, the Offsat is based on a wide angle version of the Axis Neteye™ web camera: a video camera combined with a RISC CPU compression chip and web server, all in one small body (500 grams, 4 by 12,5 by 15,5 cm). It is combined with a software for image analysis, Offsatmap, developed for us by FCI. Connected on the local IP network with standard RJ-45 cable, the Offsat sends jpeg pictures of the observed office to a distant hard disk, at specified intervals (e.g. 30 seconds).

Installation is easy: it only needs a standard power plug and a standard Ethernet network plug, which are now available in most modern offices (technically, one does just plug it in parallel with the local computer). The Offsat has its own IP address, and does not use any local resource other than standard 220V AC current. As most offices in our setting use standard 60x60 cm false ceiling cover plates, we made a few platforms of similar dimensions in a stronger material, with the web camera attached to it, so we just have to climb on a stall and substitute the Offsat to any plate in the ceiling. Therefore, the Offsat location can be chosen easily, wires go in the false ceiling, installation is quick, the office is left intact after experiment ; and all looks „ clean ". The Offsat is autonomous, silent, can be monitored with remote settings, and does not need film replacement. It can be instantly stopped by the user just by cutting power on the wire, and restarts automatically when reconnected. This solution was developed with Yann Guyonvarc'h (FCI), in order to overcome the problems encountered during a first trial using classical video on a high tripod [Conein & Jacopin, 1996], and evaluations of using 35mm camera at fixed intervals, which both were costly in film, manpower, and technically bothersome. An observation device should not be a burden to users, especially if we want them to accept it for months. We now have the device running since august 1997, and encountered amazingly few problems, except for storing the flow of data, which have to be transferred quickly from the hard disk to other media, so as to leave free space for incoming pictures (we had to stop observation during some holidays for that reason).

Present maximum resolution of images produced is 704x576 pixels, but we mainly use 352x288 (from 30k to 50k each), which proved sufficient. Images are compressed on the fly and sent directly by the Offsat through the network to a remote hard disk which is collected with delay. Ethical rules are the following: the room where the images go is locked ; images are only used for research and never shown to anyone without authorization ; before connecting „ live " to the camera, the researcher must call by phone the user for authorization ; any set of images (e.g. „ last week " will be destroyed on demand of the user (this actually happened once, for a period of one day, on a total of 52 man/month of observations). The Offsat URL is protected by password, so that only the subject and the researcher can have on-line access, through a standard web browser.

Images are cropped weekly and undergo two kinds of processing. The first is just aggregating them into mpeg movies. One then gets an accelerated view of what happened in the office. At a rate of 1 image every 30 seconds, one day (13 hours, we don't record from 20:00 to 7:00) becomes 1560 images, producing about 1 minute of film (62 s). One can then easily watch a month of activity in half an hour. Pile drift, artifact move, and general activity (e.g. stand alone computing, meeting...) are easily seen.

The second is mapping activity zones and analyzing gross activity. Images are compared in series by the software, which yields a map of zones where movement occurs. Images are then sorted by zone of activity, and statistics can be calculated (e.g. time spent in stand alone computing, number of accesses to a specific artifact, etc.)

Our design program for cognitive work, in collaboration with François Jegou and Tanguy Lemoing from Dàlt design company, used the Offsat to test the impact of some new artifacts for augmented cognitive work.

Figure 2 shows the office of two volunteers, C1 and C2, „ before " (left) and „ after " (right) implementing experimental furniture. Figure 3 shows the activity zones in the office corresponding to „ before " and after ".

**Fig.2.** Scenes from Offsat show same office before (left) and after (right) implementing new experimental furniture (Offsat position unchanged). The camera field covers about 80% of the office surface. C1 is seen on both pictures. His colleague C2 lives in the right of the office, and is hardly seen on the picture (one of his hands appears on left picture, by his keyboard). On the right image, where C1 works with a visitor, the refurbished office clearly exhibits more free space. The new „ double-deck " desks (designed by Dàlt based on users' ideas) are smaller in ground surface but have two levels, and the LCD screens are shorter. A new pile-display artifact (the „ rangepile " also designed with Dàlt, not visible on picture) cleared the floor for human activity. The file cabinet moved from the left wall (left picture) to the back wall (right picture).

C1's office was monitored with the Offsat from October 1998 to march 1999, covering the period of implementation of new furniture and information artifacts (December 1998). The Offsat was untouched, so as to compare aerial views of the office arranged as different settings. Zoning before and after was compared by analyzing two sets of 24000 pictures, before and after changes (November, and February, once new routines were installed).

158

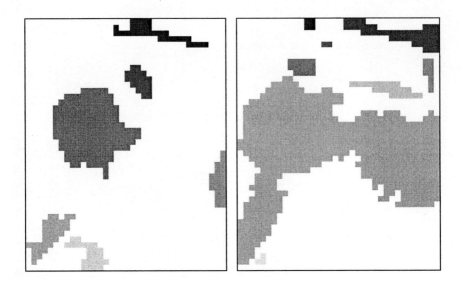

**Fig. 3.** Offsatmap outputs: zones of same office (as in Fig. 1) „ before " (left) and „ after " (right) implementing new experimental furniture (same projections as pictures in Fig. 1). The darker the zone, the more movement in it. The darkest zone on both pictures (up right) is an artifact: the window curtains move all the time because of the air conditioner. Then come small dark zones which are the computer's screens. In the center are the human life zones (left side of office for C1, and right side for C2). Bottom left is the room doorway, a crucial interface with the corridor. Increase of „ live space " after implementation of the new furniture is easily noticeable.

Notice, „ after " (right image) the much larger central zone, which corresponds to the proximal zones of C1 and C2 when seated, also melted with one doorstep zone. Detailed analysis showed significant increase of visits, of collaborative work, and of physical movements, probably due to increased available space. Whether this positively impacted production has not been evaluated, but the users incline to think so. Also the new configuration with reflection-free flat LCD screens enabled better lighting of the room. The resulting „ look and feel " of the office completely changed at ground level, due to more space and light. Users expressed strong satisfaction[2]. Some neighboring colleagues started lobbying as "me too" volunteers for the test program. One must of course be careful of test users appreciation („ Hawthorne effect " ), and it must be mentioned that one of the subjects (C1) was member of the user participative group which led to designing one of the prototypes tested here. Still, these testers proved in other testing occasions a strong critical capacity. Also, the

---

[2] This brought unexpected problems as, while the test equipment was supposed to move to another office for another test, these users expressed strong desire to „ test longer " the equipment, and reluctance to go back to their initial setting ; finally a solution was found so that they could keep at least some of the new equipment.

other tester (C2) who was at first reluctant to the experiment proved to be the more satisfied (understandable when we see the zones on Fig. 2).

Technically, zone identification is based on movement analysis, by comparing each image with previous and next image in the Offsat flow. It is a difficult problem, for technical reasons which are too long to describe here in detail, and the presence of some artifactual classes (e.g. the „ curtain " zone) shows they are not completely solved: of course, lighting changes a lot, so do colors, etc.

Counting movements in zones is another issue for which another software has been developed ; and scene analysis is under development. We hope this will help us evaluate the impact of new artifacts on office work.

## 5  Ethics and Field Preparation

These tools are powerful, and easy to plug on. But they must be used with caution, and need careful preparation and monitoring of the field. Field preparation and ethical aspects are linked. They both aim at building *trust* between the researchers and the participants, and preserving it.

At first, many people are reluctant to be observed by (any) video devices. They fear being big brotherized, they are afraid of showing "bad" behavior in some way. Technically, those fears are mostly unfounded. The Offsat view hardly allows to recognize people unless you know who might be on the picture ; there is no way of actually knowing what people precisely do (no sound, highly accelerated films). For the Subcam, the subcamer is heard on the tape, but his face is never seen, only parts of his body (hands, …). And of course both devices can be very easily and instantly turned off: "subjects" have full control all the time. The only sensitive aspect is that the social and interaction styles of subcamers are clearly exposed, and that the duration of presence in office may be known through the Offsat (but being outside the office doesn't mean you are not working !). Almost all the material collected turns out completely innocuous to users, although it may in some instances evidence big failures in the design of their environment.

Unfortunately, participants do not know this until they have actually experienced the device, and viewed some tapes ; then they relax. So it is crucial to get a first set of influential volunteers. Once people are acquainted with the devices, things go smooth. With time, it gets easier and easier to find volunteers on the same field, as people see that their colleagues did it and that no problem occurred. We now have no problems getting volunteers, and they act very naturally with the Subcam and completely naturally with the Offsat[3].

---

[3] In fact, it is quite difficult not to act „ naturally ", because action is heavily environment driven. The fact that people feel at ease is especially important for social interaction.

Ethical issues were recognized as a key issue very early, and we set up sophisticated rules for protecting individuals from any possible kind of misuse of their image or of the collected data. This has to aspects: ex ante, and ex post.

Ex ante: to avoid collecting embarrassing data (e.g. unusually aggressive gossip, private discussions, going to the toilet etc.) the subcamers are given the opportunity to turn off sound and/or image with a big, simple, clearly labeled switch. This is signaled by bright colored LED's on the front of the jacket so that other participants can also know whether they are recorded or not, and ask the subcamer to be "off record". In our experience, this does not happen often with the Subcam, and is very rare with the Offsat, except for some external visitors.

Ex post, once data are collected, the subcamers keep them first and preview them before the researchers. They always keep the possibility to destroy part or all of the recordings, with no time limit. Until now, no subcamer used this privilege. But we know that most of them only viewed a small piece of their tape, enough to realize it was innocuous, got bored at the first long sequence without strong action (e.g. long stand alone computing session) and gave us the tape.

No image is shown whatsoever without the previous informed consent of the people who may be seen or heard on the tape. If the same tape is shown to different audiences (e.g.. presentation in a symposium of a tape for which we already had informed consent for projection to an internal audience) informed consent is asked again. The procedure is very heavy and impairing for the researchers, but it does build trust on strong bases, and ethical awareness becomes a natural reflex for the researcher.

It would be too long to describe here the ethical protocol. Anyway our opinion is that although an ethical protocol is essential, it is not sufficient and will never cover all cases. The real issue is *trust*, not ethics. There is no single secret: building trust takes time. The researchers must a real sympathy for the participants, respect them, remember that *the participants' work* is more important than our research, and that observation must not be a burden for them ; having an everyday care of their interests *and also* showing it (e.g. always asking them for informed consent even for "small" occasions). It also necessitates that participants really know what is done with the tapes and why. All this is progressively built, socially, by a sum of details. We benefited of the wise advice of A. Cicourel in that field preparation. The fact that in many occasions participants could see how that the researchers really cared about the ethics ; the fact that the project is aimed at improving efficiency *and comfort* of workers, and that they could see actual outcomes in the form of prototypes ; the fact that the head of the program is an insider of the Division and that his activity could be traced long back ; that he was seen experimenting himself first all the devices, and showed widely his own tapes ; were some of the parameters that allowed building trust on the field. Also, this was a long experiment, started mid-97 and still on going. Visitors are a specific problem, as they are not warned in the same way as „ locals ", and always show some surprise or anxiety at first. Subcamers and people with Offsats in their office solve the problem case by case ; sometimes they just turn the device off.

Our experience with subcamers on other fields outside the R&D division shows that if trust between the researcher and the subcamer preexists, no other specific field preparation is necessary: The subcamer will use his own trust capital with his local social environment.

But ethics is not simply a way of building trust. Some of the material collected shows crudely the social style of subcamers, or may uncover embarrassing implicits. People *do* act very naturally, and sometimes they appear inefficient, overloaded, failing, or funny. This is why the researchers must be very careful, because, when taken out of their context, some tape extracts might be embarrassing ; however demonstrative or interesting these extracts might be for scientific purposes, those extracts will of course never shown or described. The author himself, after having viewed hours of his own tapes, and having realized how highly inefficient or socially unpleasant he appears on some extracts has become extremely benevolent and tolerant in analyzing other people's tapes. And the best guarantee of the subjects interest is that the researchers are fully aware that any use of the data which would put, directly or not, any participant in an embarrassing situation, would harm people, destroy trust, and finally end a very interesting and productive observation program.

# 6 Conclusions

Developing new environments which will help and augment cognitive workers is a great challenge for organizations. Developing good solutions is only possible with the active help of users, and a first hand knowledge of the actual usability conditions.

Solving problems is costly, so funding organizations usually want to evaluate the costs of problems, and possible benefits of new solutions. They also need evaluations of which solution is best after testing. Although this is known of everyone, appropriate methods for cognitive work investigation, cognitive environment design, and evaluation, are still few. One reason is that research funding is usually aimed at designing solutions, not designing tools to help design solutions.

We designed two complementary tools, the Subcam and the Offsat, to understand better how workers interact with their workspace. They may be handy for observing the use of experimental settings in cooperative buildings of rooms. For instance, the Offsat may be used to measure the use of "roomware" such as invented by Streitz et al (1998), the Subcam could give a realistic first-person view of the look-and-feel of settings like the ambientROOM [Wisneski et al., 1998]. More generally, the two tools, especially in connection, can be used to understand better how people use buildings, because they allow monitoring places, but also individuals moving from place to place.

These tools proved useful in our practice, in their present form, giving us access to new insights of distributed cognitive processes. Still, one must underline that many progresses have to be made. The devices themselves could be better: e.g. eye tracking, and higher resolution on the Subcam. Gathering good data requires a careful field preparation and a constant attention to ethical aspects. Finally, methods for systematic analysis long corpuses of video have to be developed.

# References

1. Autissier, D, Melkior, R., Lahlou, S. (1997) *Analyse de l'activité quotidienne de 6 chefs de groupes à la DER*. EDF/DER/MMC. Service AGT.
2. Conein, B., Jacopin, E. (1997*). Le Bureau comme espace de travail*. EDF/DER HN51/97004.
3. Fayard, AL ; Lahlou, S (1998). *The Subcam: An Insight Into the Phenomenal Flow of Office Life*. Video,7 min, EDF/DER/IPN, march 1998. CSCW '97 video proceedings.
4. Fischler, C., & Lahlou, S. (1995). *Dossiers, piles d'attente et corbeilles: la digestion quotidienne de l'information dans les bureaux*. EDF/DER. HN5195017.
5. Gibson, J. J. (1967). Notes on affordances. In : E . Reed & R. Jones (eds.). *Reasons for realism. Selected Essays of James J. Gibson*. London : Lawrence Erlbaum Associates, 1982, pp. 401-418.
6. Gibson, J. J. (1979). *The Ecological Approach to Visual Perception*. London: Lawrence Erlbaum Associates, 1986 (2nd ed.).
7. Hall, E.T. (1966). *The Hidden Dimension*. New York: Doubleday.
8. Heath, C. & Luff, P. (1991) Collaborative Activity and Technological Design: Task Coordination in the London Underground Control Rooms. *ECSCW'91*. Kluwer Press.
9. Hiltz, S. R., Turoff, M. (1985). Structuring Computer-Mediated Communication Systems to Avoid Information Overload. *Communications of the ACM* 28 (7): 680-689.
10. Hutchins, E. (1995) *Cognition in the Wild*, Cambridge: MIT Press.
11. Lahlou, S (1996). *Representations and the social co-ordination of action*. 3rd Int. Conference on Social Representations, Aix-en-Provence, 9/1996. & EDF/DER HN5196020.
12. Lahlou, S. (1994). *L'utilisation de l'information dans l'entreprise: quelques réflexions théoriques et une analyse lexicale*. EDF-DER. HN-5194055.
13. Lahlou, S. (1998a). „ La caméra subjective, une nouvelle méthode pour l'étude des représentations en contexte ". 4th CIRS. Mexico, août 1998. EDF/DER HN-51/98017.
14. Lahlou, S. (1998b). *Cognitive Overflow Syndrome: le diable est dans le détail*. EDF HN5198018.
15. Lahlou, S. (1999). Les attracteurs cognitifs et le syndrome du débordement. EDF R&D. HN51/99004.
16. Lahlou, S., Fayard, A.L. (1998). Waiting for the Paperless Office: Two Video Tools for Investigating the Paperfull Office of Today. EDF-DER HN5198020.
17. Lahlou, S., Lenay Ch., Gueniffey Y., Zacklad, M. (1997). Le COS (Cognitive Overflow Syndrome). *Bulletin de l'Association pour la Recherche Cognitive*, n° 42, Nov. 1997, p. 39.
18. Lave, J. (1988). *Cognition in Practice*. Cambridge (UK): Cambridge U.P.
19. Lea, G. (1987) *Non-users of Information Services*. Audit Report. Graham Lea & Partners.
20. Lewis, D. (1996) *Dying for Information? An Investigation Into the Effects of Information Overload in the UK and Worldwide*. London, UK: Reuters Business Information.
21. Ljungberg, F. (1996). *An initial exploration of Communication Overflow*. COOP'96, Sophia Antipolis, France. COOP group (eds.) , INRIA, France. pp. 19-36.
22. Mackay, W. (1991) Ethics, Lies and Videotapes. In *Proceedings of CHI'95 (Denver, CO)*. ACM Press. 138-145
23. Malone, T. W. (1983), How Do People Organize Their Desks? Implications for the Design of Office Information Systems, *ACM Transactions on Office Information Systems*, vol. 1, N°1, 99-112.

24. Mann, S. (1997) " Eudaemonic Eye ": " Personal Imaging " and wearable computing as result of deconstructing HCI; towards greater creativity and self-determination. In *Proceedings of CHI'97* (Atlanta).

25. Mintzberg, H. (1973). *The nature of Managerial Work.* Engelwood Cliffs, N.J.: Prentice Hall, 2nd ed. 1980.

26. Norman, D.A. (1991) "Cognitive Artifacts". In *Designing Interaction; Psychology at the Human-Computer Interface*, J. M. Carroll (ed.). Cambridge: Cambridge University Press.

27. Simon, H.A., Newell, A. (1972). *Human Problem Solving.* Englewood Cliffs, New Jersey: Prentice-Hall.

28. Simonsen, J., Kensing, F. (1997). Using Ethnography in Contextual Design. *Communications of the ACM*, Jul. 1997, vol. 40, n°7: 82-88.

29. Streitz, N. A., Geissler, J., Holmer, T. (1998). Roomware for Cooperative Buildings: Integrated design of Architectural Spaces and Information Spaces. In: Proceedings of CoBuild'98. First International Workshop on Cooperative Buildings, Darmstadt. *Lecture Notes in Computer Science 1370*. Springer: Heidelberg, 1998, pp. 4-21.

30. Suchman, L. (1983), Office Procedure as Practical Action: Models of Work and System Design, *ACM Transactions on Office Information Systems*, vol. 1, N°4, 320-328.

31. Suchman, L. (1987) *Plans and Situated Actions*, New York, NY: Cambridge U.P.

32. Uexküll, J. Von (1934) *Mondes animaux et monde humain.* Suivi de *Théorie de la signification*. Paris: Médiations, Gonthier, 1965.

33. Wisneski, C., Ishii, I., Dahley, A., Gorbet, M., Brave, S., Ullmer, P., Yarin, P. (1998). Ambient Displays: Turning Architectural Space into an Interface between People and Technology. In: Proceedings of CoBuild'98. First International Workshop on Cooperative Buildings, Darmstadt. *Lecture Notes in Computer Science 1370*. Springer: Heidelberg, 1998, pp. 22-32.

# Measuring Work Factors: A Case Study to Identify Relationships among Work Activities, Styles and an Environment

Motohiro Sakamaki[1], Fumihito Ikeda[1][2],
Shingo Takada[3], Kumiyo Nakakoji[2][4][5]

(1) Research and Development Headquarters, NTT DATA Corporation
(2) Graduate School of Information Science, Nara Institute of Science and Technology, Japan
(3) Faculty of Science and Technology, Keio University, Japan
(4) Software Engineering Laboratory, SRA Japan
(5) PRESTO, Japan Science and Technology Corporation

{samakaki, fumi}@rd.nttdata.co.jp
michigan@doi.cs.keio.ac.jp
kumiyo@is.aist-nara.ac.jp

**Abstract.** A work environment needs to be designed based on the nature and characteristics of the work activities and the work styles. Unless we have a clear understanding of what factors of work activities and styles depend on what factors of work environments and vice versa, we would not be able to modify or add components of work environments "effectively." This paper first presents our framework to measure work factors of work activities, styles and an environment, and then discusses results of our case study of applying the framework to actual work practice at NTT Data Corporation. Our framework consists of three representational models: the KPM (Knowledge Production Model) for representing work activities, the MS-GI (Mobile-Settled, Group-Individual) model for characterizing work styles, and the SOU (System-Office-Usage) model for representing a work environment. We have conducted a survey on 274 workers at an organizational unit of NTT Data Corporation by applying the three models. The result shows that the framework is successfully applied to understand the relationships among the three work factors at least partially if not completely. The paper concludes with a discussion of how the framework can be used to evolve work environments by taking into account work activities and styles.

**Keywords** work styles, work environments, measurement, case studies, office design

## 1 Introduction

Work environments need to be designed based on the working style of people who use the environments (Cross & Raizman, 1986; DeMarco & Lister, 1987). A poor fit between working styles and the work environment can result in reduced productivity(DeMarco & Lister, 1987). Therefore, the design of work environments to enhance quality and output must take into account characteristics of work activities, characteristics of working styles, and the interaction of these factors.

With this fact quite well-shared among communities, however, there has been little research on how to represent these factors; what types of work activities are performed and how they can be classified, what working styles exist and how they can be captured, what constitutes a work environment and how it should be represented, and finally and most interestingly, how these factors depend on one another.

This paper first presents our framework to quantitatively measure work factors including work activities, styles and an environment, and then discuss results of our case study that has applied the framework to actual work practice and construction of an office at NTT Data Corporation. Our framework consists of three representational models: the KPM (Knowledge Production Model) for representing work activities, the MS-GI (Mobile-Settled, Group-Individual) model for characterizing work styles, and the SOU (System-Office-Usage) model for representing a work environment. The results show that the framework partially explained relationships among the three work factors in the NTT DATA Corporation setting.

## 2 Representing Work Activities, Styles and an Environment

### 2.1 The framework

On the basis on the background described above, our goal was to identify what work factors depend on what other work factors. Such understanding about the relationships among the factors will then guide us in designing and evolving work environments including both physical (office spaces) and logical (computer tools, work policies and rules) ones.

To identify the relationships among the factors, we have taken an approach to "measure" aspects of work-related factors. Representations for each of such aspects are thus developed to achieve the goal. Fig.1 illustrates our framework for representing work. We view "work" from three perspectives: *work activities*, *work styles* and *work environments*. *Work activities* represent what types of operations and functions people perform in their work. Our approach is to characterize work activities in terms of what "information and knowledge" is produced, shared and used. We propose the *KPM* (Knowledge Production Model) for representing work activities.

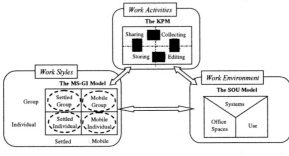

**Fig 1. The Framework**

*Work styles* represent what work settings people are in during their work. The *MS-GI*(Mobile-Settle, Group-Individual) model categorizes work styles in terms of two dimensions : whether people are mobile or settled, and whether people work within a group or independently.

Finally, *work environments* represent both the physical and logical surroundings of people in their work hours. The *SOU* (Systems-Office-Use) model is used to characterize a work environment. The *system* aspect include what types of computer tools exist in the environment. The *office* aspect illustrates how the physical office space is designed in the environment. The *use* aspect illustrates what rules and policies exist in the environment.

## 2.2   Merit of using the framework

Assuming the availability of data on the three work factors and the existence of "stable" relationships among these factors, it should be possible to use these data and relationships to guide the development of new work environments and to analyze the effect of additions to an existing work environment.

For example, when an organization builds a new work environment for a team, the organization can use the models as follows to: a) examine work styles of the team; b) identify what phase of the KPM people in each work style think is important in terms of the relation between work activities and work styles; and c) determine what elements should be incorporated in the new work environment. Similarly, when an organization adds a new element to an existing work environment(e.g., new computer system, new space, new rules), the organization can use the framework to: a) identify what phase of the KPM the introduced element supports in terms of the relation between work activities and work environment; b) examine what work style is important to the identified phase in terms of the relation between work activities and work styles; c) identify work styles of the people in the team; and d) compare the work styles identified in a) and the work styles identified in b).

The remainder of this section describes each of the three models in more detail.

## 2.3   Representation of work activities: The KPM

The work activities we have studied represent a type of work that can be described as "Knowledge Production." Knowledge production processes rely on information that people have or that may be around the people, either in other people's heads or in the world (Nonaka & Takeuchi, 1995). We have developed the Knowledge Production Model (KPM) based on how information is handled (Ikeda *et al.,* 1997, 1999; Sakamaki *et al.,* 1998). The KPM consists of four cyclic process phases:

-   *Collecting*: People need to identify information that is useful and/or necessary for the current task from a large amount of information available.
-   *Editing*: After collecting the information, such information must be put together in some coherent manner.
-   *Storing*: Information needs to be accumulated, otherwise it will be lost and become unusable.

- *Sharing*: Information needs to be shared among other people in the organization. "New" information needs to be shared among other people in the organization. "New" information provided by other people becomes a "seed" for creating new knowledge.

These four process phases may not be always distinct but may overlap. For example, one may become aware of the need for collecting more information while editing already collected information.

## 2.4   Representation of work styles: MS-GI model

We have characterized work styles in two dimensions. One is whether one performs "mobile" work or "settled" work. By "settled", we mean those who always work at fixed places. The other dimension characterizes people by whether they generally work as "individually-oriented" or as "group-oriented". Individually-oriented means work that can be conducted independent of others. Group-oriented people need to cooperate with each other for accomplishing their tasks. Looking at work styles from these two dimensions results in the four working styles:   *Mobile-Group, Mobile-Individual, Settled-Group*, and S*ettled-Individual.*

## 2.5   Representation of work environment: The SOU model

We view a work environment from three perspectives: *systems,* physical *office spaces,* and how they are *used* (Ikeda *et al,* 1997, 1999). The *systems* perspective represents computer tools and systems that are incorporated in the environment. This aspect has long been pointed out as critical in various types of works (Thadhani, 1984; Mital *et al.,* 1986), and existing research has basically concentrated on this factor in dealing with work environments.

The *office space* perspective is how the physical space is used within the work environment. This has also been reported to affect our work productivity (McCue, 1978; DeMarco & Lister 1987). The layouts of office cubicles as well as types of meeting spaces are examples of this perspective.

The *use* perspective denotes how the computer system and office space are used, including rules and policies governing people at an organization. As Grudin (1988) pointed out that computer systems may benefit only a certain type of people without benefiting others, this factor is especially important in dealing with work environments.

# 3   A Case Study: Measuring Work Factors

This Section presents results of our case study that applied the above framework in the real work practice.

## 3.1 Investigation Outline

In order to verify whether each relationship among factors in the framework is measurable, we have conducted the following three questionnaires.

A) Investigation to capture important elements of current work environment and desired elements for future environment

B) Investigation to categorize the SOU elements to each phase of the KPM

C) Investigation to classify a worker's work styles

About questionnaire A) and C), we have conducted surveys on 274 members at NTT DATA Corporation, who are engaged in sales, accounting, general affairs, planning, system development, and research. The details of subjects are that 179 subjects belonged to software research institute and 95 subjects were belonged to the Kyushu branch. About questionnaire B), we have conducted surveys on only 30 members who have worked in the Distributed Cooperative model office(see 3.8) and who have engaged in software research and development. These 30 subjects are contained in 274 subjects.

In our case study, before our conducting surveys, we have first analyzed existing work environment in terms of the SOU model(see 3.2). We have identified elements for each of the three perspectives of the SOU model based on the KPM(see 3.3). We then conducted a survey on what work styles those subjects were engaged in(questionnaire C), see 3.4). We have next asked each subject what elements of the work environments will be important currently and necessary for the future(questionnaire A)). Based on the sets of data collected in questionnaire A) and C), we have analyzed if there are relationships between work styles and characteristics of work environments(see 3.5). Then, in order to prove our hypothesis about the relationship between the SOU model and the KPM, we have conducted survey on what SOU elements was categorized in terms of what process of the KPM in questionnaire B)(see 3.3 and 3.6). At last, we have analyzed relationships between work activities and work styles based on the results from 3.3, 3.4 and 3.5(analysis result will show in 3.7).

The remainder of this section details the case study.

## 3.2 Application of the SOU model

In the analysis of the organization, we have identified thirty-one elements of computer systems, thirty-five elements of physical office space, and fifteen elements of practice (the detailed description of the elements are in (Ikeda *et al.*, 1997)). Some of the elements are:

*Systems:*
– electronic approval systems: ones that automatically identify and ask the appropriate person for approving a purchase using the organization's budget.
– tele-conferencing systems: ones that allow meetings between people that are remotely located with TV screens showing views from each site.

*Office spaces:*
- individual spaces: spaces that are segmented as booth so that people respect each other's privacy.
- large meeting spaces: meeting spaces for 10 or more people.

*Uses:*
- rules on managing information: rules instituted regarding management of information, such as how new information should be stored.
- concentration rules: rules that help people to maintain concentration, for instance, one of them states that how one should let others know that he/she wants not to be disturbed.

We have asked each subject what elements of the work environments (1) are currently important for them and (2) will be important and necessary for the future on questionnaire A). By using this application and application for the MS-GI, we can compare the difference in the SOU elements for every work styles.

### 3.3 Application of the KPM

After we have identified the elements of the work environment as described above, we have categorized each element in terms of what process phase of the KPM the element supports. Some examples of the categorization include:
- *Tele-conferencing systems: collecting, editing* and *sharing* (because such a system supports to communicate with each other, gain information from others and may produce some artifacts through communication)
- *Library spaces: collecting, storing* and *sharing* (because such a space store and share many information that can be shared among group members)

Detailed results of this survey can be found in (Ikeda *et al.,* 1997). This relationship between each elements and the KPM is only our hypothesis. In order to verify our hypothesis, we have conducted questionnaire B) which set up some routine questions by which the SOU elements are connected each process phase of the KPM. Some of the routine questions to all elements are:

- *Collecting*: has it been become easy to retrieve information?
- *Editing*: has it been become easy to come out of a new idea?
- *Storing*: has it been become easy to recycle information or/and idea?
- *Sharing*: has it been become easy to share information or /and idea?

By using this application, the KPM and the SOU model are related.

### 3.4 Application of the MS-GI model

In order to analyze what work style the subjects are categorized into, we have used questionnaire C) that contains ten questions each regarding the two perspectives: "mobile vs. settled (MS perspective)" and "group-oriented vs. individual-oriented (GI perspective)." Subjects were asked to select one of the four levels between the two extremes.

Examples of questions asked for the MS perspective include:

- *How standardized is your work?: (1) routine (2) non-routine*
- *With whom do you work together?: (1) always with the same group of people (2) always different*

Examples of questions regarding the GI perspective include:

- *How do you set up a goal?: (1) by coordinating within a group (2) by setting up individually*
- *What is the purpose of storing information?: (1)mainly for myself (2) mainly for the group*

Answers given to each of those questions are quantified and weighted sum were used to characterize each subject's work style (the algorithm used is detailed in (Sakamaki *et al.,* 1998)).

## 3.5 Relationship between work styles and work environments

From the result of questionnaires A) and C), we tried to clarify the relation between work styles and work environment in the framework. We supposed that each work styles needed each different elements of the SOU model. From the result of this investigation, we found that our hypothesis was filled mostly. The result of the survey is shown in Fig 2. In Fig 2, each SOU factors is taken along a vertical axis, and the work styles is taken along the horizontal axis. The cell which is gray is the element with which workers' need was accepted to be high. Hereafter, we will describe tendency about each work styles.

| Elements of "System" | Mobile-Group | Mobile-Individual | Settle-Group | Settle-Individual |
|---|---|---|---|---|
| Fixed-assets management system | | | | |
| Electric approval system | | | | |
| Financial System | | | | |
| Company rule-base system | | | | |
| Hours of operation calculation system | | | | |
| Library management system | | | | |
| Study and seminor management | | | | |
| Address book system | | | | |
| Schedule and meeting management | | | | |
| Task List and situation management | | | | |
| Bussiness situation report management | | | | |
| Document management system | | | | |
| WWW | | | | |
| Electric notice board | | | | |
| Subscription Service | | | | |
| Face-to-Face meeting support system | | | | |
| Computer Telephony Integration | | | | |
| TV conference system | | | | |
| Creativity support system | | | | |
| Collaborative support system | | | | |
| Work-flow support | | | | |
| Messaging infrastructure | | | | |
| Shared Information system | | | | |
| 10base-T | | | | |
| 100base-T | | | | |
| Wireless LAN | | | | |
| Intranet | | | | |
| Extranet | | | | |
| Personal cellular phone | | | | |
| Electric Outlets | | | | |
| LAN connection | | | | |

| Elements of "Office" | Mobile-Group | Mobile-Individual | Settle-Group | Settle-Individual |
|---|---|---|---|---|
| "Cave" | | | | |
| "Court" | | | | |
| Spot meeting space | | | | |
| Browsing space | | | | |
| Filing room | | | | |
| Library space | | | | |
| Temporary drops in space | | | | |
| Work room | | | | |
| Laboratory | | | | |
| Shared desk space | | | | |
| Coffe break space | | | | |
| Salon space | | | | |
| Sinking booth | | | | |
| Reception area | | | | |
| Smoking area | | | | |
| High pliability furniture | | | | |
| Ergonomics furniture | | | | |
| Bulletin board | | | | |
| Pinup board | | | | |
| Flip board | | | | |
| White board | | | | |
| Large-sized display equipment | | | | |
| OHP Screen | | | | |
| Sound equipment | | | | |
| Glass partition | | | | |
| Task-Light | | | | |
| An outside manometer and thermometer | | | | |
| coffe server | | | | |
| Refrigerator, electronic range, etc | | | | |
| Closet | | | | |
| "Cave & Court" | | | | |
| Open Office | | | | |
| Using window as a share space | | | | |
| Color scheme by the natural materials | | | | |
| Lighting plan which ca be regulated | | | | |

| Elements of "Use" | Mobile-Group | Mobile-Individual | Settle-Group | Settle-Individual |
|---|---|---|---|---|
| Event with the feeling of a season | | | | |
| Flower arrangement | | | | |
| Plant | | | | |
| BGM and BGV | | | | |
| Rule of eating and drinking | | | | |
| Hoteling rule | | | | |
| Paper-less policy | | | | |
| Library Operation rules | | | | |
| Summary into one-page rules | | | | |
| Introduction of a concentration time rule | | | | |
| Secretary | | | | |
| Librarian-support | | | | |
| Filing Clark | | | | |
| Meeting facility usage policy | | | | |
| Art | | | | |
| Hours of operation management policy | | | | |
| Manual documentation policy | | | | |
| Progress management policy | | | | |

**Fig 2. The relation between work styles and work environment**

## SOU elements for Mobile-Group

- The need for elements of office is high
- The need for informal communication is high
- The need for individual concentration is not so high

The feature of this work style is that the need for System elements and Use elements is not so high. Instead, they had demanded elements for sharing information spatially, such as *white board*, *pinup board* and *OHP screen*. Conversely, in the same Office elements, the need for individual concentration, such as *Cave*, is low. From this result, they tend to seldom pay attention to individual environment, if the spatial environment for their collaboration is prepared.

## SOU elements for Mobile-Individual

- The need for the broad access to information is high
- The need for flexible access to the received information is high

Their feature is not adhering to especially system elements and use elements but they want to access information broadly like *WWW*, *subscription service*, *personal cellular phone*, *librarian support* and so on. Moreover, as opposed to *Mobile-Group*, their needs to improve personal environment, such as *ergonomics furniture*, *Cave*, is also high.

## SOU elements for Settle-Group

- The need for flexible access to the received information is high

This work style has tendency resembled *Mobile-Individual* very well. However, since the need for *CTI*, *shared information system* is high and the need for office elements, such as *shared desk space* and *coffee break space*, is conversely low, *Settle-Group* does not desire to communicate in real space but in virtual world. Moreover, the needs to *creativity support* and *collaborative support* were high. However, we have not expected at all about this tendency. So, we need to gaze about this point.

## SOU elements for Settle-Individual

- The need for accessing to analog data is very low

There is no factor of being high in this work style only. Conversely, there are many factors that only to this work style does not have but other work styles have. Their characteristic elements are in Office elements, such as *browsing space*, *filing room*, *library space*, *salon space*, *white board* and so on. Each of these are the elements for catching information in analog. From these things, they tends to dislike the access to analog data very much. This is known also from the need for *electric notice board*, *shared information system* being high.

**Categorization SOU elements based on WS-GI axis**

Next, let us consider about the tendency of SOU elements with Mobile-Settle or Group-Individual. The needs for "Group" are *schedule and meeting management, pinup board, manual documentation policy, progress management policy.* Conversely, the needs for "individual" are *company rule-based system, Cave,* and *ergonomics furniture.* From this result, the work style classification by "Group" and "Individual" shows that there is remarkable difference in the need for the SOU model.

On the other hand, there is no remarkable difference between "Mobile" and "Settle". What does this mean? As for this, we wonder if the axis of "Group-Individual" and the axis of "Mobile-Settle" do not cross at right angles. For this reason, it may be unsuitable to consider only these two axes as an factors for representing work styles.

### 3.6 Relationship between work activities and work environments

On the basis of the result of questionnaire B), we have arranged each the SOU elements to each phase of the KPM. In this investigation, we verified only about a part of the SOU model which has introduced into the model office(see 3.8). The result is shown in Fig 3. The feature of this mapping is that "Cave & Court" covers the broad range of the KPM. "Cave & Court" is the layout which arranges some individual work spaces(Cave) around centering on a meeting space(Court). Although "Cave & Court" is classified into the elements of Office factor, it also covers the field of System and Use, such as "TV conference system", "electric white board", "meeting usage policy" and so on, broadly. This shows that in case we represent work environments, introducing SOU elements simultaneously is more effective rather than introducing SOU elements individually.

Since this mapping is the analysis only for about 30 subjects who are in the new

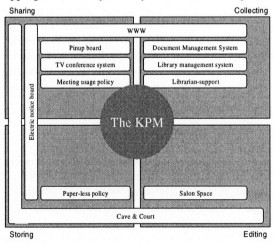

**Fig 3. The relation between work activities and work environments**

office, it is dangerous to use this result as a general solution. However, we think that this case study has suggested that relating of the KPM and the SOU model is possible.

### 3.7 Relationship between work activities and work styles

In our case study, we have not conducted evaluation which connects work activities and work styles directly. Then, we tried to clarify the relation between the KPM and MS-GI model through the SOU model by using the measured results of questionnaire A), B) and C). At the beginning, in work style which intersects perpendicularly, we think respectively that completely reverse tendency should come out. The result is shown in Fig 4.

Consequently, we found the remarkable difference between "Mobile-Group" and "Settle-Individual". This was as our expected. However, between "Mobile-Individual" and "Settle-Group", we have not found the remarkable difference. From this result, as we described in section 3.5, we have to suspect the rectangular-cross of axis in MS-GI model. However, we think that clarifying the relation between the KPM and MS-GI model has been attained to some extent via the SOU model. Therefore, our conviction that a setup of the framework by representation of work activities is effective is confirmed.

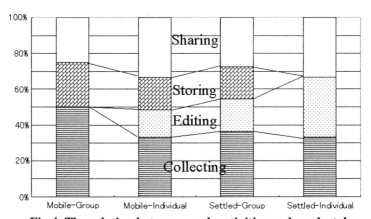

**Fig 4. The relation between work activities and work styles**

### 3.8 Construction of the Distributed Cooperative model office

We actually built a model office called the Distributed Cooperative Model Office for supporting distributed cooperative work based on our framework(Ikeda *et al.,* 1997, 1999; Sakamaki *et al.,* 1998). The purpose of constructing the model office was to prevent the decline of work efficiency that can occur in distributed environment. About 30 researchers who engaged in software development at NTT DATA participated in the model office project.

174

When we measured cooperative work efficiency using a subject's satisfaction rating, we found that satisfaction improved 30% in the model office. We interpret future offices should be built according to the framework's recommendations.

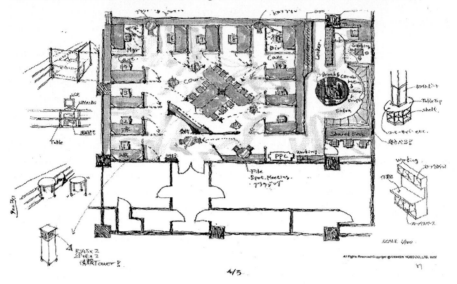

**Fig. 5 The rough layout of the Distributed Cooperative model office**

## 4 Future Work

In this case study, we could verify the validity of a framework. However, we also found that each representation model is not necessarily common and complete. We found that especially the MS-GI model that is representation of work styles could not guarantee rectangular cross of axes from the result of our case study. Therefore, we have to reexamine the axes which representation work styles.

Then, about the KPM which is representation work activities, we recognize that it is the problem that we use almost all the model of "Ikujiro Nonaka" as he wrote. However, since we cannot found the other appropriate model, we reluctantly use the KPM as representation of work activities. While verifying whether the KPM is representing work activities truly, we have to grope for other representation models for work activities.

About the relationship between the KPM and the SOU model, there are two problems to generalize it. The problems are that one is examining only SOU elements introduced into the model office, and another is that subject's work style is partial(strong Settle-Individual), and the number of subject is about 30 only. Therefore, we have to extend the verification range about the relation between the KPM and the SOU model in the future. Moreover, we may have not to prepare the general mapping but the mapping for every work styles. Furthermore, we have to form a still detailed hypothesis about it.

# 5 Conclusion

In this paper, we presented the representational models for work factors, consisting of work activities, work styles and a work environment. We have applied the framework for an organization and found that the representations are useful to identify some relationships among work factors. Certain types of work styles are dependent on determining the importance of elements of the work environment. Although the result is in some way obvious, the value of the work resides in that we could reveal the relationship based on data collected through the actual practice. The framework is found to be a promising approach to identify patterns among work factors. By using such patterns to designing work environment, we would be able to construct a useful and productive work environment by way of identifying people's work activities and styles.

### Acknowledgements

This paper was strengthened by the comments of Tom Finholt, University of Michigan and from the three anonymous reviewers. We are so thankful for them. We would like to thank our colleagues at NTT Data Corp for their helpful advice and cooperation in our studies. We are also very grateful Masayuki Inamochi and Takashi Nagase at Institute of Office Productivity and Environment UCHIDA YOKO Corporation for the valuable discussions in developing the models.

# References

1. Cross, T. B. and Raizman, M. B. (1986). Telecommuting: The Future Technology of Work, Richard D. Irwin, Inc.
2. DeMarco, T., Lister, T. (1987). Peopleware: Productive Projects and Teams, Dorset House Publishing Co., Inc.
3. Drucker, P. (1988). The Coming of the New Organization, Harvard Business Review, Jan.-Feb. 1988, pp. 45-53.
4. Grudin, J. (1988). Why CSCW Applications Fail: Problems in the Design and Evaluation of Organizational Interfaces, CSCW '88 Proc. ACM, pp.85-93.
5. Ikeda, F., Sakamaki, M., Aoki, H., Shingo, T. and Nakakoji, K. (1999). Improving software quality from the viewpoint of knowledge production and the work environment, 6th European Conference on Software Quality.
6. Ikeda, F., Sakamaki, M., Aoki, H., Shingo, T. and Nakakoji, K. (1997). Toward an environment to support distributed work by integrating information technologies, physical spaces and practice, Information Processing Society of Japan, SIG Notes, GW-24.
7. Iivari, J. (1996). "Why are CASE Tools not Used?", Comm. ACM, Vol.39, No.10, pp.94-103.
8. McCue, G. (1978). IBM's Santa Teresa Laboratory −Architecture Design for Program Development, IBM Systems Journal, Vol. 17, No.1.

9. Mital, R. M., Kim, M. M. and Berg, R.A. (1986). A CASE Study of Workstation Usage During the Earlry Stages of the Software Development Life Cycle, Proc. ACM Symp. on Practical Software Development Environments, pp. 70-76.
10. Nonaka, I. and Takeuchi, H. (1995). "The Knowledge-Creating Company", Oxford University Press.
11. Sakamaki, M., Ikeda, F., Aoki, H. (1998). Research for evaluation of an environment to support distributed cooperation work by integrating information technologies, physical spaces and practice, Information Processing Society of Japan, SIG Notes, GW-29.
12. Thadhani, A. J. (1984). Factors Affecting Programmer Productivity during Application Developments, IEEE Software, Vol.6, pp. 15-22.

# Video Mediated Communication for Domestic Environments —
## Architectural and Technological Design

## Stefan Junestrand\*,\*\*,\*\*\*, Konrad Tollmar\*,\*\*

Interactive Institute (\*)
Center for User Oriented IT-Design (\*\*)
Dept. of Architectural Design and Technology (\*\*\*)
Royal Institute of Technology
100 44 Stockholm, Sweden
s.junestrand@arch.kth.se / konrad@nada.kth.se

**Abstract.** This paper presents different solutions for the integration of Video Mediated Communication (VMC) into the home environment considering primarily architectural and technical aspects. The context is entitled comHOME, a concept dwelling of the future designed and built as a full-scale model in collaboration with a telecom operator. The principal problem investigated is the various aspects of private and public zones when using VMC in a home environment. The solution concerns the integration of different comZONES (communicative zones for VMC), where the resident can be seen and heard at different levels varying in time and space. The comZONES presented include, for example, a "videoTORSO" - a large vertically mounted flat screen for informal everyday communication and a "mediaSPACE" - a set-up consisting of a wall of screens permitting shared activities in both time and space. The comZONES are mainly described from an architectural (form and function) as well as technological (hardware and software) perspective.

**Keywords.** architecture, communication, comZONE, design, dwelling, home, ICT, intelligent building, media space, smart home, video mediated communication, VMC

# 1  Background

This paper presents a piece of work based on the idea of a changing society where work and other activities at home become more closely integrated in both time and space (Junestrand & Tollmar, 1998). The core argument is that information and communication technologies (ICT) are a prerequisite for the transformation process from a society focused on industrial production to a society dominated by information processing and based on communication (Dahlbom 1997). Based on a theoretical framework for how our living could change due to new social movements and new use of the domestic environment, we have designed a concept apartment entitled comHOME, demonstrating a set of design solutions for the integration of VMC into a dwelling. In this way the home becomes, in some aspects, a public place accessible through VMC, while still retaining its private nature for several traditional everyday activities. ICT, directly or indirectly, will free us from a large part of the mechanical work we have been used to for a long period of time. Future work activities will consist even more of talking and interacting with other people (Dahlbom 1997). This and other novel ways of working will be possible from almost any location and will be, to an increasingly extent, supported by ICT. Telework from the home, supported by information technologies, is one of the new ways of working predicted to increase in the near future (Bangemann 1994).

It is without doubt an important consideration that the way to live in our homes in the information society is becoming more complex with increasing integration in both time and space between work, shopping and traditional domestic activities. The actual time we spend in our homes is also on the increase. For many of these activities, ICT can support the process despite a separation in space and time. However, since several of the possible ICT supported activities have a public, or semi-public, character, the limits of private and public in the spatial organization of our environment will have to be opened up (Graham & Marvin 1996). The earlier public character of the traditional farmer's house disappeared in modern planning practices. The dual concept of public and private has developed and become something clearly important during the industrial age. The border between the public and the private sharpened up. Compare, for example, the public character of a staircase in an apartment building and the privacy of the apartment hall in a typical residential building of later decades. However now, in the infancy of the information society, it appears that the creation of public spaces in the private dwelling must be considered once again (Junestrand & Tollmar 1998).

## 2  Video-mediated communication in domestic environments

The development of information technologies is very rapid and several trends and tendencies indicate that VMC will become an important part of communication - in our homes as well as our offices (Kraut and Fish 1997). Communication can, in this context, support and complement a wide range of home based activities such as professional work, studies, care of the elderly and leisure activities. Our particular focus is on the integration of architectural and technical designs. Dwellings all over the world are generally not very well suited for VMC due to e.g. unsatisfactory acoustics, light conditions, technical installations, floor-plan layout and spatial design. On the other hand regular VMC solutions used in traditional professional work environments seem to be unsuited to the home without profound redesign. In spite of the great difficulties experienced in establishing a market for video-conferencing in the professional field, we still believe that VMC is a future technology for domestic environments. This is mainly based on the fact that VMC primarily supports social and emotional aspects of communication (Whittaker 1995) and this is the primary requirement for a VMC system in a home environment. It should also be observed that all currently available VMC solutions so far lack significant qualities such as the capacity to transport information concerning gaze awareness, smell, taste and touch among many physical cues that we use. This is an extremely interesting area, but one for which it is no place in this paper or our research at the moment.

# 3 Theories and related work

The complex design of the VMC solutions presented in this paper have been created by a multi-disciplinary group and span over a number of academic fields, each field with a number of theories and interesting works as possible references. Here, we will limit ourselves to presenting the theories and related work that we have found to be most important, inspiring and encouraging.

## 3.1 Design theory

The theoretical framework of the project presented in this paper is based on the ideas of the sciences of the artificial, introduced by Herbert Simon (1969) and further developed by Bo Dahlbom (1997). Dahlbom writes: "When we realize that the world we live in is an artificial world, a world of human creation, made up of artefacts of all kinds, becoming even more complex and intertwined, our attention will shift from studying nature to contributing to the design of artefacts." In this future science we become, as designers, a part of the design. Our intention is to investigate what is possible in the design and thereafter structure, analyze and share that information.

## 3.2 Architectural design

Considering architectural design issues in home environments, the work has a methodological relationship to the explorative and creative development of the functional period of international architecture. This primarily refers to the development of new conceptual and practical ideas for the dwelling that took place at the beginning of this century. A period when the house was referred to as "a machine for living in" (Le Corbusier 1923) instead of being a more traditional central place in peoples' lives. There is also direct reference to the more formal aspects of architectural design as far as cognitive and psychological aspects are concerned (i.e. Hall 1966 and Weber 1995).

Architectural projects and research related to the use of IT in the home environment, intelligent buildings or smart homes appear to be more focused on the technology than on the architectural design. One exception is the work done by Olindo Caso (Caso & Tacken 1993) that concerns the analysis and classification of different IT supported activities which can be carried out in the home environment. These strictly theoretical studies aim at presenting a conceptual organization and allocation of IT supported activities in time and space within the home.

### 3.3 Computer Supported Cooperative Work (CSCW)

Within the area of CSCW research, the importance of a medium that could support informal communication has been debated for a long period of time. The presence/absence of a social context deeply influences how conversations proceed and their results. Kraut (1990) suggests that informal communication is an essential form of human communication. Studies of video-communication have suggested that the main contribution of the video-media is the rich social context (Tang and Isaak 1993). Consequently we believe, as is highly likely, that informal network building will become even more important when part of working time is moved to the home, i.e. that VMC will become one of the major communication media when most of us also work at home.

Naturally, as VMC moves from the office environment to the domestic environment, we could learn many important lessons from CSCW research. In the context of video communication for remote collaboration the major focus has been on whether the video media actually improve conversation or not. Much work in this field has moved along the specifics to find and separate variables that could be used in studies to solve the issue – exactly how valuable is the video media. In some cases researchers have been able to separate variables that move along deterministic paths – but overall has it turned out to be very difficult to generalize these results into a wider context (Whittaker 1995).

In more current research in Mediaspace (Bly 1993) we could see a trend towards non-quantitative studies in an attempt to specify users' perception and awareness of others presences (Dourish 1995). Furthermore, mediaspaces appear to be specially well suited for informal communication (Bly 1993ibid.).

### 3.4 Social aspects of everyday technology

In our new societies, the worlds of work and play, education and entertainment, industry and the arts and the public and private sectors are no longer strictly separated, neither at home nor at work. Transactions and communications continue around the world at the same pace, whether day or night, whether we are awake or asleep. At home too, we perform many activities at the same time. This has become possible partly due to technology. We cook while watching television, monitor children sleeping in the bedroom while entertaining friends in the living room, and work while listening to music (Venkatesh 1997).

Hughes et. al. (1997) has described the role of technology in the home environment from a mainly sociological viewpoint. The authors mean that the effect of using new technology in home environments is increasing. In their studies they found that "The presence of technology within the home is absorbed so completely into the routine practice of homelife that it becomes yet another way in which those routines can be articulated". Although it cannot be said that technology places non-breakable scripts on daily activities. On the contrary the situated nature of home activities is very strong but they are also constrained by negotiated as well as unspoken rules. So even if re-configurations of rooms often occur, this is carried out within some given boundaries. Hughes et. al. also found that in the cases where technology was a major part in the re-arrangements, this caused great stress and the technology was perceived as being badly designed and less user friendly.

## 4 Research questions related to VMC use in homes

The research project carried out here aims at exploring, making proposals and defining further relevant research questions about how VMC solutions should be designed and integrated into the home environment. In the longer run of course, also some general conclusions or results might be drawn from the work. From this standpoint the general research problem could be described as follows:

- How should architecture and technology be designed to support VMC in future domestic environments?

Some central sub-issues are then possible to define from this perspective:

- What processes of future everyday activities in home environments could realistically be supported by VMC?
- How should the speciffic VMC set-ups be designed for the activities it is supposed to support?
- How can the demands of private and public spaces be fulfilled in this context using architectural and technological design?
- What interfaces should be used to facilitate interaction with the system?
- How should the VMC be integrated in other advanced domestic technolgies?

In this paper we are describing what has been done and visions of what is going to be done in the near future in the design of the comZONES in the comHOME apartment. We are trying to provide a general overview of the project and the description below does not aim to provide specific answers to each one of these questions, rather to construct a framework in which to place the themes discussed. The design goals are exemplified as short scenarios when we describe the different VMC set-ups. The key part of the remaining text below discusses how to deal with public and private spaces.

## 5 comHOME - A vision of an apartment of the future

The comHOME apartment is a dwelling of the future, used both as a laboratory and a as a showroom. The comHOME project covers several aspects of future dwellings. Our primary goal in the comHOME project has been to develop and integrate VMC solutions into a home, although we are also working with making the home smart. The authors bear the primary responsibility for the design of the dwelling while the project has been carried out in cooperation between our research lab, a telecom operator and a company providing and developing Lon-Works home-automation technology. We would initially like to point out that the comHOME apartment is not a complete dwelling. It lacks a bathroom and the general floor-plan layout is not suitable for a real apartment. It is best described as a full-scale model constructed from a number of scenario-like room set-ups standing each by itself. As an example the activity "Telework" from the home environment cannot be limited only to a specific area as in the design below, but rather, the whole dwelling should be seen as a potential place for work (Junestrand & Leal 1998). Neither is it intended that anybody should live in this apartment for any extended period of time.

## 5.1 Architectural design concept

The spatial design of the dwelling is based on the idea of creating different comZONES to support the demands of both private and public digital spaces within the home environment. In an inner zone, a person can be both seen and heard through VMC equipment. In the middle zone the individual can be seen but not heard. In the outer zone the resident can neither been seen or heard. In this way the inner zone is a public zone, the middle zone is a semi-public zone and the outer zone is a private zone. (Junestrand & Tollmar 1998). The zones may vary in time and space. These zones indicate places that Mitchell describes as "places where you can hear and be heard, or see (on a display) without completely relinquishing the privacy and controllability of the home" (Mitchell 1995).

The principal architectural issue was the establishment of the mental and physical boundaries between the public and the private in the VMC supported communication zones, i.e. to uphold the absolute demand of being secure from being seen or heard when so desired. It can be assumed that locating activities in a way that a good balance is attained with other everyday activities, as well as for the arrangements for general technical installations, will also be important. The design also takes into consideration both the inside-out and the outside-in perspectives. Meaning that it is of interest how the outer world is perceived through VMC from within the home as well as how the dwelling is perceived from places outside the dwelling supported by VMC.

The different comZONES are expressed by technical solutions such as screens and cameras but also by the use of architecture - spatial forms, colors, light, materials. The architectural space can then, in combination with ICT solutions, form an interface to the digital world. Figure 1 shows a drawing of the conceptual floor plan to be compared to the more traditional floor plan sketch in Figure 2. Both these plans have been used to communicate the basic conceptual idea during the design process.

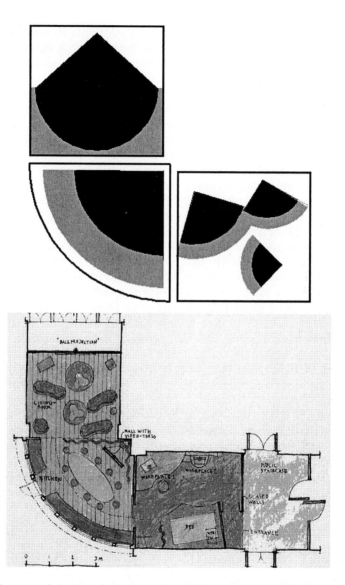

**Figure 1.** Conceptual design of the floor-plan indicating the comZONES. In the inner black zone the individual can be both seen and heard by the VMC equipment. In outer gray zone the resident might only be seen but not heard. In the sorrounding white zone the person can neither be seen or heard. These zones can vary in time and space.

**Figure 2.** Floor plan sketch of the dwelling. The entrance is at the lower right. The middle room at the bottom is a combined telework and sleeping room. To the lower left is a kitchen, and to the upper left is a living room.

## 5.2 Technical design concepts

The technical challenge in deploying VMC in comHOME uncovers multiple layers of complexity. The major difference to be considered is that a home is a radically different place to the more controlled office environment, e.g. poor lighting and audio conditions should be considered as normative rather than rare exceptions.

The technical design of the video and audio space in comHOME is based on several short-range cameras and microphones being mapped and routed through a common media switch. This media switch could be seen as the heart of all incoming and outgoing media streams. The control of the media switch is carried out either via a remote control or a GUI on a terminal. or automatically by the central logic of the smart home. Furthermore, automatic pre-settings could be activated by the central logic of the smart home based on sensor data directed to the media-switch. The video and audio space is hence also closely linked to the design and automation of comHOME as a smart-home. In other words an incoming video call might cause a dimming of the lights or activate the mute command on the radio.

The creation of the different comZONES into the rooms of comHOME is a major technical undertaking. Early works have proposed the use of physical metaphors for control of the video and audio space in VMC systems. One approach, suggested by Kawai (1996), used a GUI with a floor plan to control the field of view of the cameras. Most of these methods suggest using an explicit and direct control of the cameras. In our case, the variation of the zones in space will mainly be controlled by a spatial recognition system that links the physical position with the identity of the person/people in the rooms.

By control of focus depth and field of view combined with the placement of cameras in the rooms we could, using a simple model, fairly well adjust the video space in the different zones. The control of the audio space is actually more complex. Our primary solution is to mix wide range microphones, such as PZM microphones, with directed microphones. Unfortunately the fairly precise video-space is not matched by equally well-defined boundaries in the audio space. We are aware that array microphones and spatial directed loudspeakers might solve part of this puzzle, but these technologies have not yet become available to us. Similarly prototypes of realtime image manipulation that could, e.g. extract actions or allow people in the background be removed from the videostream do not yet exist.

# 6 The comZONES in comHOME

The *comHOME* dwelling has three rooms: a living room, a kitchen and a combined telework and sleeping room. In our attempt to explore the usability of the comZONES concepts we have designed a set of six places and scenarios for which we are attempting to describe different design solutions.

A **videoTORSO** for informal everyday communication while standing and talking is placed in the kitchen. This VMC system explores the possibility of supporting informal full screen communication standing up, on a vertically mounted flat screen. The area around the kitchen shelves is normally a semi-public zone where the individual can be seen but not heard. However this could easily be changed into a public or a private zone. The public zone is normally located a little closer to the videoTORSO so that the resident must take a step forward to be heard. The screen can also be places in a horizontal position by twisting it. Ongoing activities aim at integrating the camera and the microphone into the videoTORSO at each side of the screen. In this way they are exposed and in function when the screen is in a vertical position for communication, and hidden and not functioning when the screen is in a horizontal position. The twisting of the screen is motor driven and controlled by the central logic. In this way the user can indicate with e.g. a gesture or a voice command, that he/she wishes to communicate and the screen automatically assumes the correct position. The speakers are placed above the screen and are always visible since the screen in the horizontal position can be used as a television, a web browser or ambient media. In this setting the core problem is to zoom into the audio space to a suitable range. This could perhaps be achieved by directed microphones which normally peak at a distance of 2 m and fade off rapidly at distances greater than 2.5 m.

A **comTABLE** located in the kitchen contains a computer and screen. The current uses for this table are two-fold. Firstly it enables a virtual dining guest to be a part of dinner through a video conference session that is displayed on the screen. Secondly it also make it possible to read for example a digital morning paper that appears in the table. This has two results.

Firstly, by placing a large display in the one of the table's unfolding parts it will become easy to adjust the screen for multiple use. In up-folded position the screen could be used for a remote invited dinner guest. In down-folded position could the screen be used for reading the morning paper or doing on-line ordering of groceries.

Secondly, by integrate the camera and microphone into the unfolding part control of the visual view becomes very physical (one interpretation of the ComZoon). By placing the camera into the frame we are hoping to find a natural syntax of adjusting the ComZoon – up-fold the display and the camera will view across the table, down-fold the display and the camera will stare into the roof.

The screen is located in a mobile frame on the rear end of the table. This VMC set-up can be used to read your interactive digital morning newspaper when seated at the rear end. Or the screen could also be placed vertically as a video representation of a guest on the screen during Sunday dinner. The integrated camera is located in the mobile frame so the control of the public space can be manipulated by lifting the frame up and down. This very physical interaction with the comTABLE provides an alternative to software and sensor based solutions.

A **deskTOP** and a **lapTOP** workplace, both for professional work in the home environment, are located in the combined home office and sleeping room. These two workplaces are held together with two boards completing the spatial definition. The public zone, where the resident can be seen and heard for example while participating in a video-conference, is indicated with a false ceiling equipped with integrated illumination. In these two settings, two cameras are used at each place. One is a dedicated handheld document camera for showing physical objects and the other a fixed camera that is adjusted so as to provide the talking head of the person.

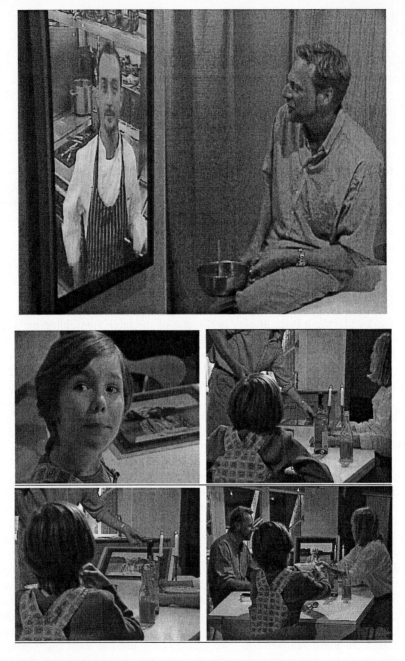

*Figure 3.* A videoTORSO for informal everyday communication.
*Figure 4.* ComTABLE for VMC in a dinner situation.

*Figure 5.* The deskTOP workplace with the wooden panel and lowered ceiling that indicates the *private zone.*

An **internetTV** with video communication facilities as well as connection to Internet services is located in the ceiling at the bed place. The border of the public is indicated and expressed by the shape of the wooden structure around the bed and a curtain behind it. Also in this setting, fixed cameras are used to simply define the fixed boundary.

A **mediaSPACE** located in the living room is the extension of the physical room creating a larger social space with the digital representation of another space. This is done on two parallel mounted 80" screens seamlessly integrated into one wall of the small living room. This comZONE is extended, and merged, with another room at distance. This space is primarily a public zone when in use and is limited by a curtain on its back wall. Realizing that this room is a mostly public space – when the VMC is in use - turns the problems upside down. In this case it instead becomes a challenge to both keep a broad overview and provide close-ups within the scene. Here we use a technique from the VideoCafe system (Tollmar et al. 1998) and provide a dual video stream that could be used for both overviews and close-ups.

## 7 Conclusions from VMC in comHOME

The construction of the comHOME dwelling was finished during late 1998 and has since been taken into use as a laboratory. At this stage, rather than presenting results from specific evaluations, the points below can be considered as a number of ideas tested within the limitations of this full-scale experiment with no contradictions so far identified. Some early tentative conclusions from the design phase are:

- It is possible to introduce architectural expressions into the dwellings in order to support the resident in his/her understanding of, as well as experiencing the limits of, comZONES in the dwelling as far as the public (where you can be seen and heard) and the private (where you can not be seen nor heard) VMC issues are concerned

- It seems to give an added value to dwellings if information technology and architecture together can support the integration of VMC

- The changing use of the dwelling and the introduction of new ICT technologies seem to demand both new concepts for the general floor-plan layout as well as the specific spatial design

- Solutions for both sound and images are very complex and tend to be crucial for a successful integration of VMC set-ups in homes.
- Using none wearable microphones only, it appears to be difficult to create zones for audio which are as sharp and easily controlled as those of the video.

- In order to achieve a successful result, the development of new VMC set-ups for home environments should be closely linked to the general design of a smart home, both from a user and producer perspective.

- During the complex design process we have experienced, naturally several trade-offs have had to be made in both the general concept and the details of every specific VMC set-up. It has been very difficult to evaluate the effects many of these selections will have on the final real-life situation.

## 8 Future work

We still have a lot of work to do both regarding the hardware and software designs in order to make the VMC settings working properly. New directions in our research also include the use of sign/gesture language tracked by video to interact with the technologies in the room. Further integration with the general smart environment is also underway.

Although lacking technical functionality we are at the moment performing user studies evaluating the architectural and technical design of some specific settings. A video, using professional actors and film-team, has been recorded and is now being edited. This video demonstrates putting the different VMC set-ups into a social context of everyday life.

## Acknowledgments

This work has been performed with the kind collaboration of S-lab at Telia Networks in Farsta to whom we are deeply grateful, especially to Roland Bohman and Lasse Lindblad. We would like to thank our professors Ulf Keijer and Yngve Sundblad at the Swedish Royal Institute of Technology for their guidance. We would also like to thank Ingvar Sjöberg, Director of our Smart Things and Environments for Art and Daily Life Group at the Interactive Institute, as well as our other colleagues for their collaboration and invaluable support during this work.

# References

1. Bangemann, M., (1994), Europe and the Global Information Society: Recommendations to the European Council, Cordis Focus Supplement 2, Luxembourg.
2. Bly S., Harrison S. and Irwin S., (1993), "Media Spaces: Bringing People Together in a Video, Audio and omputing Environment", Communications of the ACM, 36(1).
3. Caso, O. & Tacken, M., (1993), TELEMATICS IN RESIDENTIAL AREAS - Spatial Effects for Dwelling and Neighbourhood, Publikatieburo Bouwkunde, Delft University, Netherlands.
4. Dahlbom. B., (1997), Going to the future, in J. Berleur & D. Whitehouse (eds) An Ethical Global Information Society: Culture and Democracy Revisited. London: Chapman & Hall 1997, and www.informatik.gu.se/~dahlbom
5. Dourish P., Adler A., Bellotti V. and Henderson A., 1996, "Your Place or Mine? Learning from Long-Term Use of Audio-VideoCommunications", Computer Supported Cooperative Work, 5(1).
6. Finn, K., Sellen, A. & Wilbur, S., (1997), Video-Mediated Communication, Lawrence Erlbaum Associates, publishers, New Jersey.
7. Hall, E., T., (1966), The Hidden Dimension, Man's use of Space in Public and Private, The Bodley Head Ltd, London.
8. Hughes, J., O´Brien, J. & Rodden, T., (1998), Understanding Technology in Domestic Environments: Lessons for Cooperative Buildings, in Streiz, N., Konomi, S., Burkhardt, H.-J. (Eds.), *Cooperative Buildings - Integrating Information, Organization and Architecture, Proceedings of CoBuild'98.* LNCS 1370. Springer, Heidelberg, pp. 248-262.
9. Junestrand, S. & Leal, I., (1998), The Home Office - a new architectural perspective, Man Machine Environment & Nordic Ergonomics, 4/98, Karlskrona, Sweden.
10. Junestrand, S. & Tollmar, K., (1998), The Dwelling as a Place for Work, in Streiz, N., Konomi, S., Burkhardt, H.-J. (Eds.), *Cooperative Buildings - Integrating Information, Organization and Architecture, Proceedings of CoBuild'98.* LNCS 1370. Springer, Heidelberg, pp. 230-247.

11. Kawai, Bannai, Tamura, (1996), Argus: An Active Awareness Systsem Using Computer-Controlled Multiple Cameras, in CSCW´96 tech. video program.
12. Kraut and Fish, Prospects for Videotelephony,
13. Kraut, R. E., Egido, C. & Galegher J., (1990), Patterns of Contact and Communication in Scientific Research Collaborations. In Intellectual Teamwork, Galegher, J. and Kraut, R. E. (Ed.), Lawrence Erlbaum Ass.
14. Le Corbusier, (1986), (orig. 1923), Towards a new architecture, Dover Publications Inc. New York.
15. Mitchell, W. J., (1995), City of Bits, The MIT Press, Cambridge, Massachusetts, London, England.
16. Tollmar, K., Chincholle, D., Klasson, B. and Stephanson, T., (1998), VideoCafé – Virtual Espresso-Cafés and Semi-Located Communities, Technical report TRITA-NA-D9905, CID, May 1998. http://www.nada.kth.se/cid/pdf/cid_47.pdf
17. Tang, J. and Isaak, E., (1993), Why DoUsers Like Video?, In Computer Supoorted Cooperative Work, Vol1 No3, Kleuwer Academic Publisher.
18. Weber, R., (1995), On the Aesthetics of Architecture, A Psychological Approach to the Structure and the Order of Perceived Architectural Space, Avebury, Hants, England.
19. Venkatesh, A., (1996), Computers and other Interactive Technologies for the Home, Communications of the ACM, 39, No 12.
20. Whittaker, S., (1995), Rethinking video as a technology for interpersonal communications: theory and design implications, Int. Journal of Man-Machine Studies, 42.
21. *Visions of the Future*, (1996), Philips Corporate Design, V + K Publishing, Bussum, Holland & www-eur.philips.com/design/vof/toc1/home.htm

# The Aware Home: A Living Laboratory for Ubiquitous Computing Research

Cory D. Kidd, Robert Orr, Gregory D. Abowd,
Christopher G. Atkeson, Irfan A. Essa, Blair MacIntyre,
Elizabeth Mynatt, Thad E. Starner and Wendy Newstetter

College of Computing and GVU Center
Georgia Institute of Technology
Atlanta, GA 30332-0280, USA
{coryk,rjo,abowd,cga,irfan,blair,mynatt,thad,wendy}@cc.gatech.edu

**Abstract.** We are building a home, called the Aware Home, to create a living laboratory for research in ubiquitous computing for everyday activities. This paper introduces the Aware Home project and outlines some of our technology- and human-centered research objectives in creating the Aware Home.

**Keywords.** Home, ubiquitous computing, context-awareness, sensors, applications, evaluation

## 1 Introduction

As the trend to broaden computing away from the desktop continues, new research challenges arise. One unifying research theme is to focus on computing needs in our everyday lives, specifically, that part of our lives that is not centered around work or the office. For this reason, we have initiated an effort to investigate research issues centered around computing in the home. Because we feel that any significant research in this area must be conducted in an authentic yet experimental setting, we are building a home that will serve as a living laboratory for ubiquitous computing in support of home life. The experimental home will be called the Aware Home, signifying our intent to produce an environment that is capable of knowing information about itself and the whereabouts and activities of its inhabitants.

### 1.1 The Prototype Home

The Aware Home prototype is currently under construction. This home will have two identical and independent living spaces, consisting of two bedrooms, two bathrooms, one office, kitchen, dining room, living room and laundry room. In addition, there will be a shared basement with a home entertainment area and control room for centralized computing services. We expect construction of the house to be complete by the end of the 1999 calendar year.

The reasons for building two independent living spaces are to allow for controlled experiments with technology and to allow inhabitants to live on one floor while prototyping or providing demonstrations on the other floor. We anticipate that the initial occupants will be students involved in the research project living in only one floor of the house. A longer-term goal is to have both floors occupied by a family or elderly occupants, as these are the targeted groups of our research. These occupants will give more realistic feedback on the performance of systems within the house.

We anticipate that the house will not be ready for us to occupy for nearly nine months from the date of this writing. We are moving ahead with the research project in this interim period. In order to test some of the systems that we plan to use in the house, we have constructed a prototype room in our lab. The room was constructed using standard house construction techniques to resemble the actual house as closely as possible. We expect to implement some systems immediately to test their effectiveness in the house. These systems include human position tracking through ultrasonic sensors, RF technology and video, recognition through floor sensors and vision techniques.

**Fig. 1, 2.** First and second floor plan, front elevation of house

## 1.2 Our Background

Rather than provide an exhaustive survey on home automation, intelligent environments and other related work,[1] we provide a brief summary of our research backgrounds and relevant work we have conducted at Georgia Tech on living laboratories for ubiquitous computing research and computing in the home.

The research interests assembled to work on this project cover a wide spectrum. These interests include HCI, ubiquitous computing, ethnography, machine learning, computational perception, augmented reality, wearable computing, wireless networking, security, distributed systems, software engineering and sensor

---

[1] Interested readers can explore a Web-based collection of this related work at http://www.cc.gatech.edu/fce/seminar/fa98-info/smart_homes.html.

technology. In this paper, we will outline some of the specific research goals for the Aware Home project that cover this wider spectrum of research interests.

One of the reasons we are committed to this experimental model of ubiquitous computing research, in which a living laboratory is created for experimentation within some specific domain, is that it has proven a very successful model for us in a different domain. Since July 1995, we have conducted research on ubiquitous computing in support of education through the Classroom 2000 project, as described by Abowd (1999).[2] One of the main goals of that project has been to instrument an actual classroom environment to enable the recording of live lectures. This captured experience is then made accessible to students and teachers afterwards. Extensive experience using this system has greatly informed our understanding of the general ubiquitous computing problem of automated support for capture and access to live experiences. This deep understanding would not have been possible had we not gained authentic experience with many different users over an extended period of time.

We have been interested in ubiquitous computing as it applies to the home for a number of years. Our earlier efforts were covered in the Domisilica project, an attempt to build a bridge between the physical home environment and the electronic world of a virtual community or MUD environment (Mankoff et al., 1998).

In the rest of this paper, we will present our research agenda in two parts. The first part will deal with research topics focussed on technology in the Aware Home. In this part we introduce the types of technologies that we plan to use in our research. The second part will deal with more human-centered research issues. It is here that we discuss the possible applications that this environment could have in the future. In our final section, we discuss the social implications that we foresee in this research and address possible difficulties that will have to be overcome in this research.

## 2 Technology-Centered Research Agenda

Our research in the Aware Home covers many different areas. In this section, we provide a summary of some technological themes being investigated. We will not directly address some of the networking and distributed computing themes here. This research is being conducted by other Georgia Tech researchers to provide high bandwidth wireless and wired networking throughout the home and to provide appropriate security mechanisms for the middleware within the complex high performance computing environment we are building. Instead, in the next section we discuss application and evaluation research themes.

### 2.1 Context Awareness and Ubiquitous Sensing

Humans, in general, are quite successful at communicating complex ideas to each other, due in part to an implicit shared understanding known as context. When humans interact with computers, there is very little shared understanding or context.

---

[2] Information on Classroom 2000 can be found at http://www.cc.gatech.edu/fce/c2000.

However, it is becoming increasingly possible to build sensors that can help a computational environment to interpret and begin to understand the contextual cues of its occupants. In augmented environments, such as the Aware Home, we need to provide the capability for computational services to take advantage of these soon-to-be ubiquitous sensing capabilities. For example, we have built vision-based sensors to track multiple individuals in an environment (Stillman et al., 1999) and we are trying to use similar signal processing techniques to build a smart floor interface that can identify and track people walking across a large area. There are many compelling applications for these sensing technologies throughout a home, such as support for the elderly or finding lost objects, or in specialized spaces within the home, such as the front door or the kitchen.

However, progress in the sensing technologies needs to be matched by progress in supporting the rapid development of applications that use sensed information. These applications are what we call context-aware applications, and we are building a software infrastructure to assist in their rapid development (Salber et al., 1999). To date, the context-aware development infrastructure has been applied to controlled situations in an office environment and we see the Aware Home as a very valuable resource for exercising much of the capabilities we want to provide in a robust and programmable software infrastructure.

## 2.2 Individual Interaction with the Home

One interesting direction of this work occurs when we consider sensing on the body, as is done in wearable computing, in conjunction with sensing off the body, as is typical in an instrumented environment. In this environment, human-home symbioses becomes important as a means to provide as seamless interaction as possible with the home. Wearable computers and intelligent environments allow the delivery of convenient, personalized information and entertainment services at almost any time and in any context. However, there is very little work on how wearable computing and any computing infrastructure attached to the home environment should interact together on behalf of a user. By learning about users' habits and behavior, embedded systems in the home may perform complex, seemingly intelligent tasks automatically. Part of the technological and social challenge is determining where to put various interaction and sensor technologies for maximum benefit.

The Aware Home infrastructure is an excellent chance to obtain general information about a user while at home, and a wearable computer can gather data wherever the user may go. The home can contain a large amount of computation and infrastructure for sensing at a distance, while a wearable has the advantage of immediate and intimate contact with the user. The data gathered on the wearable might then be filtered and released to the environmental infrastructure as appropriate. On the other hand, the wearable may draw on the house's data resources to cache important information for the mobile user when away from the house. Thus, an automated wireless collaboration between the platforms seems appropriate, with the user placing limits on the type and level of information transferred between his personal and environmental infrastructure. We will develop such infrastructure interactions and explore some of the technical and social benefits.

## 2.3   The Smart Floor

In ubiquitous computing, knowing *who* is *where* and *what* they are doing is central to enabling intelligent behavior. In the Smart Floor project, we are addressing the *who* and *where* aspects of this problem: we have created a system to identify and locate a person based solely on his or her footsteps[3]. In this system, we will place ten strategically sized and located force-sensitive load tiles throughout the Aware Home to gather footstep data from occupants. The tiles are flush with the floor and consist of a metal plate supported by four industrial load cells; the data we gather from these tiles are known as *ground reaction force* (GRF) profiles. We have gathered sets of training data to create footstep models for each person; we then compare each new GRF profile against these models and search for the best match. We have used two techniques to create models for each user: Hidden Markov Models (HMMs), and simple feature-vector averaging. Work similar to our HMM approach was described recently by Addlesee, et al. (1997). For a reasonably sized user population (on the order of 10 people), the GRF profiles are unique enough to correctly identify the user over 90% of the time. We are currently characterizing the system more fully, including examining the effect different shoes have on GRF profiles, and comparing the Smart Floor to identification technologies such as face recognition. We are also investigating the relevance and robustness of the particular features chosen for our feature-vector models, and are studying other methods for creating and evaluating the user models, such as neural networks.

As mentioned above, we will strategically size and locate our Smart Floor tiles throughout the Aware Home. In addition to the tiles, we are exploring other technologies to track users more finely throughout the house; we are evaluating systems based on grids of piezoelectric wires, grids of deformation sensitive optical fibers, and networks of vibration sensors attached to the underside of the flooring. In this tracking system, we will establish identity and a location landmark using the Smart Floor tiles and track the movement of users with the finer grained system.

## 2.4   Finding Lost Objects

One of the applications of the tracking and sensing technologies in the Aware Home will be a system for finding Frequently Lost Objects (FLOs), such as keys, wallets, glasses, and remote controls. The system will use small radio-frequency tags attached to each object the user would like to track and a long-range indoor positioning system to track these objects (Werb and Lanzl, 1998). The user will interact with the system via LCD touch panels placed strategically throughout the house (for example, by the front door). The system will guide the user to the lost object using spatialized audio cues (e.g., "Your keys are in the bedroom."). While we hope that the FLO system will be able to keep track of objects 100% of the time, we know that these expectations are not realistic; another person may walk off with the keys, or the batteries in the tag may fail. In these exceptions, the other tracking technologies in

---

[3]  More information on the Smart Floor project can be obtained at http://www.cc.gatech.edu/fce/smartfloor/index.html.

the house, such as the Smart Floor, can assist in locating the objects. For example, if the keys were last seen with Jane at the front door at 8:30am, the system can inform the user of these facts and the user can conclude that Jane accidentally took the keys with her to work.

# 3 Human-Centered Research Agenda

An important question to address in the Aware Home is what purpose does the technology serve from the occupants' perspective. We have suggested that we intend to support everyday activities, but that is too vague. Our initial studies on home life have revealed several research topics. The first presented here is support for the elderly and the second is the need for qualitative studies of home living. We conclude this section with an example application used for finding lost objects in the home.

## 3.1 Specific Application: Support for the Elderly

There can be no denying that the U.S. population is aging. As the baby boom approaches late middle age it seems clear that this maturing mass of humanity will impact this country both financially and emotionally. One question concerns how to care for a population that lives many years longer than any preceding generation. A part of this question involves where one lives as one ages. Assisting a person to remain in familiar surroundings as they age not only improves the quality of their life but also increases the length of that life. But the increased mobility stemming from the industrial revolution has forever changed American society. People no longer live in the same community all their lives. Aging parents no longer live close to their adult children. The current practice of institutionalizing elderly people into assistive living centers is expensive and often an unsatisfactory experience for all involved.

As people get older and find it more difficult to live on their own, they are often forced to move out of their homes, though they do not require any type of constant physical assistance. This is done not only to provide peace of mind to their family members, but also to themselves. Moving out to some form of assisted living provides the security of frequent monitoring and the availability of medical assistance in the event of an emergency. If these people were able to keep that "peace of mind" while still living in their own homes, they would not be forced away from the familiarity and friends to which they are accustomed. The goal of this project is to design a system that provides a type of monitoring currently supported by an assisted living center for those individuals that do not demand frequent medical help or services that could only be provided by another person.

In our preliminary investigations we have identified three areas for interface design and sensing technology research.[4] First, we want to support social connections between elder parents and their adult children promoting peace of mind for family members. These persistent connections will convey activity in the respective homes

---

[4] Further information on the Support for Aging in Place project can be found at http://jrowan.cc.gt.atl.ga.us:8080/JimzMondoSwiki.62.

as well as trends over time. Second, we hope to support "everyday cognition" by augmenting those aspects of memory that decline with age and planning capabilities of elder residents. Third, we also plan to sense and identify potential crisis situations so that appropriate outside services can be contacted as needed.

## 3.2 Evaluation and Social Issues

As we explained earlier, the reason we are building the Aware Home with two independent living areas is to allow at least one region of the home to be occupied at all times. Our experience in Classroom 2000 has shown the value of everyday use of a ubiquitous computing environment, both for informing the iterative design cycle and for understanding how technology and people co-evolve.

An important issue that must be addressed in the context of this project is the consideration of privacy. The home is constantly monitoring the occupants' whereabouts and activities, using audio and video observation methods, and even tracking its inhabitants' medical conditions. There is a clear need to give the occupants knowledge and control of the distribution of this information. This is a concern that we expect to become more prominent as we develop the systems that will be collecting various types of sensitive information. One method that we may use for insuring the privacy of an individual's information is to store personal information on a wearable computer and allowing access to be controlled from there. Other programmatic security mechanisms are the direct concern of distributed computing researchers involved in the project.

## 4 Future Challenges

### 4.1 Qualitative Understanding of Everday Home Life

Designing the next generation of applications for homes is different from designing for offices. In offices, time and how it can be used is determined by the rhythms and culture of the organization. Movement is restricted and often monitored. Tasks and activities are circumscribed and determined by the organization. Work is generally couched in terms of productivity, efficiency and profit, emblems of Tayloristic notions of work. But what are the frameworks that guide activities at home? Can we apply such notions as productivity and efficiency or are there home-based concepts that guide the way people use space and existing artifacts? There we are free to use time as we wish, to undertake the kinds of activities that we like, to come and go as we please, and use resources as we see fit. At home we are free to choose how space and time are structured, what activities are undertaken and who is involved. For these reasons, homes are what we call "free choice" environments. Because designing for such environments is challenging, it is critical that we develop methodologies that ensure that the latest technological advances are being funneled into useful applications. This thread of research will apply more qualitative techniques for uncovering applications for technology in the home.

Using qualitative techniques, one specific activity we will attempt to understand deeply is how people lose and find objects around the home. This study will be used to support our Frequently Lost Objects project mentioned above. We will use ethnographic techniques to study what people lose frequently, why these things become lost, how people go about finding these objects, and how other people in the household may assist in finding what has been lost. While we have already outlined a technical solution to the problem of finding lost objects in the Aware Home, we are not irrevocably committed to this solution and we hope that our qualitative study of this problem can help to direct modifications or our existing system or help inform the design of another solution altogether. We also hope to use the relationships with the families who take part in this narrow study as a jumping-off point for additional broader studies of home life.

## Acknowledgements

We would like to acknowledge the support of the Georgia Tech Broadband Telecommunications Center, and specifically its director, Dr. John Limb, for the initiation of the Aware Home project. The Aware Home is being initially funded through the State of Georgia Research Alliance. Further information on the project can be found at http://www.cc.gatech.edu/fce/house.

# References

1. Abowd, G. D. (1999). Classroom 2000: An Experiment with the Instrumentation of a Living Educational Environment. *IBM Systems Journal.* Special issue on pervasive computing. To appear.
2. Addlesee, M.D., A. Jones, F. Livesey, and F. Samaria. "ORL Active Floor." *IEEE Personal Communications*, Vol.4, No.5, October 1997, pp.35-41. IEEE, Piscataway, NJ, USA.
3. Mankoff, J., J. Somers and G. D. Abowd (1998). Bringing People and Places Together with Dual Augmentation. In the proceedings of *Collaborative Virtual Environments – CVE'98*, Manchester, England, June, pp. 81-86. Also available as a PDF document at http://www.cc.gatech.edu/fce/publications/CVE.pdf.
4. Salber, D., A. Dey and G. D. Abowd (1999). The Context Toolkit: Aiding the Development of Context-Enabled Applications. In proceedings of *CHI'99*, pp. 434-441. Pittsburgh, PA, May 15-20.
5. Stillman, S. R. Tanawongsuwan, and I. Essa (1999). A System for Tracking and Recognizing Multiple People with Multiple Cameras In proceedings of *The Second International Conference on Audio- and Video-Based Biometric Person Authentication – AVBPA'99*, Washington D.C., March 22-23.
6. Werb, J., and Lanzl, C. Designing a positioning system for finding things and people indoors. *IEEE Spectrum 35*, 9 (September 1998), 71-78.

# The Importance of Homes in Technology Research

Debby Hindus

Interval Research Corporation
1801 Page Mill Road, Palo Alto CA 94304
hindus@interval.com

**Abstract.** This paper argues for the importance of home-related research on technology. Several important differences between researching homes and researching workplaces are described, and several issues in conducting home-related research are discussed in the context of specific research efforts. Ways to advance home-related research as a discipline are presented, including an existing course on technology design with a home focus.

**Keywords.** Domestic technologies, residential technologies, personal computing, home computing, consumers, homes, computer-human interaction, CSCW, media spaces, design.

## 1 Introduction

Computing is being dramatically affected by the adoption of technology by the mass market of consumers and the infiltration of computer technologies into everyday lives—over 50% of American households now own a computer, for example, and the Internet is accessed at least weekly by 40% of U.S. residents.

Yet, technology in homes has to date received little attention within the research community. A quick check of the ACM Digital Library shows that there is at least an order of magnitude more papers about offices and workplaces than about homes and consumers (and the latter totals only a few dozen publications in the last decade).

As the discussant for the CoBuild'99 session on "Networked Home Environments," I shall argue for the importance of homes in technology research. The two other papers in this session (Junestrand and Tollmar 1999, Kidd et al. 1999, this volume) are the springboard and inspiration for the specific topics discussed here.

The remainder of this paper starts by addressing why homes are an important topic in technology research and the relationship between CSCW and home-related studies. Next, I focus on a few key issues with home-related research that are raised by the papers in this session, and close by describing activities that will advance home-related research as a legitimate and respected research discipline.

Throughout this paper, I draw upon several years of researching domestic technologies and their interaction with family and domestic life, with examples from the Casablanca project, which explored new forms of home-based communication. I also draw upon my experience teaching a seminar on domestic technologies at Stanford University.

The primary goal of this paper is to inspire this community to question our deeply rooted assumptions about what is known about the role of technology and where that knowledge is applicable. Secondarily, I intend to acquaint readers with the existing body of work on homes. Finally, I add to that body of work by briefly describing my own home-related work.

## 2  Why Study Homes?

Why be concerned about homes at a conference about cooperative buildings? I cannot say whether homes are an appropriate topic for any specific research conference. However, I see homes as an important topic for research from a number of perspectives. The first perspective is that homes are, of course, technology-filled buildings. In the United States, there are 106 million households, and they each already contain technology for entertainment, communication and household infrastructure.  Most U.S. households will have access to high-speed Internet connections within five years, and industry watchers estimate that 20% will have selected this service by then.

Furthermore, homes and technology are too important economically to ignore, and will become more so. For example, according to the Consumer Electronics Manufacturers' Association (CEMA), the average American household spends $800 each year on consumer electronics. More and more of these devices incorporate computing technology, and even traditional items such as televisions and stereo components will soon interconnect digitally, thus creating the opportunity for new forms of home networks and consumer interaction generating billions of dollars in revenue.

Another reason to study technology in homes is that it is a rich research field, and has the potential to improve everyday life for millions of users. Also, work and home are intertwined now, and even if workplace concerns are paramount, it is difficult to ignore the work that gets done in homes (Junestrand and Tollmar 1998). Finally, homes are a challenging design venue, and deserve the attention of talented practitioners and innovators.

## 3  The Relationship of CSCW to Home-Related Research

Even starting from the premise that homes are a worthwhile technological venue, it can be argued that the diffusion path of technology is from workplaces to homes and so CSCW technologies will naturally migrate to the home. In this section, I describe several important aspects of how homes are fundamentally different from workplaces. I hope to provoke discussion of the implicit assumptions of much CSCW research and how they are, or are not, applicable outside of workplaces.

### 3.1 Homes are not workplaces

It is obvious that houses are not workplaces with respect to construction. Workplaces are designed to accommodate technology. Data networking is built into every component of a workplace. In contrast, houses are not designed for technology, at least not on a large scale. Furthermore, there are no standards for technology infrastructure in homes, though CEMA is working on a technology rating system for residences.

Also, commercial buildings benefit from professional planning, installation and maintenance of technology and its supporting infrastructure. For consumers, these activities can represent significant investments of time and money, and are hurdles to adopting new technologies. Another important difference is that adults of working age primarily occupy workplaces, whereas home technologies must safely reside with babies, children, elders and pets.

### 3.2 Consumers are not knowledge workers

A key difference between workplaces and homes is that consumers are not knowledge workers. That is, motivations, concerns, resources and decisions can be very different from those found within workplaces. Buying behavior is perhaps the most compelling difference. Consumers make purchases based on aesthetics, fashion, and self-image in addition to practical considerations of cost and utility. In workplaces, buying decisions are driven by productivity concerns. The ways that consumers think about technology are also specific to the home setting (Mick and Fournier 1998).

### 3.3 Families are not organizations

In the past 50 years, the study of families has been the purview of sociology, and there is a large literature on family dynamics and home life (e.g., Coontz). Family structures are complex and not hierarchical, at least not in the sense that corporate organizations are structured. Decision-making and value-setting are quite different within households.

Until recently, there have been minimal collaborations between computer scientists and sociologists, and technology has received scant attention. John Hughes at Lancaster University in the U.K. has pioneered cross-disciplinary studies (Hughes, O'Brien and Rodden 1998), as has Sara Kiesler at CMU in the United States (Kraut et al. 1996). Some social science methods have been incorporated into industrial research, such as Tony Salvador's highly influential "garage ethnography" efforts within Intel (Mateas et al. 1996). The use of time in households is also salient to technological research (Robinson and Godbey 1997).

# 4 Issues in Home-Related Research

The previous section presents fundamental framing differences between workplaces and homes. In addition, the papers in this session raise a number of methodological issues about creating and studying home technologies. The most obvious issue is where the research is conducted. Interestingly, the approach that we took in the Casablanca project differs from either the Aware Home or comHome projects. Another predominate issue is how to obtain meaningful consumer input and feedback. These issues are discussed in the remainder of this section.

## 4.1 Obtaining consumer input

Workplace technology design and user feedback techniques have received considerable attention over the last decade, and the mechanics of such projects have been refined. Those mechanics have to be modified for projects involving homes, to take into account issues of informed consent, boundaries and safety.

Informed consent is trickier for homes, because of the presence of children and the centrality of children to home life. Children need to be treated with special care in studies. Boundaries and rapport are also more challenging in homes; the social norms of being a guest are at odds with the inquisitiveness required for in-depth home visits.

Once the mechanics of home qualitative studies are understood, the problem arises of predicting how innovative technologies will be viewed by potential consumers. This is especially challenging for unfamiliar applications, as acknowledged by both papers in this session. At Interval Research, the consumer research group has developed techniques for home ethnographic-like interviews and subsequent analyses that have been widely applied to research efforts, both internally and in collaborations such as with HomeNet (Ireland and Johnson 1995).

## 4.2 Designing for homes

After a need has been identified and a solution has been roughed out, prototypes can be created at various levels of fidelity. The issue of fidelity can be very powerful in home settings. We noticed when deploying an early set of Casablanca prototypes that homes do not easily accommodate the numerous pieces of equipment, cables, phone jacks and electrical outlets required for desktop conferencing, as illustrated in Fig. 1.

While trial users may make accommodations temporarily, good industrial design is a vital component of a serious

**Fig. 1. An early Casablanca desktop conferencing prototype in a user's kitchen.**

prototyping effort. A later Casablanca prototype of an awareness device illustrates this point, shown in Fig. 2.

### 4.3 Conducting participant-observer-designer studies

When a prototype is available, the question arises of how to get experience of it in use. Doing the research in one's own home is one approach to situated trials. The participant-observer approach can be quite informative when the participants are part of the design team (Adler and Henderson 1994). The Adaptive Home project at the University of Colorado was conducted in Prof. Michael Mozer's own home (Mozer 1998).

**Fig. 2. A later Casablanca prototype of a home awareness device.**

As we experienced in the Casablanca project, the participant-observer-designer approach has some unique implications. The system under study was derived from mediaspace work (Bly 1993) and featured a custom desktop conferencing application on standard personal computers.

Several issues arose. One issue was introducing housemates and spouses to the formalities of informed consent and intellectual property; the consent form was crafted to be complete yet not intimidating. Another issue is that of dwelling alterations. Making permanent changes for a temporary trial study was discomforting; the home-owning participants were concerned about resale value and home décor, and the renting participants had to negotiate with landlords.

Having a trial system in our homes caused the work-home boundary to become blurred, though not necessarily in a negative way; housemates enjoyed understanding our work better. As participant-observers we wound up learning a fair amount about each other's home lives, things that we would not have learned otherwise. This may not always be perceived as a positive consequence.

### 4.4 Situating the research

A critical issue in home-related research is where to conduct the work, especially for experiential studies. Previous work has taken various forms, including true ethnographic studies, conventional usability tests in simulated home environments, and situated deployments of prototypes into real homes for limited or sustained trials. The two other papers in this session both approach home technologies in a situated way, though they represent somewhat different philosophies.

The Aware Home project (Kidd, et al. 1999) is taking the step of building an actual house, designed from the outset to accommodate technologies, technology trials and studies of technologies in use. Their eventual goal is to have people actually live in part of the house and have sustained experience with technology prototypes. Building a house solely for research purposes is an ambitious undertaking, and will no doubt lead to significant new results. I look forward to seeing updates on the Active Home.

The comHOME project at KTH has quite the opposite intent; their dwelling is, as they state, "... best described as a full-scale model constructed of a number of scenario-like room set-ups," (Junestrand & Tollmar 1999). The IHome project at University of Massachusetts also uses the simulated dwelling approach (Lesser et al. 1999).

## 4.5  Extending the research to real-world residences

Neither of the above approaches replicates the home environment of the vast majority of people who live in existing dwellings; these structures do not readily accommodate the built-in technologies envisioned by designers. In the United States, about one million new homes are built each year, less than one percent of the existing housing stock. Existing residences are considerably more difficult places to add infrastructure technologies, such as the sensing mechanisms planned for the Aware Home.

Another concern is the limited validity of single-family residences. Over 20% of American dwelling units are multi-family units, or MDUs. MDUs can be quite different environments for technology, because of the greater density of both people and technology. Privacy, installation, and conflicting technologies can complicate the successful use of many new technologies in MDUs. Sensors and wireless technologies are particularly vulnerable to errors introduced by density.

# 5  Advancing Home-Related Research as a Field

To this point, I have been arguing for homes as a topic of research, and I have addressed some of the particulars involved in conducting such research. Now, I would like to focus on a few activities within the research community that I believe are integral to establishing home-related research as a legitimate and respected discipline. These activities include integrating homes into educational curricula, building a community of practice around home-related research, and forging strong ties between industrial and academic efforts in this domain.

## 5.1  Appreciating the multi-disciplinary nature of home-related research

This field will by necessity be multi-disciplinary; project teams need to be familiar with the history of technologies, the nature of home life, examples of recent work in domestic technologies, and the pros and cons of specific technologies. Other relevant topics include industrial design, home automation and home networking, along with issues of infrastructure and the economics of technologies. Policy and regulatory issues are salient areas, as are home architecture and décor.

I particularly like Aware Home's multi-disciplinary team description. In my own research, the team included sociologists, user interaction designers, computer scientists, engineers, and industrial designers with varied backgrounds.

## 5.2 Teaching design with a focus on homes and consumers

In early 1999, I inaugurated a course at Stanford entitled "The Design of Domestic and Consumer Technology." This course emphasizes the social context of the home with respect to technology design; other courses have been product design-oriented like one offered at the Royal Institute of Technology, or technology-oriented like one offered at Georgia Tech, or feminist-oriented like one offered at Simon Fraser University.

Fellow researchers presented recent studies of consumers and wired communities, and discussed the methodology behind their work. Topics included the social history of household routines and appliances; demographics; consumer market research (Wostring, Kayany and Forrest 1996); homes and family life (Marcus, Coontz 1992) and interactions between home life and work life (Nippert-Eng 1996). Methodological material included online demographic resources, learning from one's own experiences as consumers, techniques for doing lightweight situated research, interviewing, structured approaches to data, and how consumer studies could inform design work (Norman 1998).

For term projects, these computer science graduate students conduced small qualitative studies. Project topics fell into four general categories: recreation and technology, communications in everyday life, computers in the home, and children and technology. The projects were successful, and although the small number of interviews limited external validity, the students did uncover original insights.

Students readily came to examine their implicit assumptions about consumers, domestic environments and the role of technologies in homes and everyday life. This experience convinced me of the value of teaching home-related research. This course could be sequenced with a general qualitative methods course; indeed, workplaces, homes, schools and other specific domains could all be options for students to apply general skills.

## 5.3 Converging on a body of practice

There is not yet a consensus within the community as to how home-related research is best accomplished. This issue exists within the CSCW and CHI communities as well, of course, although they have had over a decade of shared experience and have formed norms about what constitutes good-quality work. This leads to the question of how we can share work. There is enough ongoing work, and enough interest, to justify some kind of academic and industry workshop or gathering in the near future, and to justify serious consideration of creating a topic-specific publication venue.

Additionally, there is no textbook or a readily identified body of literature on domestic technologies. For course readings, I drew upon CHI-related work, including CSCW, CoBuild and DIS. I also drew upon sociological and behavioral research, market and consumer research, technological histories, feminist studies and design philosophy.

## 5.4 Building strong ties between industry and academia

Over the last four years there have been CSCW and CHI workshops targeted at domestic technologies and studying people in their homes (Scholtz et al. 1996, O'Brien et al. 1996, Tollmar and Junestrand 1998). Many of the participants have been industry researchers; the topic has not achieved a critical mass of interest within the research community.

There are currently a handful of academic research projects devoted to the home, including the comHome project at KTH, the Adaptive Home project at Colorado (Mozer 1998), the Future Computing Environments project at Georgia Tech, the IHome effort at U. Massachusetts, HomeNet at CMU, and the Counter Intelligence initiative at the MIT Media Lab. These efforts do involve industry partners, of course.

However, this is an arena in which industry is well ahead of academia; consumer-oriented companies such as telecommunications firms have been using living-room simulations in consumer research for years. Mainstream personal computer companies such as Microsoft, Intel and Hewlett-Packard have all recently invested significantly in consumer-oriented R&D, even to the point of altering their business organization to focus more on the mass market.

It will therefore be essential that the community form sustained, deep relationships between academic and industry research efforts. This will require outreach and adaptation by all involved. For example, academics will benefit from recognizing the salience of industry trade events such as the yearly Consumer Electronics Show (CES) sponsored by CEMA, with attendance of over 100,000. Indeed, at a CHI'99 informal special interest group on domestic technologies (organized by Beth Mynatt and me), CES emerged as the venue that would be most attended by those present.

# 6  Closing Comments

In this paper, I have just touched upon the complex nature of home-related research and how it relates to existing bodies of practice and research. I hope that this is just one early example of what will be a long and rich stream of thinking, writing and designing for technologies with the home sphere in mind.

### Acknowledgements

I'd like to thank Interval Research for its support of this work. Thanks also to Terry Winograd, my students, guest speakers and commentors for making my course a success. I especially thank Sara Kiesler for her support and advice. Many, many people at Interval contributed to the Casablanca work, with special thanks to Scott Mainwaring. Finally, I very much appreciate the CoBuild'99 program chairs' willingness to expand the domain of cooperative buildings to homes.

# References

1. Adler, A. and Henderson, A. (1994). A room of our own: Experiences from a direct office share. In *Proceedings of CHI'94*, pp. 138-144.
2. Bly S., Harrison S. and Irwin S. (1993). Media Spaces: Bringing People Together in a Video, Audio and Computing Environment. Communications of the ACM, 36(1): 28-47.
3. Coontz, S. (1992). The Way We Never Were. BasicBooks.
4. Hughes, J., O'Brien, J. & Rodden, T., (1998). Understanding Technology in Domestic Environments: Lessons for Cooperative Buildings, In Streiz, N., Konomi, S., Burkhardt, H.-J. (Eds.), *Cooperative Buildings - Integrating Information, Organization and Architecture, Proceedings of CoBuild'98*. LNCS 1370. Springer, pp. 248-262.
5. Ireland, C. and Johnson, B. (1995). Exploring the Future Present. Design Management Journal. pp. 57-64.
6. Junestrand, S. and Tollmar, K. (1998). The Dwelling as a Place for Work. In Streiz, N., Konomi, S., Burkhardt, H.-J. (Eds.), *Cooperative Buildings - Integrating Information, Organization and Architecture, Proc. of CoBuild'98*. LNCS 1370. Springer, pp. 230-247.
7. Junestrand, S. and Tollmar, K. (1999). Video Mediated Communication for Domestic Environments -- Architectural and Technological Design. In Streiz, N., Siegel, J., Hartkopf, V., Konomi, S. (Eds.), *Cooperative Buildings - Integrating Information, Organizations and Architecture, Proceedings of CoBuild'99*. LNCS 1670 (this volume). Springer, pp. 176-189.
8. Kidd, C. D., Abowd, G. D., Atkeson, C. G., Essa, I. A., MacIntyre, B., Mynatt, E., and Starner, T.E. (1999). The Aware Home: A Living Laboratory for Ubiquitous Computing Research. In Streiz, N., Siegel, J., Hartkopf, V., Konomi, S. (Eds.), *Cooperative Buildings - Integrating Information, Organizations and Architecture, Proceedings of CoBuild'99*. LNCS 1670 (this volume). Springer, pp. 190-197.
9. Kraut, R., Scherlis, W., Mukhopadhyay, T., Manning, J. and Kiesler; S. (1996). The HomeNet field trial of residential Internet services; Commun. ACM 39, 12, pp. 55-63.
10. Lesser, V., M. Atighetchi, B. Benyo, B. Horling, A. Raja, R. Vincent, T. Wagner, P. Xuan, and S. XQ.Zhang; (1999). The UMASS intelligent home project In *Proceedings of Autonomous Agents conference*, pp. 291-298.
11. Marcus, C. C. (1995). House as a Mirror of Self, Conari Press.
12. Mateas, M., Salvador, T., Scholtz, J. and Sorensen, D. (1996). Engineering Ethnography in the Home. In *Proceedings of CHI96*, pp.283-284.
13. Mick, D. G. and Fournier, S. Paradoxes of Technology: Consumer Cognizance, Emotions, and Coping Strategies. (1998). Journal of Consumer Research. 25, Sept. 1998, pp. 123-143.
14. Mozer, M. C. (1998). The neural network house: An environment that adapts to its inhabitants. In M. Coen (Ed.), Proceedings of the American Association for Artificial Intelligence Spring Symposium (pp. 110-114). Menlo, Park, CA: AAAI Press.
15. Nippert-Eng, C. (1996). Home & Work: Negotiating Boundaries.
16. Norman, D. (1998). The Invisible Computer. MIT Press.
17. O'Brien, J., Hughes, J., Ackerman, M. and Hindus, D. (1996). Workshop on Extending CSCW into Domestic Environments. In *Proceedings of CSCW'96*, November 1996, p.1.
18. Robinson, J. P. and Godbey, G (1997). Time for Life: The Surprising Ways Americans Use Their Time, PA State Univ Press, pp. 3-23.
19. Scholtz, J., Mateas, M., Salvador, T., Scholtz, J. and Sorensen, D. (1996). SIG on User requirements analysis for the home. In *Proc. of the CHI '96 conference companion*, p.326.
20. Tollmar, K., and Junestrand, S. (1998). Workshop on Understanding Professional Work in Domestic Environments. In *Proceedings of CSCW'98*, November 1998, p. 415.
21. Wostring, C. E., Kayany, J. M., and Forrest, E. J. (1996). Consuming technologies at home: New consumer research techniques. In Edward Forrest and Richard Mizerski (Eds.), Interactive Marketing: The Future Present (Chapter 19, pp. 269-281). Ntc Business Books.

# A Swivel Chair as an Input Device

## Michael Cohen

Spatial Media Group, Human Interface Lab
University of Aizu
Aizu-Wakamatsu 965-8580, Japan
mcohen@u-aizu.ac.jp
http://www.u-aizu.ac.jp/~mcohen

**Abstract.** A pivot (swivel, rotating) chair is considered as an input device, an information appliance. The input modality is orientation tracking, which can dynamically select transfer functions used to spatialize audio in a rotation-invariant soundscape. In groupware situations, like teleconferencing or chat spaces, such orientation tracking can also be used to twist multiple iconic representations of a seated user, avatars in a virtual world, enabling social situation awareness via coupled visual displays, soundscape-stabilized virtual source locations, and direction-dependent projection of non-omnidirectional sources. The Internet Chair, manifesting as personal LBE (location-based entertainment), has potential for both stand-alone and networked applications.

**Keywords.** Audio windows, information furniture, soundscape stabilization, mixed reality.

## 1 Introduction

There are more chairs than windows, desks, computers, or telephones. According to a metric of person-hours used, and generalized to include couches, stools, benches, and other seats, the chair is the most popular tool on earth, with the possible exceptions of its cousin the bed or eyewear. The Internet Chair (Cohen, 1998) begins to exploit that ubiquity.

The direction one's body is oriented differs from which way one's head is turned (a primary parameter for auditory directionalization), which in turn differs from which way one's eyes (and also often one's attention) point. Nevertheless, a chair tracker, which senses and transmits the orientation of a pivot (swivel, rotating) chair, provides a convenient first-order approximation for all of these attributes. Informal experiments suggest that seated body tracking alone provides adequate parameterization of dynamic transfer function selection for auditory directionalization (Koizumi et. al., 1991) while serving as a cue to others in groupware contexts (virtual conferences, concerts, and cocktail parties) about directed attention. The propriocentric sensation is linked with soundscape stabilization (invariance preserving the location of virtual sources under reorientation of the user).

# 2  Implementation

A stand-alone instance of the Internet Chair can use orientation to adjust presentation of lateralized audio. The full prototype software is a (very thick) client (Cohen and Koizumi, 1992), bundling the chair tracker, graphical user interface, and sound directionalization, connected to a multicasting conference server for CSCW. The prototype computing platform is a Fujitsu MicroSparc S-4/Leia running NextStep. The prototype "backend" is an ordinary swivel chair retrofitted with an azimuth sensor. The spinometer uses a Polhemus 3Space IsotrakII electromagnetic tracker deployed as a yaw sensor, but alternatives would be more appropriate for different simultaneous contexts, like GPS-based systems for vehicle-mounted seats or factory-installed mechanical sensors.

An important feature of an interface for such a chair exploits forked presence, the ability of an individual user to have multiply instantiated avatars (vactors, delegates, …) across arbitrary soundscapes. The Internet Chair allows a lone human to drive the orientation of multiple iconic representatives. Reality is separated into layers which can be superimposed. Parallel research explores the interface potential of multiple representations of a user in virtual space, made explicit through an exocentric paradigm (Cohen and Herder, 1998). Such a feature finds application in situations for which a user desires presence in different contexts--- monitoring, for example, an ongoing teleconference, a side-conference, an intercom connected to a nursery, …

# References

1. Cohen, M. (1998). The Internet Chair. *Proc IEEE International Workshop on Networked Appliances,* Kyoto, Japan (November 1998).
2. Cohen, M. and Herder, J. (1998). Symbolic representations of exclude and include for audio sources and sinks. *Proc. Virtual Environments*, Stuttgart, Germany (June 1998).
3. Cohen, M. and Koizumi, N. (1992). Iconic control for audio windows. *Proc. Eighth Symp. On Human Interface*, Kawasaki, Japan, October 1992.
4. Koizumi, N., Cohen, M., and Aoki, S. (1991). *Japanese patent application #3194281*: Voice reproduction system, August 1991.

# Progress of MUSE (Making User Friendly Spaces): A Context-Aware Assistant for Orientation

Matina Halkia, Jaime Solari

Starlab Research Laboratories
Excelsiorlaan 40-42, Zaventem, Belgium 1930
{matina, jaime}@starlab.net

**Abstract.** We describe a prototype system of work in-progress that combines remote sensors with presence detection to address the orientation needs when confronted with unfamiliar spaces. The goal is to explore how these technologies might together make interactive spaces that can support users in their everyday interactions with the world. An application that presents information about our office space using environmental sensing hardware and infrared badges is introduced. An explanation of how the prototype is used, and a description of the rationale behind designing its software infrastructure and hardware selection is provided.

**Keywords.** context awareness, computer based guidance system, context relevant assistance, personal orientation guide, environmental monitoring, information enhanced spaces, dynamic information signs.

## 1 Introduction

This project, Making User Friendly Spaces (MUSE), addresses the orientation challenge faced by people entering a new space. The spatial arrangement of workspaces reveals information about the structure and hierarchy of organizations, the methods of work, the amount and types of collaboration, the distinction between private and public, the various degrees of accessibility, and even reveals the disfunctionalities in the workplace. In physical space this is the work of the architect. The designer prompts human behavior by providing spatial cues. A building however by its physical structure can only communicate timeless messages. Information enhanced spaces can prompt spatially relevant human behavior that changes dynamically with time. The system conveys the contextual information of space (namely environmental conditions, presence and location of people) through sensing hardware, and provides thus a dynamic graphic sign for spatial and contextual orientation, using information filtering techniques and customized visualization tools.

**Fig. 1.** Environmental Sensors (TEABoard)

## 2 Related Work

Loomis et al. (1994) developed a system that makes it possible for blind users to navigate a university campus by tracking their position through GPS to present spatial sonic cues. Petrie et al (1996) have field-tested a GPS-based navigation aid for blind users that uses a speech synthesizer to describe city routes. Feiner et al. (1997) developed a mobile user interface to overlay 3D graphics through augmented reality and thus provide campus information. More recently, Starner (1999) and Mann (1998) developed wearable systems and intelligent signal processing tools for contextual awareness. Our project on the other hand embeds the surrounding environment with the sensors and processing units freeing up the users of having to carry hardware on them. The only required hardware the users must wear is the active badge location emitters.

## 3 Overview

The system aims at enhancing awareness and therefore people's ability to *adjust* to new spaces effectively. By awareness we mean an understanding of the activities of others, which provides a context for one's own activity as pointed out by Dourish and Belloti (1992). A case study using Starlab's main headquarters is in progress, with visitors and staff as the evaluators.

There are two factors that are important in this project:

i. context sensitive information (according to the number of people and environmental conditions in each room)
ii. customized delivery (according to the types of visitors and their needs)

i. *Adjustment* presupposes context-awareness. By context we understand the information the user is surrounded by, her emotional state, focus of attention, location, orientation, and time of the day, objects and people in the users' environment as well as the user's personal model of them. Therefore, the *adjustment* of a visitor to an unfamiliar space must take these factors into consideration. We have kept these in mind in the development of the prototype, and the development of the scenarios.

ii. The system can distinguish between the different types of users, and be able to adjust its guidance to the different needs and interests of the user. For visitors the case study will be a new environment while for the employees quite familiar.

These goals are accomplished by providing information to the visitor about the activities and current environmental state of the offices, through light, sound, pressure, infrared sensors and active badge locators. Therefore the needs of the visitors have been divided into three categories:

Orientation
Activity tracking
People tracking

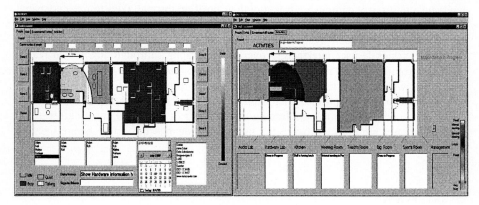

**Fig. 2.** Prototype Interface

## 3.1 Orientation

The basic functionality that the system provides is orientation through the office. Based upon the activities and the user profile, a 3-D representation of the office will display the pertinent activity information and suggested behavior. For example, if a demonstration is in progress, the user is informed of the demo and depending on the information filters, he or she is directed towards the location where the activity is taking place.

## 3.2 Activity tracking

Activity tracking is done with environmental sensors and the infrared badges to inform the visitor where and what activities are taking place in order to propose an action. The activities are inferred according to the type of room, the time of the day, and by comparing the room's usual number of occupants with those present at a given time (i.e. more than average people in the kitchen during noon means the staff is having lunch).

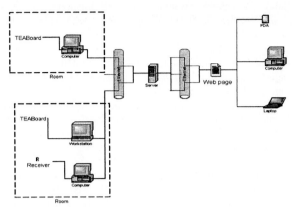

**Fig. 3.** Architecture of the system

### 3.3 People Tracking

While the activity tracking is event-driven, the tracking of people is continuous. Each employee wears a badge that emits an infrared signal to the receivers that are mounted on each doorframe. This way the identity and number of people for each room can be inferred. The information is represented dynamically in a plan of the office with abstract representations of the staff located in it. The functionality listed below is shown in the interface screenshot in Fig. 2:

1.  Informs about room activities in an office environment
2.  Helps orient the user through the different spaces
3.  Informs about people density and environmental conditions in each room
4.  Interprets environmental data and positioning information
5.  Delivers customized behavioral recommendations according to the user's profiles

## 4  Architecture

The hardware components of this system consist of sensing hardware -- TEA boards described by Albrecht et al. (1999) and IR receivers -- which detect the environmental changes in the office rooms and location of people. These signals are processed on the client machine for variations and changes in state, which trigger events that are transmitted via TCP/IP over the network to a server. The server is running a pattern recognizer, which detects the activities being represented by the events coming from the different clients. These activities are then displayed on the interface running on the welcoming computer located at the main entrance to the office.

# References

1. Dourish, P. and Bellotti, V. (1992). Awareness and Coordination in Shared Workspaces. In: *Proc. of the Conf. on Computer Supported Cooperative Work CSCW 92, pp.107-114.* ACM Press, New York.
2. Feiner, S., MacIntyre, B., Hollerer, T., Webster, A. (1997). A Touring Machine: Prototyping 3D Mobile Augmented Reality Systems for Exploring the Urban Environment. In: *Proc. ISWC '97 (Int. Symp. On Wearable Computing),* Cambridge, MA (October 13-14, 1997).
3. Loomis, J., Golledge, R., Klatzky, R., Speigle, J., Tietz, J. (1994). Personal guidance system for the visually impaired. In: *Proc. First Ann. Int. ACM/SIGCAPH Conf. On Assistive Technologies.* Marina del Rey, CA (October 31-November 1, 1994).
4. Mann, S., (1998). Humanistic Intelligence: 'WearComp' as a new framework and application for intelligent signal processing. In: *Proceedings of the IEEE, Vol. 86, No. 11, pp.2123-2151*
5. Petrie, H., Johnson, V., Strothotte, T., Raab, A., Fritz, S., Michel, R. (1996). MoBIC: Designing a travel aid for blind and elderly people. *Jnl. Of Navigation, 49(1):45-52.*
6. Schmidt, A., Aidoo, K.A., Takaluoma, A., Tuomela, U., Van Laerhoven, K., and Van de Velde, W. (1999). Advanced Interaction in Context. In: H. Gellersen (Ed.) *Handheld and Ubiquitous Computing, Lecture Notes in Computer Science No. 1707, p.p89-101.* Springer-Verlag Heidelberg.
7. Starner, T.E., (1999). Wearable Computing and Contextual Awareness, Doctoral Dissertation, pp23-25. Massachusetts Institute of Technology, Cambridge, MA.

# Design of the Swisshouse: A Physical/Virtual Cooperative Workspace

Jeffrey Huang, Muriel Waldvogel, Surapong Lertsithichai

Harvard University
Graduate School of Design
48 Quincy Street, Cambridge, MA 02138, USA
jhuang@gsd.harvard.edu

**Abstract.** This paper describes the design of the Swisshouse, a physical/virtual cooperative workspace to foster networking and knowledge exchange among a distributed community of Swiss scientists, with business people, lawyers, doctors and politicians. The physical "cooperative building" of the Swisshouse, will result from the transformation of an existing 3,200 sq.ft. large retail store located in Cambridge, Massachusetts, into a wired loft-space, to be completed in December 1999. The design encompasses both a physical building and an intimately connected Internet-based web-space. In this paper, we describe our work-in-progress on the design of the interfaces between the two worlds. We present our current design of the embedded information devices that connect the virtual community, and -as architectural elements- define the physical cooperative loft space: an interactive information wall, stackable videoconferencing chairs, a knowledge café, a media space and a kinetic arena.

**Keywords.** cooperative buildings, videoconferencing, distance learning, shared workspaces, virtual communities, roomware.

## 1 Introduction

What does it take to create a strong virtual community of like-minded participants? This paper gives a short overview of our current, design-oriented approach to the above question. Our research is predicated on our belief that essentially a community can *not* be designed. Yet we argue that what *can* be designed is the infrastructure to make communities happen. We detail our approach via the example from our on-going design of the Swisshouse, a virtual/physical infrastructure to foster the creation and growth of the virtual Swiss scientist community.

The paper is organized as follows. In the next section, we provide the background of the project. Next, we present the underlying design concepts, and describe in detail the individual pieces of the project. In section 5, we outline the precedents and related work. Finally, we conclude by discussing the contributions we expect to make and suggest an agenda for further research.

## 2 Background

The Swisshouse is a new type of Consulate. It originated as a donation by Lombard-Odier, a Swiss private bank to the Swiss Government. The objectives of the Swisshouse are (i) to facilitate networking and knowledge exchange among the Swiss-American scientific community, (ii) to build a bridge to the Swiss university network, and (iii) to provide a platform for transdisciplinary interaction among participants from academic research, industry, business/finance, law, politics, and the arts (Comtesse 1998).

The original program called for a physical building only. But in order to expand the scope beyond the limits of the physical boundaries and enable the geographically dispersed community to actively participate and cooperate, we proposed a concept that comprised not only a physical but also a virtual component. The physical building will be located in Cambridge, Massachusetts and the virtual on the Internet. Both worlds, the virtual and the physical Swisshouse, will be intimately linked together. The scientific, cultural, political and business exchange will happen physically and digitally. The physical space will give a sense of place and belonging to community, and act as a forum for face-to-face interaction, intellectual exchange, and the creation of entrepreneurial opportunities. The digital world will integrate into the physical space and allow the Swisshouse to reach out far beyond the defined physical walls to become a "global village." The virtual space will provide a platform for matching distributed interests in the community and fostering continued synergetic exchange over the Internet.

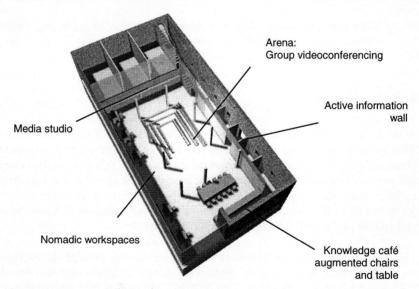

Arena:
Group videoconferencing

Active information
wall

Media studio

Nomadic workspaces

Knowledge café
augmented chairs
and table

**Fig. 1.** Map of the information devices in the Swisshouse.

# 3 The Physical Building

We conceived the physical building as 3,200 sq.ft. large, wired loft-space for meeting, exchanging, nurturing and developing ideas and projects. The programming and articulation of the interior spaces of the Swisshouse reflect its unique nature as a physical/virtual construct. The underlying design principles were:

1. Embedded Information devices. The information appliances that make the connection to the virtual world are embedded in the architecture and furniture of the building, and become space-defining elements themselves. The devices are social and cooperative in nature.
2. Intimate link between physical and virtual space. The physical building is conceived as a spatial interface to the virtual community. Particular attention has been given to the different types of spaces and elements needed to connect with the virtual community.
3. Deliberate use of the senses of perception (acoustic, visual, touch and smell) for enhancing the physical and the virtual space.

The main elements are the kinetic arena, the knowledge café, the open and closed workspace, and the active information wall (Figure 1). They are described in the following.

## 3.1 The Kinetic Arena

The convergence point in the physical Swisshouse is the «Arena». The «Arena» is a rectangular shape that slowly steps down 3 feet into the floor slabs. The arena makes the landscape of the Swisshouse: it is a hydraulic device that can be leveled at the street level, sunk into the basement, or elevated to form a small podium, based on acoustical requirements. For example, it can be sunk for seminar-type discussions (1-20 participants), and elevated for far-reaching speeches (1-2000 spectators). Activities happening in the arena are transmitted in real-time onto the virtual sites via a "net-eye" mounted onto the ceiling of the Swisshouse.

## 3.2 The Knowledge Café

The Knowledge Café opens directly to the arena. The tables of the Café are networked media objects, large and long, creating informal groupings and enabling geographically dispersed brainstorming. The chairs are stackable low-cost video conferencing chairs that enable different groupings: empty chairs suggest the presence of distant participants (Figure 2). A small kitchen located in the brick back wall can be used for small snacks and coffee. The senses of smell and taste are added deliberately to the knowledge café to enhance brainstorming by reaching deeply into personal and intimate experiences.

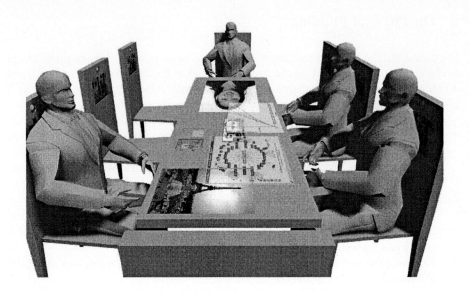

**Fig. 2.** The Knowledge Café with the stackable video conferencing chairs and active table.

### 3.3 Nomadic and Closed Workspaces

Open nomadic workspaces are distributed throughout the loft-space. A visual partitioning system (eleven22, USM Haller system) will be put in place, while the acoustic link will remain open. The wooden floor will be wired and provide plug-and-play access to a local area network with fast connection (T1) to the Internet. On the galleries, overlooking the arena, glass office spaces hover 8 feet above. The gallery offices can be closed off acoustically, yet still maintaining their visual link to the large open space.

### 3.5 Media Space and Video Conferencing Spaces

The media rooms are located under the gallery. The spaces provide efficient screen displays, and remain open to the hall and the arena. The wall panels integrate large screens for computer projections to be used for cooperative work and interactive presentations. Translucent windows provide the spaces with a direct link to the loft.

### 3.6 Active Information Wall

The service zone includes kitchen, restrooms and storage. It is attached to the existing brick back-wall. The service zone is separated from the loft space by an active information wall that will serve as a large interactive display for exhibitions, real-time information and asynchronous connection with the distributed virtual community.

## 4 The Virtual Swisshouse

The Virtual Swisshouse is the virtual counterpart and extends the idea of the Swisshouse into the Internet by offering a platform for exchange of information, networking among individuals, distant education and creation of a virtual community. A high-speed computer server, located in the basement of the physical Swisshouse, will host the web-based environment, and facilitate networking and interaction among the Swiss-American scientific community.

The general structure of the site is that of a marketplace in which ideas and expertise are exchanged. Authorship of content is decentralized: everyone contributes. Community members post and retrieve information based on their interests. Market mechanisms automatically determine which information will persist. The role of the swisshouse is to act as the information broker.

The graphical interface is personalized to meet the habits of the individual user. The underlying structural elements correspond to the physical elements and are interconnected: Arena, Knowledge Café, Information Wall, Donuts, etc. Information is pushed to the appropriate sections based on predefined user profiles.

## 5 Related Work

The following research efforts and developments are related to and inspired the design of the Swisshouse:
- The idea of ubiquitous computing (Weiser, 1991)
- Early prototypes of media spaces (Harrison & Minneman, 1990) and ClearBoard (Ishii & Kobayashii, 1992)
- The roomware and cooperative buildings concepts (Streitz, 1997)
- Virtual Communities (Rheingold, 1993) (Kollock , 1997)
- Process Handbook (Malone et al., 1993) (Huang, 1999)
- Tangible Media (Ishii & Ullmer, 1997)
- Augmented Surfaces (Rekimoto and Saito, 1999) and Holowall (Matsushita and Rekimoto, 1997)
- Integration of the Senses in Design (Waldvogel, 1999)

## 6 Discussion

We have presented our current design of the Swisshouse, a new prototype embassy/workspace combining physical and virtual technologies. The Swisshouse is conceived as a physical interface to a distributed community, augmented by a parallel virtual world. The work has been inspired and follows thoughts similar to research done within the emerging field of cooperative buildings (Streitz 1997) and related research areas. What distinguishes our approach from the precedents mentioned above, is our perspective, which is distinctively architectural in nature. The structure of our approach follows typical stages of architectural design thinking: needs analysis, site analysis, program definition, schematic design, etc. Accordingly, the success of our project will not only be determined by verification of our research hypotheses, but also, and in particular, by the ability of our design to fulfil the future users' needs. Possible measurements could include, for example, the number, frequency and "stickiness" of visits. We see the Swisshouse as an emerging, important platform for empirical evaluations of such issues, and, more broadly, for potentially providing answers to questions about the possible and desirable role of cooperative buildings in society.

# References

1. Comtesse, X. (1998). Swiss House for Advanced Research and Education: SHARE, White Paper.
2. Harrison, S., Minneman, S. (1990). The Media Space. In Proceedings of the Conference on Participatory Design, CPSR Seattle; 157-166.
3. Huang, J. (1999), "How do distributed design organizations act together to create a meaningful design? Towards a process model for design coordination." In Eastman, C., Computers in Building - CAAD Futures '99, Dordrecht: Kluwer Academic.
4. Ishii, H., Kobayashi, M. (1992). ClearBoard: A Seamless Medium for Shared Drawing and Conversation with Eye Contact. In: Proceedings of the Conference on Human Factors in Computing Systems (CHI'92), New York: ACM Press, 525-532.
5. Ishii, H., Ullmer, B. (1997) Tangible Bits: Towards Seamless Interfaces between People, Bits and Atoms. In: Proceedings of CHI'97, ACM Press, 234-241.
6. Kollock, P. (1997), Design Principles for Virtual Communities. In: The Internet and Society: Harvard Conference Proceedings. Cambridge, MA: O'Reilly & Associates.
7. Malone, T.W., Crowston, K., Lee, J., and Pentland, B. (1993), "Tools for inventing organizations: Towards a handbook of organizational processes," Working Paper, Cambridge, MA: MIT Center for Coordination Science.
8. Matsushita, N., Rekimoto, J., (1997), "HoloWall: Designing a Finger, Hand, Body, and Object Sensitive Wall", Proceedings of UIST'97.
9. Rekimoto, J., Saitoh, M. (1999) "Augmented Surfaces: A Spatially Continuous Workspace for Hybrid Computing Environments", Proceedings of CHI'99, ACM Press.
10. Rheingold, H. (1993). The Virtual Community. Reading, MA: Addison-Wesley Publishing.
11. Streitz, N., Konomi, S., Burkhardt, H.-J. (Eds.) (1998). Cooperative Buildings - Integrating Information, Organization and Architecture. Proceedings of the First International Workshop on Cooperative Buildings (CoBuild'98), Darmstadt, Germany (February 25-26, 1998). Lecture Notes in Computer Science, Vol. 1370. Springer - Verlag, Heidelberg.
12. Waldvogel, M. (1999), Le Sense du Toucher dans l'Art et l'Architecture, PhD Dissertation, ETH Zurich, Switzerland.
13. Weiser, M. (1991). The Computer for the 21$^{st}$ Century. Scientific American, 1991, 265 (3), 94-104.

# Author Index

# Keyword Index

# Lecture Notes in Computer Science

For information about Vols. 1–1622
please contact your bookseller or Springer-Verlag

Wentworth - Alumni Library